Investment Euphoria and Money Madness

The Inner Workings of the Psychology of Investing—for Financial Advisors and Their Clients

Harry "Bud" E. Gunn

Glenlake Publishing Company, Ltd.
Chicago • London • New Delhi

Fitzroy Dearborn Publishers
Chicago and London

© 2000 The Glenlake Publishing Company, Ltd.

ISBN: 1-888998-82-2

Library Edition: Fitzroy Dearborn Publishers, Chicago and London
ISBN: 1-57958-257-5

Printed in the Unites States of America

GPCo
1261 West Glenlake
Chicago, IL 60660
glenlake@ix.netcom.com

Dedication

To my wife Vi, my soul mate and partner in all I do. Also, to my sons, Bud and Bill, great sources of joy and encouragement,

and

To a very important person in my life, My Friend, My Pal, My Brother, Bill Gunn.

Table of Contents

About the Author

Harry "Bud" Gunn is a Clinical Psychologist who has helped individuals deal with their fears, conducted workshops for stress management and improving communications skills and has applied psychological techniques to improve investing. He is the author of numerous publications including *The Test for Success Book, Fear of Success and Guilt over Success,* and *The Test Yourself Book and Manipulation by Guild* among others. Dr. Gunn was educated at Beloit College, Purdue University, The University of Chicago, and received his Ph.D. from Loyola University, Chicago.

Introduction

Many people in the world of investment might question the need to study psychology. Some argue that they are "numbers" people, not social reformers. Still others, disavowing any emotional problems, feel they don't need to engage in self-analysis. Many firmly believe they make only rational or logical—never emotional—decisions.

However, for everyone there is an intertwining of reason and emotion, so that the demarcation is not always clear. Money has a way of stirring the emotions and clouding higher thought processes. Money also changes people. The nice, quiet, compliant person can become a screaming maniac when investments are not successful.

There are three main reasons why the broker needs to understand psychology:

1. To understand his or her own individual equation of the broker and thereby maximize performance.
2. To improve rapport and understand the client's covert strategies.
3. To avoid liability because of failure to detect a client's emotional deterioration.

Psychology is in part the study of human behavior, which includes perception, decision making, goal setting, motivation, and social interaction as well as emotional expression and adjustment. Psychologists are not primarily interested in simply finding something wrong with people but rather helping people become even bigger winners at their trade.

That is why I have written this book. I wish success to all who deal with investments—after all, you might be making one for me one day!

Chapter I
Understanding Yourself: The Key to Better Performance

The most difficult person to take a good look at is yourself. Yet your personality will play a major role in how you perform in the investment world. If you can know yourself, you will have a significant advantage.

Personality and Performance

Why is self-knowledge important? There are two primary reasons:

1. Our personalities determine how we relate to others, and of course that means to clients.
2. Our personalities heavily influence our investment approach.

Consider the following examples:

A broker who could be described as flamboyant, exuding confidence, likes to make decisions on his own. He tends to look for investments that could make the big gain. He is likely to seek the more risky investment and then hang on too long, at the top as well as the bottom. Little gainers do not appeal to him, but by waiting for more profit he may register a loss.

Another broker overly identifies with his investment work. He empathizes with the market to such an extent that when it goes down, he gets down. Depression robs anyone of the ability to make sound business decisions. When everything looks unfavorable to a depressed person, a number of bad things can happen. At one extreme the broker may just lose interest, become withdrawn, and fail to keep up with current events.

At the other end the broker may feel helpless; in order to feel in control he may make impulsive decisions, selling stocks that are down without waiting for a rebound or even selling those that are already on the upswing. Of course, when the market is noticeably on an upswing, there may be a tendency to overbuy.

Another has a personality type that is pessimistic. Though this may seem like the one before, it isn't. Here the emotional state is related not to external conditions but rather to personal disposition. When a stock starts to go up, the pessimist will sell quickly because of concern that it will soon tumble. Potentially big profits are lost with the quick sale. But of course losses are also not as severe.

The optimist, on the other hand, expects things to go well. As a result gains can be maximized—unless he stays with the investment the whole way. At the low end, though, there is the expectation that things will bounce back. Losses can easily be high.

There is another personality type that makes a major impact upon investment strategy. This person suffers from the "fraud complex." She suffers from low self-esteem; whenever things go well, she expects a turnaround. She usually experiences heavy anxiety when she is success-ful because she thinks she's a fraud. She's sure she doesn't deserve it. You have to watch this type because you never know at what point the com-plex will set in. Can she gain 10 percent? 25 percent? 30 percent?

She's like the golfer who has a career round going but is just waiting for his game to fall apart. She brings on her own defeat, either by taking excessive chances or by creating inner tension that disrupts thinking and rhythm. With investments, the problems for this personality type are pri-marily at the high end; she can be very accepting of failure because it does lower anxiety.

The real issue is how much success you can comfortably expect. Some may deny the prevalence of this complex, yet how many times have we heard someone say, "Things are going too well." There is a common myth that we can jinx things by being excited when things go well. That is most unfortunate because rewards increase motivation, and we all need that.

Then there's the analyzer. He won't make an investment without ana-lyzing every aspect. He may even have several systems that cancel each other out. He may be so slow in making decisions that he falls behind the trends. Usually, too, people who are highly compulsive are not good lis-teners. Following what is logical to them, they don't expect others to understand their logic.

Which brings us to the non-listener. She may also have a mixture of other traits (e.g., heavily introverted), but she just does not focus on what others are saying, or for that matter feeling. Whatever the causes, this approach has two main weaknesses; she doesn't get enough information from others, and she doesn't share enough information with the client. If client and broker are not on the same wavelength, that could mean serious legal problems down the road.

Just as it's possible to identify with the market, it's possible to over-identify with a client. I once worked with a broker who took an almost parental role with his clients. Their problems became his. When a client felt a need for the stability of long-term investments, the broker pursued that goal. When that same client suddenly wanted money for a lavish vacation, the broker went along by selling some of those long-term investments. The broker changed his investment strategy constantly at the whim of the client.

"Just think what that means, Dr. Gunn," the broker said. "I need a new plan of attack every time my client's needs change." No wonder he looked depressed and tension-ridden. The opposite can also be the case: These are people who can never make any commitment. One such broker went through three wives, several homes, and a variety of dress styles. Call him a compulsive change seeker. Sometimes he would make an investment in the morning and sell it by noon. He couldn't even commit to a stock buy. The very complicated plans he would make on Monday morning rarely made it through the week.

Another personality type is Mr. Bravado. This person keeps a batting average of all his "bets," though he avoids any talk of his misses. Taking a loss is unthinkable to him—he'll hang on for years rather than admit a mistake and move on. Until a stock is sold, he feels it's not in the loss column. Of course, while waiting for that low stock to rise in value, he's missed dozens of stocks moving upward. Better to just admit the mistake; no one hits them all.

Some brokers come on very strong. I've noticed that among those who make sales phone calls; as soon as you answer there's a barrage about some stock, prior recommended, that has soared.

We can all agree that confidence has value. The trouble is that like everything else, it can be overdone. There may also be problems if there is not a clear understanding of what is expected. Some clients tend to think that a broker who hits once can do it again. Not so—and if things don't work out there might be legal action.

Those who invest are no different from the rest of humanity. When things don't go well, we look for some excuse, someone else to blame it on. How many times has a losing football coach said, "We got a few bad calls and that killed us"?

The world of finance can be greatly influenced by just a few comments by key people, but this should be taken into account when dealing with financial matters. The broker who continually makes excuses is not allowing himself to evaluate his own investment philosophy. He would do well to ask himself instead what he might have done to produce a better result.

Many people seek magical paths to success. For them a tip has a divine quality: It just can't be wrong. This reaction is primarily emotional; reasoning as well as planning may be totally ignored. At one extreme there is no evaluation of the person who gave the tip. The tip approach may also heighten a broker's dependency; he may not be relying on his own judgment as he should. The broker who relies increasingly on tips is likely to become indecisive. Instead of giving advice, he seeks advice.

Selective perception is a term I once applied to a broker who sought my help. Though this broker made some excellent stock selections, he also made many that were very unsuccessful. Did the losers have anything in common? He didn't think so but was asked to list his investments. Looking at the listing, one factor jumped out. The vast majority of stocks he bought were medical; so were the big losers.

My client didn't realize he was so heavily into that area, but added, "They all seemed so exciting."

"John, could that be related to the fact that you started in pre-med?" I asked. John frowned, "You know, it could be. I still think about being a doctor," he said. Later he told me that he began to realize that his selection process had been focused on what was interesting to him, not on the best buy.

A very delicate problem can be communication between client and broker about investments. Some brokers feel uncomfortable if they have to disagree with a client. A friend once said to me, "I find it difficult to tell this client not to buy a stock he favors. He gets real angry when I don't support him."

I responded, "He'll be a whole lot more angry when the stock goes down and you didn't tell him you saw an unwise purchase."

Difficult as it may be, if you want long-term clients you must be a leader. A broker should not try to force his opinion but he should explain his reasoning. It would be a mistake to simply go along—just as it would be to assume that a client could never come up with a good investment idea.

Finally, we need to talk about the effects of some key emotions. These are depression, anxiety, and guilt. We'll go into more detail about these emotions later. At this point we're interested in what happens to the broker who is burdened by these feelings.

Depression is a very painful emotion that affects millions of people at one time or another. Its key effect is to cut off interest in the outside world—including people. A depressed broker is less likely to study investment indicators or to share information with colleagues. Investments are extremely sensitive to world events, something depressed people pay little attention to. Generally depression slows down the decision-making process even though less information is incorporated into the process.

Sometimes besides depression there are mood swings from high to low. On the high, or manic, cycle, decisions are made so rapidly that judgment and reason are impaired. Unlike the depressed person the manic individual does respond to the external world, but so rapidly that misinterpretations abound and information cannot be adequately processed.

Guilt, the third most common negative emotion, can also be destructive to the broker, who may cave in to the requests of others even when reason says he's right. He will question his own judgment and perception. Decisions will be slow and often changed midstream. When things go too well, the guilt-ridden broker will unconsciously invite failure, becoming either too conservative or too risk-prone. He is likely to lose big profits because of lack of faith in his own judgment.

Anxiety is probably the most common negative emotion. It is a crippler of cognitive functioning. We have all had the school experience that caused us to say, "I got so nervous I forgot everything." We recognize that memory suffers. Because immediate memory suffers more than long-term memory, current information goes first.

Anxiety also causes problem-solving to become stereotyped. The same approach is used over and over even when it fails to bring success. A broker who has learned a variety of strategies may use only one because anxiety has narrowed her scope. Fearfulness, which anxiety is, causes doubt in the decision-making process. Buying and selling activities become much less logical. Then the lack of decisiveness further impairs the broker's self-confidence.

These are ways that explain how personality type may influence the broker's performance. This next section describes how personality style may influence how a broker interacts with clients. We must always keep in mind that investing deals not only with numbers but also with people.

Influences on Relationships

What if the broker swings from high to low? The poor client will not know how to approach him. When he is on the low side, he may be very difficult to communicate with at all! He may project disinterest because feeling low has drained his energy.

What about when the broker is on a high? One of my clients made a good observation of that, you can't get a word in edgewise; they will claim infallibility, they are quick to spend *your* money. If you want to communicate you should wait for them to come down.

Some people, including some brokers, are very argumentative. How does that affect a client? Often the client will feel crushed by all the information the broker uses to win his argument.

The trouble is that no one really wins arguments. The client may never want to ask questions because he may feel his broker won't listen to him, and so he may leave, find a broker who will.

A similar situation is set up by the broker who never listens. He doesn't argue, he just doesn't talk. Or he tosses out a trivial comment: "We'll have to wait and see." "I'll be watching your investment." What does that mean? Watch it go down? A client who doesn't know what is going on or what is expected can get pretty angry. There can be no unified investment program without communication.

Some brokers have a personality that combines several types that melt together. Consider the broker whose attitude is high and mighty. He may be a high-pressure salesman, or a build-them-up, let-them-down type. These types all blend into a similar pattern: The client gets the impression that a wonderful purchase has been made, but the client doesn't know why it's wonderful because she doesn't have enough information to appraise the investment. She's on a high because her broker is. Next thing she knows is that it "never quite panned out." Now the poor client doesn't understand what went wrong. After a few experiences like this, someone is going to generate a lot of anger.

Finally what happens to the client who perceives the broker's anxiety, depression, or guilt? He may feel sorry for his broker and not wish to "burden" him. He may listen to the broker's problems instead of asking important questions. He may pick up the broker's anxiety and feel anxious himself. That causes fears of market performance and an overly emotional investment strategy.

When people are around others who are depressed or anxiety-ridden they usually begin to feel the same way. We don't want clients to start dealing out of fear and not out of reason. If anything, the broker should be a calming, steadying force.

Imagine what would happen to one of my counseling clients who said, "Oh Doctor, I don't know what I am going to do" and I answered, "I don't know either." That client would jump out of his skin and out of the office, probably.

Getting to Know Yourself

We know how hard it is to get an objective view of ourselves, but there are some important ways to make it easier. A major reason why getting to know ourselves is hard is that we have preconceived notions of what we want to be like. For example, a man who is afraid to be seen as passive and indecisive will tend to avoid evidence that he has those traits. In fact, if others suggest he does, an argument is likely.

To help yourself observe yourself more accurately, try to avoid making judgments. Think not in terms of what's good or bad, but merely in terms of what is. Learn to accept first of all what you are, because you can't change something until you see it. Being aware of a trait allows you first to better control it and then, if you wish, to change it.

Sometimes a little quiz may point us in a new direction. In a later chapter we have a more complete "brokers' quiz," but for now try this simpler version.

1. Would your spouse or another special person say that you listen well?
   Yes ___   No ___

2. Do you feel irritated when a client points out an unsuccessful investment?
   Yes ___   No ___

3. Do most other people find you easy to approach?
   Yes ___   No ___

4. When you have a conflict with others, what do you do?
   a). Nothing ___   b). Avoid the issue ___
   c). Talk about it ___   d). Try to say what the other person wants to
                                hear ___

5. Would your spouse or another special person say you face issues directly?
   Yes ___   No ___

6. We all have people who dislike us. What would those people say about you?

a). You are too direct ___   b). You are a "know it-all" ___
c). You avoid issues ___   d). You are too difficult to approach ___

7. How would your close friends appraise you?
   a). Easy to rely on ___   b). Hard to reach emotionally ___
   c). Too giving a person ___   d). All of the above ___

8. When you were a child, how did your parents respond to your achievements?
   a). Gave great praise ___   b). Gave material reward ___
   c). Didn't pay much attention ___   d). Always demanded more ___

9. What sort of discipline did you have as a youngster?
   a). Explanatory approaches ___   b). Physical ___
   c). Loss of rewards ___   d). Rather harsh ___

10. How did you feel with your parents?
    a). Very important to them ___   b). Never had time for me ___
    c). We seldom talked ___   d). They didn't know how to do
                                          things with me ___
    e). Important when I achieved ___

For the time being we won't score the quiz, but think about what you might conclude from your answers. Getting an opinion from others can provide a useful check on our own perceptions. You might want to try a little more of that. Then compare your results on this quiz with the results on a later one.

Chapter II
Improving Rapport with Your Clients

The basic goal is to make successful investments. Not many people become unhappy when they are making money.

The investment world, however, is more complex than that. No one makes money all the time. There can be differences in what people believe constitutes success. One person is concerned with long-term results; another wants to make gains the quickest way possible.

Evaluating investment performance is not simple because there are so many changeable factors. What one client feels is good another may feel is below average. What is a good investment gain in January may be poor by March, or what is good in January may be outstanding in March. The investment market is nothing if not changeable.

There is another intangible to be considered in gauging performance. It seems to me that any time you make an investment you're trying to predict the future. Major questions then are how much risk you're willing to take and how much profit margin you want, and how do you define risk? A big risk to one client will be minimal to another. Communication between client and investment advisor is crucial to answering these questions.

There are two primary factors that may impair communication: (1) People often don't know what they want, and (2) They have difficulties telling others even when they do know. Only a very safe environment will encourage adequate open communication.

What can you do to build rapport with your client? The very first step is one that could improve every area of anyone's social functioning. That is to become a good *listener.* Before we look at what people want, let's look at an actual encounter between a broker and his client. It started with the client yelling at his broker that all his investments were lousy.

•

The broker could have become angry. He could have yelled back. He didn't. Instead he invited the client into his office to take a look at his investments. He asked his client which particular investments bothered him.

The client pointed to one that had gone down by about a third. What was interesting, though, was that this particular investment was the client's idea. The broker had raised an objection when they discussed buying it, but the client insisted because he had a tip from a golfing buddy.

The broker could have shifted the blame but he knew that would alienate his client even more. As he listened, he was able gradually to get his client to look at his other investments. He did this in a gentle, non-pushy way: "Can we look at the other investments for a minute?" In short order the client did admit that the overall picture was good. He brightened and became more open.

Knowing that people transfer feelings from one situation or person to another, the broker gently asked how other things were going. The words were hardly out of his mouth before the client began a verbal torrent about how bad his life was. His work had been cut back. He had had a fight with his wife, who had referred to that "lousy stock you bought." Little wonder that he was upset.

The broker performed a miracle because he knew what his client really wanted: to ventilate his feelings. A basic human need, this should be accepted as entirely normal. When we're upset we want to be able to share that with someone. The first goal before any remedial act can take place is emotional expression.

What if the broker had immediately objected to the client's anger? Because the emotion would not have been ventilated, the intensity of the anger would have increased. That client didn't want to hear how well his stocks were doing. He wanted to tell someone how angry he was.

What if the broker had quickly showed him how good his investments were? The client would have found something else wrong. Haven't you seen people who find one thing wrong after another? The new information can only get in after the anger has gotten out.

There is another approach that should be mentioned, and it's a bad one. When someone says to an obviously anxious person, "You have nothing to worry about," that will slam the door. You're saying the anxious person is stupid for feeling what he's feeling.

The best approach is to listen and ask for more information. You're trying not only to find out what the other person is feeling but also what has contributed to it. You're looking for the "why" of the feelings. People will generally not tell you that until they have ventilated some of their emotion. People will also not open up if they feel they are being judged. Try to understand, not criticize.

Most people have trouble dealing with the anger of someone close to them. If another driver cuts you off, you may quickly verbalize how you feel about that person. You may even use hand signals. But generally that approach is unsuitable in most other situations. If you try not to become defensive or take it personally but instead side-step the anger, you will be much more effective with emotional people. Don't call names back, don't defend your position, until the angry person has become more specific. This is the art of side-stepping, working around the other person's feelings.

Another emotion often used in our culture can also cause havoc. That is guilt, an emotion often used to manipulate others. While it may control some people for a time, it's likely to be damaging in the long run. People encouraged to feel guilt are likely to feel uncomfortable with and to avoid the instigator. Sometimes their anger becomes covert; they may, for example, bad-mouth the manipulator. It's also true that any time we dominate someone, we take responsibility for them—and they can become very demanding and angry if their needs are not met!

Just as using guilt on a client is unwise and usually destructive, so is it destructive to allow clients to manipulate you. Among the destructive consequences: You may not want to be around that client. You may be eager for him to pick the wrong stock. Something that allows you to say, "I told you it was a bad investment." Because a broker encouraged to feel guilty will not want his client to be successful, he may not warn him as he normally would when disaster can be foreseen.

Another possibility is that the investor helped to feel guilt-ridden will become afraid to make a move. If an investment goes down she may be overly afraid to sell or to take a chance with a potential winner. Fear of failure will sooner or later produce failure. The investor may try too hard and perhaps hang on too long, hoping for a big winner. As an investment counselor, you owe it to your client, and to continuing rapport, to not let him foster guilt feelings.

One trait that will help you establish rapport is being a fun person. All of us tend to be drawn to people who are pleasant to be with. Have you ever known a person who seems to always be in a bad mood? Someone who complains all the time about something? This is not a people person, one who attracts other people. In fact, people will make any excuse they can to get away.

If you find yourself in a bad mood, try to find some way to get into a good mood. Exercise away the tension. Find someone to talk to. Whatever you do, try not to show your bad mood to your clients.

People generally learn by example. If you're to build good rapport with your clients, you must set a good example. A broker, like a leader, needs to be a stabilizing influence. It should go without saying that when you work with a member of the opposite sex, little flirtations are very much out of place. The pocketbook nerve is a very sensitive one. Interaction must be businesslike. You can enjoy the interaction but it shouldn't be frivolous.

A broker should also be a stabilizing factor in regard to market or investment ups and downs. Many clients will become unreasonably excited when the market is on the rise. They may call to advocate a buying spree. Expecting the market will just keep going up, they want to be in on the big profits.

Or you have the opposite picture: All of a sudden everything seems to be dropping. Instead of over-enthusiasm you now have panic to deal with. The phone calls come in to "sell before we lose it all." Even investments that are up become suspect.

Often the very ones who were yelling for you to buy will now scream for you to sell. Keep in mind that those with less experience are going to be more emotionally upset than those who do this work every day for a living. The key thing to remember is that investments must be bought and sold with reason, not emotion. There are profit opportunities in both up and down markets if the decisions are made with intelligence. It is up to you as the investment counselor to provide a measure of stability and not allow an overreaction to investment trends.

There is one very delicate situation to avoid: getting caught between family members. This could be Lawsuit Territory!

Let's assume that the husband is conservative and the wife more daring. You as the advisor suggest an investment that might be regarded as medium risk. The wife sides with you, beginning an argument with the husband. Now you will be caught in a marital conflict, probably of long standing because of different philosophies. What do you do? I would suggest that you carefully point out the positives of both sides, then defend their right to disagree. As an advisor you need to give your opinion carefully. You might declare that you have not achieved infallibility.

There are even more delicate situations. Imagine a woman broker, a husband with a similar investment philosophy to the broker, and a jealous wife. I have seen situations where every agreement between husband and broker caused more anger in the wife. There were even accusations about

—well, we don't need to write it, do we? Again the advisor must be very careful to stay neutral, perhaps pointing out that the opinions of both should be heard.

That brings up the importance of listening again. Near the top of a list of human needs is the need to feel important. This need goes by many different labels, among them "self-worth," "confidence," and "self-esteem."

I saw this need most lucidly expressed in the days when I was doing marital counseling. I remember one charming couple who had presented themselves because of "frequent marital arguments." Jack felt that he never did anything right in Betty's eyes. He said he was close to the point of just giving up. Her complaint was that she was never involved in making decisions.

Betty and Jack were asked to give some illustrations. Betty wanted Jack to go first and Jack obliged. He described all the work he had done to plan a really nice vacation. He had to get extra work done at the office in order to be able to take time off. Then there was the job of finding just the right facilities. Because Betty liked golf, Jack found a city where there were many different golf courses. She liked swimming, so the place he selected had a pool or ocean available. Jack knew Betty would like the food (mainly seafood). As could be imagined, this location was not cheap. Jack stated, however, that Betty still found things wrong. There were quarrels. He couldn't understand Betty's discontent.

When it was Betty's turn to present what had displeased her, her scenario was approximately the same as Jack's. She simply stated that her husband did everything without consulting her.

There was an interesting ending to all this. Ten months later when Jack and Betty were having a quiet dinner at home, they started to talk about a possible vacation. Jack remembered some of what he had learned in his counseling. He asked Betty where she wanted to go. Betty mentioned the hotel Jack had picked. She wondered if they could get the same room. "It had such a beautiful view of the ocean," she said. "And, oh, the food—I'm going to have to go on a diet," she added.

Well, they duplicated the trip of a year earlier, but this time with no quarrels, just fun. Betty sent me a post card telling me how happy she was and how well the counseling had worked.

To some this doesn't make sense, but from another perspective it does. We all want to feel important and to see that others value our opinion. If someone asks about our feelings, they care about us. Much of the time it doesn't matter if they follow our opinion if they at least consider it.

You will generally find that if you ask the opinions of your clients, they will respond favorably. You as the advisor do not have to agree with your client's opinion. If you do and the investment fails, the client will be angry. He will insist that he doesn't need a "yes person."

What do you do when the client has a definite preference for a particular investment? I don't recommend that you argue. No one wins arguments. The one who seems to prevail loses because he will lose friends, and clients. No one enjoys being whipped in a really emotional argument. Just think of how much we love to see the champion lose!

People who lose arguments usually do not change their opinions. How often have you found people during elections listening to an argument and then changing their opinions? Very seldom, and for a good reason: People do not listen. Generally because their minds are made up they hear only what they want to hear. They may become angry with the other person's arguments but they won't change. So why make them angry and create enemies for no reason?

Does that mean you should just go along with the same old concepts? Can't you help people find new approaches? You can, but not by emotional arguments. If you want change, you need to help the other person take a look at some of his or her ideas and opinions. The more you attack, the more the other person will refuse to listen.

A very helpful approach is to ask the other person what her opinion is. It gets right back to the idea that people want to feel important; having someone interested in your opinions and feelings makes you feel more important. That in turn creates positive rapport.

A useful approach with business relationships is to defer your opinion until you hear the other person's. Others will often ask you how you feel about, let's say, an investment. Try asking how they feel. Then you know what they base their attitude on. If the basis is illogical, once they have heard themselves state their opinion they may begin to realize that. Listening first may allow you to ask other key questions. With this approach you may soon find more readiness for change on everyone's side.

Dealing with differences of opinion is always one of life's major difficulties. I would suggest that you not say things like, "Oh, but you're wrong," or "That's a bad idea." Instead, after you listen see if you can suggest another way of looking at something. "Can we consider this other approach?" is an opening that makes it more likely that the customer will at least consider the new approach.

Memory is another mental ability that can greatly help build rapport. Can you remember going to a restaurant you haven't been to for a while and the hostess greeted you by name? It probably made you feel good. The same is true in the investment world. Here it would help to know something of the client's likes and dislikes, family situation, and investment preferences. You might want to keep a file on important information in your clients' lives—birthdays, golf scores, anniversary, kids' names— all the things that might help clients feel cared about.

There is one approach I've never cared for: the overuse of praise. Some insincere people try to manipulate by indiscriminately telling others how great they are. These phonies don't really touch others. They don't really empathize with them. It may take time but usually people figure out how shallow these people are.

So be sure that when you congratulate someone on something, they also see it as an accomplishment. A short interaction at a well-known golf course illustrates this. The first golfer said with a smile that he just shot 91. The second golfer remarked that he felt sorry for him as he knew he was much better than that. The first man shot right back at him, "What do you mean? That's the first time I broke 100 on this course!"

So while praise is good, it should be honest. Overpraising suggests that others see the recipient as pathetic. Find what people are proud of about themselves and support that.

Another trait that will help build rapport is honesty. When you make an investment error, admit it. See if there is something you can learn from it. When things didn't go as you had expected, it certainly doesn't hurt to evaluate your expectations. Share what you learn with your client and redirect your strategies for the future. Where do we go from here? should be the approach. That should help alleviate some of your client's anxiety. Don't make excuses, but be reassuring.

There are plenty of situations when the investment world will be filled with tension. That means that anxious clients may become quick to express their displeasure. You need to know as an investment advisor what you can tolerate. You can say, "I can understand how you feel," and that may help the client ventilate, but you don't want to allow any client to become abusive to the point where you start to lose control. Set your limits and hold the line. We all must have boundaries.

To have really good rapport there must be sound communication. People's life goals, including their investment goals, often change without their realizing it. There are also times when we think we know what someone desires and we are totally wrong. A client may say, "I just want security," and then become unhappy when his short-term profits aren't big enough. Many may say "I just want a good profit," but what is that?

The only way we can answer the question is by building good communication with the client. We must realize, though, that changes in people's goals must be recognized or the once happy investor may become unhappy.

For the best of rapport between you and your client you may have to educate them. Anxiety is often rooted in ignorance. As an investment counselor you must have some leadership input, but you can't comfortably lead until you know where your client is. A part of the educational program should be getting to know what the client really wants. You need to be clear about what the client means by investment terms like "risky," "secure," "long term," and "good profit."

You need to educate yourself about the client's entire life. Is she married, and if so, is her husband to be included in the investment discussions?

I am reminded here of a situation that confounded a good friend of mine who was an investment advisor. His name was Bob. His clients were George and Louise. Bob told me he had excellent rapport with George and greatly enjoyed working with him. "He's such an easygoing guy. He's always very appreciative when you do well for him," Bob said with a smile.

"Seems like a pleasant man from what I've seen, Bob," I said, "but I don't know him well."

Bob went on to relate how he had met George: George was unhappy with his current advisor, mainly because of poor communication. He felt that he couldn't question the rationale for some of the investments he had made. George had given his consent for his advisor to make some purchases without asking him. That had gotten to be a sore point because there was no explanation later as to why these purchases were made. The advisor had done well financially, but George wanted more information.

So George recalled having met Bob at a dinner party and felt very comfortable with him. They started working together immediately and things had gone well.

Shortly after my conversation with Bob, something apparently changed. The next time I saw Bob, he told me that now he sure was confused about his relationship with George. I asked what was happening that caused the concern.

George said, "Well, in my office he asks a few questions, I go over the changes I would suggest, and then he agrees or disagrees. Then he goes back home and I get a phone call. That's happened almost every day that George has stopped in."

"Is that unusual?" I asked.

"Somewhat," Bob answered, "but what's strange is that his whole demeanor has changed. Now on the phone he's angry and much more aggressive."

What was surprising to Bob was that many of the investment purchases that were being reversed or outright canceled were ones suggested by George. No one could hazard a guess as to what caused this sudden shift.

Then one day George was talking to Bob about some rather daring investments. He had read about several companies that he felt would turn a good gain. He seemed excited as he told Bob about his ideas. Bob shared his enthusiasm, but George began to hedge when it came time to make the purchase decision. He became silent. Then he asked Bob if he really felt these would be a good buy. Bob agreed they were but he also suggested a quick purchase.

"Stocks like this move quickly," he said.

George decided to call home. Bob had to hear the one-sidedness of the conversation. His wife was apparently reviewing the stocks and passing judgment on them. Bob could hear her voice over the phone, even standing five feet away, and she sounded very aggressive indeed. George clearly let her make the final decisions.

Bob didn't say anything after George hung up. He felt George might feel embarrassed. The two of them just looked at each other awkwardly for a few moments. Then Bob felt he had to break the ice.

"Is your wife interested in the stock market?" he asked.

With that George started talking about his wife and her amazing stock record. She let George do all the actual buying, but Louise found nearly all the good buys.

Bob suddenly realized that he should have invited Louise to a meeting when George and he first started working together. Hoping that it wasn't too late, he extended an invitation for Louise to come in. He said he'd love to see how she obtained her information and how she made her decisions.

Louise did come to the brokerage house with George. Bob kept hearing about her wonderful record in the stock market. When Louise showed him a record of what she felt were good stock buys, Bob was impressed. Louise was pleased that Bob accepted her. She said perhaps she had been hard on George, but she was tired of never being included in investment planning just because she was a woman. Bob didn't allow her to feel excluded any longer—and he had to admit that on occasion she had some wonderful tips!

Whether to include a client's spouse is, of course, a very touchy subject. If a woman investment counselor invites the wife, both the husband and wife may object. Or the client's wife may feel that his advisor is being competitive with her.

My advice is to never do any inviting directly. I like the idea of people working together but the approach doesn't work for everyone. The client may not want the spouse there and the spouse may not wish to be there. If you invite someone who has not expressed an interest, you may wear out your welcome

I would suggest that you say nothing at all unless your client brings something up. For example, a male client might at some point say, "Gosh, my wife would be interested in this investment." That may be just the opening you need to make some casual comment like, "If you think she'd like to meet with us, it's fine with me."

I know of one situation that is opposite of our typical stereotype. I have a friend, a neurologist, who is extremely involved with his work. He works very long hours and probably would not even take vacations if it were not for his wife. He is a man who truly loves his work.

Early in his practice he was in a group with some other doctors. At that time he began a retirement fund, but he paid no attention to it. When the group broke up, it became necessary to change some of the financial programs. Someone had to take care of some of these new problems and the doctor didn't want to.

His wife asked if he minded if she took over that responsibility. She had a little card shop that took up some of her time. Her husband was happy that she had the skill and the interest. So his wife did take over. The first few times she placed orders, her broker asked if her husband knew about these investments. "No, he doesn't, and he doesn't want to know about them," she answered with indignation.

Isn't it funny how some stereotypes take so long to change? In this particular case the problem was quickly resolved; the lady found a new investment counselor. The point is, however, when you have a legal arrangement with any adult, that is the person to whom you are responsible.

There are a number of other techniques that have worked well for my own clients. First I try to be brief when explaining something to a client. People tune out whenever the conversation gets lengthy. It sounds like a lecture and people hate being lectured. Along the same line, don't pile up arguments to make your point. Never do overkill with your argument.

In fact, I recommend that you avoid arguments. Discussions and differences of opinion are fine but no one wins arguments. Even if you get the best of other people, they won't like you for it. They may even lie in wait to get back at you in the future. That may sound childish, but a person who suffers ego damage can carry a grudge a long time. Others who may have been offended by your views may show it only by withdrawal. You can pick that up by noting the suddenly taciturn client. That may start an interactional trend where no one is aware of how the problems originally started.

A similar issue is being overly competitive. It's not uncommon for client and advisor to have social contact sometimes in a competitive atmosphere, such as a golf game. For instance, Phil, an investment counselor, and Ron, his client, had actually become good friends and often went out to dinner together. Their wives also became friends and that made for even more enjoyment. They talked about other things that they might do, and when Phil made a big investment their planning heightened. They decide to take a trip together. In fact, they decided on a golf holiday.

Now Phil is an excellent golfer while Ron is close to—well, a dub or "hacker." Ron never knew just how competitive Phil was until he played against him at the resort with two other golfers they hadn't know before. The first day Phil's golf score was about half of what Ron shot. The two golfers who joined them wanted to play for money and so did Phil. Ron lost $87 and he was not happy. It was not the money but the feeling of humiliation over being badly beaten.

The next day was more of the same. Finally Ron asked why he was never paired with Phil. Phil decided that might be a good idea. But Ron played so badly that Phil couldn't carry the team. Ron became increasingly uncomfortable and Phil never said much to him. He didn't complain about Ron's game but he didn't support him either.

Back at home Ron found another advisor. After about six months, though, he came back to Phil and Phil was overjoyed to be working with his investments again. They still play golf together but not against each other. And Phil gives Ron golf tips when he's asked for them.

Was it a mistake for the two men to play golf together, especially in a competitive situation? Possibly, but the answer is who really knows? Could Phil have been more supportive? Could he have said something like, "Hey, Ron, it's just a game?" Perhaps when he became quiet, that too sent an unwelcome message to Ron.

There is another type of competition that can impair a workable investment relationship. We all like to be winners. Sometimes we can become angry (and jealous) when we see others making a big profit and we aren't. What about when others are making a big profit and we're taking a loss?

One stockbroker I knew, wanting to look good, bragged about some of the big profits he had turned for some clients. He had a tendency to make comments such as, "I made this client an 18 percent profit in only two months." Well, that's fine, but how does it sound to the guy who just took a loss? My advice here is that you not brag about other clients' gains in front of those who have lost. Granted, there may be reasons for the difference but your losing client only cares about what you did for him.

Along the same line, I doubt that you will improve your client rapport by badmouthing other advisors. That will sound like jealousy to your clients, and they will wonder if the ones you criticize have some great ability. They may turn to them for advice. Other clients and potential clients may become fearful of investing because they begin to feel there is too much danger out there.

Predicting disaster is another way to scare off investors and ruin rapport. Good rapport means, among other things, that you help people become comfortable. All of us have known people who always see things ending badly. "Everything bad happens to me" is their constant comment. Sometimes I want to look to see if a black cloud is hanging over their heads.

In the investment market they are likely to always expect big losses. If they make a gain, they're sure it will be erased the next day. As an advisor you need to reduce unfounded anxiety and fear. If you truly believe there will be a down market, say it just that way. You can ask clients if they want to wait the market out for a time. Or you can say, "We should have a turnaround here in a short time, but not as yet." But they don't want to hear that "the sky is falling."

Then there is the whole question of how to recruit new clients. Many more stockbrokers now make phone calls to attract new clients. My experience has been that many people resent the approach because they consider it intrusive, though in today's world it may be necessary. Since we're writing here about building rapport, I would offer a few suggestions:

- When the prospect says he's tied up, accept that and see if there is another time available.
- I suggest that you not announce how many thousands you have made for others. The prospect will probably not believe you.
- I still have not become convinced that calling prospective clients by their first name is advisable.

- I doubt that arguing is helpful.
- I may well be off base, but my thought is that you offer a tip for the customer and say that if that turns out well, you would like to call him again.

As far as recruiting, I feel it can best be done by establishing a relationship. You can build rapport by using the attitude that you are interested in offering a service to people who are successful. You are then telling the prospective client that you see him as an important person. You may use this approach for people who are friends of a friend. For that matter you may wish to extend the offer of help to sons and daughters of your client when they become of appropriate age.

From time to time your clients may seek advice from someone else. You don't have to have an exclusive contract with them. Also clients get stock tips from a variety of sources. It is easy to feel threatened then, becoming concerned that you will lose your client to another advisor.

When your client receives such advice two things are likely:

1. It will turn out badly. There may at times be an inner push to say, "I told you so," as if to announce that you would not have given such advice, but whatever you do, don't gloat or you'll likely destroy your rapport. Who really likes an "I told you so" person? Having good rapport is based on caring about someone, so in this case empathize with your client's pain. Don't say anything about the one who gave the bad advice.

2. It will turn out well. That success may pose a threat to you as an advisor. The concern may be that whoever gave the successful tip may have others that will prove attractive to your client. What should you do? My advice is that you keep to the theme of this chapter, improving rapport with your client. Support what took place and congratulate him. Don't warn him that next time he will probably be a loser. Not only is he is likely not to believe you but he may resent your apparent inability to share in his joy. Do everything you can to show that you have an interest in this person.

Keith, an advisor friend of mine, was a very hard-working professional. He had a wealthy client, Arnold, who had earned big profits with Keith's guidance. The two seemed to have a really solid relationship, having been associated together for a number of years.

Then one day Arnold was given a stock tip by a man with whom he had just played golf. They sat around having drinks and comparing investment ideas. The tip turned out very well and Arnold made a very large profit. That tip was followed by three more over the period of a month. Each one did better than the one before. Arnold finally asked his new friend where he obtained all of those "wonderful tips." Arnold began using the advisor he named.

Funds were transferred from Keith's office to the new advisor's office and Keith told me he felt sorry for the loss. But he quickly added that he was pleased that investments were going so well for his friend Arnold. "Maybe I should ask his advisor for some tips," Keith said goodnaturedly.

Keith was very friendly to Arnold whenever he did see him. Keith never acted as if he had lost interest in Arnold and several times they had a drink together. One day Arnold called Keith and asked him to check out a stock for him. "I hate to do this when I'm working with another advisor," he said, but his advisor was out of town.

Keith assured him that it was no problem and got the information. He assured Arnold he would be happy to help any time and wished him luck. Arnold thanked him and left.

Keith didn't hear a word from Arnold for seven months. Then Arnold called to say he was transferring his account back to Keith.

Nothing was ever said that would explain the move back and Keith never asked. What this shows is that if the rapport stays good, anything is possible. Had Keith expressed his feelings of loss, the two may never gave gotten back together again.

Maintaining good rapport means, among other things, knowing how the client lives. Someone who loves entertainment and travel may have entirely different needs than someone who wants only to be secure in old age. Someone who is now retired on a good pension may want a more conservative investment approach.

People need information to be comfortable with their investment situation. I believe that it will help your rapport with clients if you have regular informative meetings with them so they can talk about their needs, goals, and life changes. It lets you explain where you are with your investment goals. It can also be an important assessment time to determine among other things how the communication is doing. People usually feel better when they know where they stand.

You want good rapport with your client and that is in turn related to ability to communicate and to feel support, but a word of caution seems indicated: Some clients have a strong need for support and even guidance. In a later chapter when we discuss the dependent personality, perhaps that will remind you of what is mentioned here.

The danger is that as clients begin to talk about problems, they also begin to look at the listener as a kind of magical person. Perhaps when a married couple disagrees, one may start saying, "You're the only one who understands me!" When you hear anything like that, be very careful.

The rapport you want is one adult relating to another. You won't have that if the relationship gets to the point of doctor/patient. Then one of two things is likely to happen.

1. The client will begin to push you into a situation where you make all the decisions but are supposed to perform like a super hero. Then when things don't go so well, the client becomes disillusioned.

2. The client will begin to talk about problems other than financial. You may be pushed to give advice and even to take sides on marital problems.

This is a common difficulty for those who do psychotherapy and it's hard to handle. On the one hand the therapist doesn't want to be emotionally cold, but he can't be too involved either. Once the relationship with the client gets entangled, it's hard to change it back again because at that point there may be a good deal of anger because the dependent one feels rejected.

So what do you do? Try to not let it get to the place where it becomes entangled. Stay away from taking sides or giving advice, especially about key relationships. When inappropriate advice is requested, don't give it, just gently express the idea that this is not your field of expertise. You can also turn some of this off by not commenting. That way you lessen the buildup on the sticky relationship.

There are a number of things you can do to develop interpersonal skills. These make it much easier to develop excellent rapport.

One is to avoid rapid or loud talk. We present an air of thoughtfulness when we do not act in an impulsive manner. Rapid speech gives the impression that you may go into things in a superficial manner. Loud talk seems to indicate a less controlled person.

Try not to be a worrier. If you are, you're likely to transmit that to your client, who may gradually lose faith in you. That doesn't mean that there's nothing out there to worry about. There is, but try to be reality-oriented. Also realize that any event can be looked at in a variety of ways. That is important to remember, because it means you don't have to be negative all the time.

A well-known coach, Ken, was a marvel at getting his football team motivated both in and out of the classroom. The final game was to decide the conference championship. As fate would have it, the day dawned with heavy rain showers—just the sort of day that makes complainers.

At the team meeting Ken gave his players no chance to complain. "Do you realize what a break this is for us?" he asked with his warm smile. Some of his players looked confused. That didn't stop Ken. He went on to explain that since his team didn't mind rain, they wouldn't be inclined to fumble, and that is exactly how it went. By having their minds made up that they could play in the rain successfully, they handled the challenge.

In investing, too, if you can develop a positive mind set it will help you become a winner. There are times when all of us feel that we want to take our money out of the market. Perhaps the timing is wrong because investment values are down. That may be just the time for our investment advisor to give us a pep talk, and persuade us that if we can just hang on, the values may well go back up.

A few other things will help you build good rapport with your clients. One of the most important is to project a feeling of importance or confidence. If you're going to be a leader and educator, you must see yourself as an important person.

In recent years we've had a tendency to play down financial success. We've heard comments like, "You can't buy health." I agree that health is the most important asset we can have. It may be that you can't buy it, but it sure is expensive to maintain it.

There are many other important activities that are directly related to your financial success: where your children go to school, when you retire, how well you live, and what quality time you spend with your family. All these depend on your financial position. Consequently we can comfortably state that one of the most important persons in our lives is our financial advisor. So out of pride as an advisor, you have a motivation to do your job well.

It's important that you inspire confidence in others. I knew one advisor who did just the opposite. He was unkempt in his appearance, coarse with his language, often poorly groomed, and known to have alcohol on his breath. (In his defense it should be stated that he never arrived at work under the influence.) He had been known in the past as a brilliant advisor but that was during a period when investment decisions were made over the phone.

What gradually began to happen was that he couldn't get his clients to trust his investment suggestions. People clearly didn'thave great faith in him. With the more conservative investments they followed his advice, but with the quick profit type they did not. They waited to see movement; usually by then a major part of the quick gain was lost.

His situation changed dramatically when he married a woman from his office. Also a gifted advisor, she apparently encouraged him to look better. His advice was followed and his whole practice suddenly picked up.

What factors help someone build rapport with *you*? It seems legitimate to ask yourself this question, because what you like, others will probably also like, so listening to your own needs may give you a good start on relationship-building.

All of us need to feel special somewhere, so when your client arrives at least act like you're happy to see him. Try to smile and show some warmth. Perhaps ask a few questions about his life in general. Be happy with him about anything good, like a low golf score. Show a little sympathy for a high score. Then as much as possible be available to discuss his investments.

Try to have each client's personality in mind as you start your interaction. In time, this will become automatic. What that will do is tell you, given current market conditions, how to start your conversation with that client. For example, in a down market, if this is Nervous Nellie you know you will need to try to calm her down. If this is Bold Bob you may need to slow him down; he needs to be aware that a low doesn't always bounce right back.

If you have recommended what turns out to be a poor investment, you will likely harm rapport most by trying to deny it or make excuses. Always try to go back to what now seems reality and be as honest as you can. In the long run, none of us is perfect. If your client shared responsibility for the purchase, reassure him also.

Our last suggestions for building rapport all relate to the same general theme, that people enjoy fun and they like people who help them have fun. Isn't making money fun? You haven't seen too many sad people who have just made a killing. I don't ever remember someone coming to see me, all depressed because "my stock went way up." If they did, I would send them to another shrink. I wouldn't want that attitude to rub off on me!

Try to think of investing as fun and make it that way. Rejoice because you're in a field where you can help people, in fact you can help many people at the same time. Use rewards by permitting at least a little happy reflection when you make a profit. Share your success and reward your clients for their success. At the very least they can be congratulated for listening to you.

In the long run, if you enjoy being with people, if you can use humor at times, if you like what you're doing, and if you like helping people feel good, you'll have excellent rapport with others.

Chapter III
How People Function

There are many different ways to look at human behavioral patterns and underlying personalities. In fact, almost every person regarded as an expert (e.g., Freud, Jung, Adler, Erickson) has a different system. Sometimes there is so much disagreement we might wonder if they're all talking about the same species.

Our goal in this book is to enhance your investment success and to improve your relations with others, especially in the business world. We do not aim to improve, e.g., marital functioning, although financial success has often improved marital interaction.

This chapter presents information to help you understand what various people are trying to do. A word of caution: Nothing muddies the waters as much as labeling something as "abnormal." By implying that a person is disturbed, it fails to answer the question, "What is he trying to do?"

In order to talk about people's behavior, we must believe that there are similarities common to all persons. Otherwise we could not generalize from one person to the next. There could be no common rules of behavior. We would have no common ground of knowledge to enable us to understand basic human needs and desires, and there can't be scientific rules where there are no common elements.

Yet we know that people are not identical. If they were, prediction might be much easier but no one would care because "if you've seen one, you've seem them all." People would be boring and there would be little or no creativity.

How, then, shall we know people? We do it by understanding what we refer to as the individual's "personality." For our purposes, personality can be defined as "an individual's habitual approach to some goal." The goal is an attempt to solve a problem, whether simple or complex.

It can range from eating a candy bar to making a lucrative investment and beyond.

Our behavioral patterns tell something about our basic personality. Can you not, for example, say something about two people, one eating a rich chocolate dessert and the other a diet food supplement?

But let's talk first about similarities. Take the concepts of human needs, desires, and motives. A need is something required for comfort and well-being, even existence. A good example would be food. A desire is something we want (like variety); it has less pulling power. A motive is something that drives us toward some goal, and is the source of the term "motivation."

We can make predictions about people because human needs are so similar. Yet there are differences too, because those needs are handled in such a variety of ways. Though food quells a particular need, hunger, what is appetizing varies from country to country. Basic needs, desires, and motives all push us in a direction but in most cases we still make the ultimate decision, one that is based on how we function psychologically.

Psychological needs or motives are highly complicated for a number of reasons. There may be several that contradict one another, and they all may involve unconscious motives, ones of which we are unaware. For example, an individual who begins to overeat believes that he does so because he is working harder and needs the food. The real reason may be that he is depressed and is looking for diversion.

The bad consequence of being ruled by unconscious motives is that a measure of control is lost. The individual is often pulled in a direction that he or she really doesn't want to go. The direction may even place the person in jeopardy.

Take, for example, a young woman I saw who appeared to many to be self-destructive. There were hints she might have made a number of suicidal gestures, though she denied it. An interview with her husband failed to shed any light; he seemed genuinely concerned. He felt his wife's behavior had changed when he got a job promotion and started working longer hours.

That piece of information helped us understand what was happening. The young wife admitted that she had been happier when she could spend more time with her husband. He reminded her a little of her father, who had also worked long hours. The difference was that her father didn't raise her very much and didn't respond to her needs when he was more available.

"When did he?" I asked.

She paused for a few moments and then she said, "I remember that my dad was always there when I got hurt. He spent a lot of time with me when I twisted my knee badly in soccer. It felt good having him there!"

She had learned to associate closeness with pain. Her motive was not self-harm but getting more attention. We were able to suggest some techniques to help her reach that goal more constructively.

Most people use a logic system that is built on either/or type thinking. Human nature would be more fathomable if that were true, but life just doesn't work that way. We are all aware that we can both be drawn and repelled by something. That's where ambivalence comes in.

Take a simple example most of us have experienced. We've been dieting and feel really good about the way we look. But that piece of rich chocolate cake looks very good. We love it for the taste we know it will have. We hate it for the calories it will give us.

Most of us find that when we gratify one need we rebuff another. That frequent conflict can lead to indecisiveness. Perhaps another illustration will help clarify this type of conflict: Tom as a normal, healthy man has social needs. He desires conversation with those who are important in his life, and he needs affection from them too. He loves talking politics, business, and especially sports. Tom is generally regarded as a good conversationalist and is respected for his vast fund of knowledge. Some of the people who seek conversations with him do so because they desire business information. Many of Tom's stock tips turn out to be winners.

Tom's sons also like to talk to him and love doing sports activities with him. Their faces reflect a good deal of joy every time they go to the back yard to play catch.

Spending time with his wife is also very important to Tom. He enjoys her company, likes to talk to her about her work and his, and the two exercise together regularly.

Tom enjoys his work. He feels that the other employees are very compatible with one another and with him. Tom likes his boss and feels that he is given ample time to fulfill his creative needs. Tom has the opportunity to work with people, which gratifies his social needs.

From an outsider's view, what could possibly be objectionable? Time spent with wife, children, fellow employees, boss, and co-workers all seems highly rewarding. From time to time Tom has been elected to positions at his social and athletic clubs, so any need for political control was met. However, a clue that something was wrong showed itself first in that arena and then with his job.

Tom always felt a great obligation to provide for his family. He came from a poor family and felt that had it not been for his athletic scholarship he could not have afforded a college education. He wanted to be sure his sons had whatever education they wanted. He knew it could be expensive: One son talked of being a doctor, the other a graphic artist.

Tom was offered another job that would pay much more but would require a move. He knew his family loved their current location—but still it would be more money. Tom also realized that he would have to work longer hours and this gradually became more unacceptable. He had resigned all his political positions to see if he could work longer hours and still have family time. He was attempting a trial run and he didn't like what he saw.

Tom now began to realize that he was caught between various needs so that when he fulfilled one he neglected another. For example, he loved his sons and yearned to spend more time with them, and his sons couldn't understand why he worked so hard. The older boy even showed a guilt reaction when he told his father he didn't need "more toys and stuff." College was so far away they couldn't see why all the hard work was needed now. They offered to baby sit and save money themselves.

Tom's wife, Cindy, didn't like the limited time they spent together. She felt Tom wasn't as affectionate as he once had been, probably because he was so drained. Cindy also mentioned that Tom had lost the time for himself that he once cherished so much. Cindy noted they were successful but not as happy or fulfilled as they had been.

When Tom sought professional help, he was asked to list all the needs that he recognized and see where the conflict came in. His listing looked like this:

Need		Opposite Need
1). Spending time with children	-	Working long hours
2). Wanting to be a good father	-	Earning more money
3). Being affectionate with Cindy	-	Needing more money
4). Wanting to develop his "self"	-	Needing more money
5). Socializing with friends	-	Need to be with family
6). Moving away to higher earnings	-	Need to be with family
7). Talking with his children	-	Need to earn more money
8). Going out with Cindy	-	Need to earn more money and needing to be with friends and fellow workers

When the various needs are presented in this manner, it becomes easy to see how people are pulled in a number of directions at the same time. Sometimes there appears to be no way out. A man has a need to be a good father and that means spending time with his children. But a father needs to be a provider too.

Realization of self is a crucial part of an individual's development. I believe that it's impossible to feel complete without a solid self-identity. Yet society does not recognize the importance of that and is quick to call people "selfish" or "self-centered." We see that in particular with women. We know women generally have a need to nurture, but can't they also wish for self-actualization in employment and achievement?

Tom was instructed to make a hierarchy of his needs as best he could. Then he was asked to try to balance his life out; for example, what income figure did he really need? He realized that he was resentful when socialization outside his family took away his personal time. He increased his physical activity and included his boys in it a little more. He had more private dinners with Cindy, and during one of these he got a surprise: Cindy wanted a business of her own. As Tom listened he was sure it would be successful. He helped her get started and 15 months later he was working with her. They have now become successful (able to meet their needs) from a number of perspectives.

Life is a great balancing act. We must all recognize that what works for one will not work for another. It's hard, for example, to decide what's an adequate amount of socializing. The person who's strong on socializing may well enjoy entertaining for his business; the person who values private time will likely feel resentful about a great deal of business entertaining.

Added to this balancing act is the fact that psychological needs, desires, and motives often over-lay other need systems. Earning money, for example, can be related to the realistic need to pay expenses, (e.g., college) but it can also respond to a psychological need to prove adequacy. Doing things differently can be the result of a creative bent or the psychological need to rebel. How can we determine which are the predominant motives? For now let's just say it relates to how compulsive the person is and the extent to which he is self-defeating. When one need predominates to the exclusion of all others, the time to be suspicious has arrived.

More on that later. At present we wish to comprehend basic human functioning, what causes people to behave as they do. To do that, we need to understand a person's basic personality so that we can at least somewhat predict future behavioral patterns. Toward that goal the following definitions and models seem helpful as used here:

- The term personality refers to habitual approaches to problem-solving. Some may regard this as too superficial; they would prefer to mention all those traits that make us unique. This observation has merit, but all those unique traits are used for goal-directed behavior which in turn necessitates problem-solving to reach the goal. Therefore we offer the following model:

- Where E refers to our ego and DM to our defense mechanisms.
- Ego refers to our concepts about our "self," to those processes through which we make our contact with the outside world.
- Defense mechanism refers to those techniques that our egos use to defend themselves. A look at the model shows us that the circle around the ego has some holes in it; it is not solid. The same is true of the circle defining the defense mechanism. These holes indicate a vulnerability, and the arrow shows a place of attack or threat.

We have all at one time or another seen examples of this. We have all known someone who knew just where another person was sensitive. I recall a man who knew just when to point out that some woman had gained a few pounds. He never seemed to do this to those who were not insecure about their weight. Several women tried to fight back but it never bothered him. I suggested making reference to his hair loss and that hit pay dirt!

People are not all bothered by the same thing. In fact many are hurt by something that the rest of us think unimportant. One person is often surprised, amazed, even shocked at what upsets another person. A prime reason for this is that people try to hide those things that upset them, using the various defense mechanisms.

Let's return to the model. If the ego is strong it can handle threats directly, so it doesn't need powerful defense mechanisms. The threat is seen more as a challenge that the strong or healthy ego can handle. The primary sign of threat not readily handled is anxiety. Anxiety is a type of fear where the object or source of fear is not known. People can more easily deal with what they can see; the unknown is more frightening.

The weaker the ego, the greater the anxiety when a threat is perceived. In fact, if the threat is far more than the ego can handle, there is a tendency to escape by losing contact with reality. The ego is saying, "I can't stand the pressure from the world, so I will withdraw from the world." The ego shatters and the person withdraws from social and often even physical contact with the world.

While this may seem impossible, I have seen several people who counted their computers among those who plotted against them. Their problems started with people problems and the feeling that no one could be trusted. Then, when they had programming problems, even the computers became enemies. In short order these people were in a power struggle, and feeling helpless, they felt vulnerable to outside forces.

There are basic misunderstandings about the strong ego. Some might ask, "If someone had a powerful ego, wouldn't they be self-centered and would they have *any* anxiety? The anxiety would depend on the situation. The world can be a threatening place, but if the threat emanates from reality it's realistic.

People with strong self-identities don't need to constantly toot their own horn. Being comfortable with yourself let's you be genuinely interested in others. You bridge the gap between them and yourself and find it easy to empathize. Strength allows you to see the other person's viewpoint. The person with ego strength will use defenses as needed, but realistically. She will want growth, challenge, social contact, and new experience. She will look at herself rather than quickly blaming others.

Now let's consider the person with a weak ego. First, he will not like new experiences because they may pose a hidden threat. For the same reason, he will forever be distrustful of others. Consequently, he will not be the open person that someone with a strong ego will be. Others will see him as distant, guarded, inflexible, and quick to reject them. People interacting will find that they never really know him; often he may be playful to the point of being evasive. While he may joke, serious intimate talk poses a threat. Finally, he will have a rigid, defensive approach. We can conclude that our defense mechanisms help reduce loss of reality contact, ego deterioration, and anxiety, but they also reduce our ability to live a full and involved life.

Note the outer circle in our model denoting the defense mechanisms. We don't plan to mention all of the defense mechanisms that can be employed because the reader will easily get the idea from these:

1. *Denial.* This is one of the most popular mechanisms. The individual reduces his anxiety by disavowing his thoughts and feelings.

For example, a man who is angry at his mother can't face the feeling and pushes the impulse out of his mind.

2. *Reaction formation.* Here the person's behavior patterns are just the opposite of what he feels. For example, a person who actually has great hostility toward others in order to hide his anger becomes a very gentle nurse. Though acting as a protector, he unconsciously feels rage. The clue is an over-zealous attack on something he says he's against—like other people's anger.

3. *Compensation.* This is an attempt to make up for a weakness. For example, a student, feeling inadequate because he lacks athletic ability, may overwork obsessively in the classroom.

4. *Identification.* With this mechanism a person attempts to pattern himself after someone else. We see this to a lesser degree whenever we watch a sporting event, for there are many who unconsciously attempt to behave like their hero.

5. *Projection.* Here a person experiences a feeling or thought that is unacceptable to her. She then attributes that thought or feeling to someone else. For example, a person who can't face her jealousy of a fellow worker who is very productive convinces herself that the fellow worker is jealous of her. This is a very important defense mechanism because many tests, called "projective tests," are based on this principle. Quite often when people think they are describing someone else they are really describing themselves.

6. *Conversion.* Freud found this mechanism common in his time. It turns ideas into bodily symptoms. He reported paralysis with no physical basis that made it virtually impossible for the person to do something unacceptable to her value system.

7. *Dissociation.* Here the affect surrounding some object or event is separated from that object. Many may recall stories of people who were abused as children dissociating the feelings from the acts.

8. *Undoing.* Remember the game children played: "Step on a crack, break your mother's back?" That might have meant that some hostile act or impulse took place and now the person tries to do something in the opposite manner to undo or reverse the original act.

9. *Sublimation.* With this defense the person switches from something not highly acceptable to something more acceptable. This all sounds very comfortable until you see all the unanswered questions. Case in point: I saw a young man who had plenty of talent but just could not get ahead. He was aware that he always seemed

to do something to disrupt his success, usually by becoming very passive and draining too much energy by giving to others. He just didn'tknow why. When he began to talk about his father, he described him as having a dislike for anything that was unacceptable to others. His father never wanted to offend anyone. My patient was taught that people won't like you if you do too well. Consequently, when he came near success his anxiety level rose until he failed or at least became less assertive. Freed from the indoctrination of father's ideas, he was able to be successful and still do an adequate amount for others.

10. *Rationalization.* This is a defense mechanism often used by bright, well-educated people. It gives a phony reason for something that was done; the real reason is not acceptable so you invent another. The best example I ever heard came from a fellow therapist. He said one day a patient of his came in and announced that he had just given up smoking. Without being asked he gave nine reasons for the decision. His therapist said, "O.K. what's the real reason?" The client seemed to sink in his chair. He paused and then said, "Well, my wife wanted me to."

This list will be adequate for our general purposes but to be complete, we should recognize that there is no universal agreement on the list. Professionals with different theoretical positions often disagree among themselves.

There is one other necessary word of caution; most of human behavior has multiple motives. For example, earning money can be motivated by a need for power, to feel important, to feel more secure, because of love for the activity that brings it, and to be able to give to others. All these can exist together.

With that understanding it should be helpful to describe some examples of different ego structures.

Case 1: Jim has never felt important to his parents. When he did accomplish something, there was either criticism or no reaction at all. He often said that the latter was probably worse. Because his parents were quiet people and often very busy, they didn't talk to him very much, though at least they didn't abuse him, so as a result he didn't see the world as dangerous. Jim's parents were hard-working, productive people who gave him many material things. They sent him to wonderful summer camps. They also let their son know that they did a lot for him by spending on his schooling, musical education, and any sport in which he excelled. Fun activities were not stressed because his parents didn't do things "just for fun."

When Jim did experience failure, his parents still didn't say much: they just looked at him as if to say, "How could you?" Jim was not happy to have his parents watch him in sports but he did want more attention from someone.

Here then is Jim's ego model:

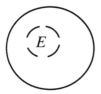

We note holes in the ego that denote the lack of a strong self-concept. Because Jim never felt important to his parents, he never felt important himself. He was the classic lack-of-confidence type of guy—everything posed a threat to his self-esteem. His defenses were so rigidly strong that they didn't allow him to try anything new. He was afraid to accept challenges and even more afraid to make decisions. He shifted responsibility to others and then became angry when things turned out badly.

He recalled that when he started dating he either didn't go out or he sought the girls no one else asked out. Once he went out with a girl who asked him for a date on a "girl's choice" event. They had a good time but Jim never asked her out again. Why? He said he knew he wouldn't be able to impress her once she knew what he was really like. Later when he did get married he gave his wife a hard time, alternately feeling she too must be defective or was too good for him. As you would guess, he was a very jealous man!

Jim's rigid defense mechanisms were denial, projection, compensation, and rationalization. He said other people were critical of him when he was actually the critical one. He said he was too busy to deal with the pettiness of others, he denied any feeling of inadequacy, and he substituted money for strong social skills and intimacy. He often criticized men in general because he felt they wanted to dominate women—just the way his wife said he behaved.

Jim's behavior around business and particularly investments was most revealing. First, money-making was vital to his adjustment. It served to build his ego, made him feel important, and gave him something to say he was better than others.

But nothing makes up for feelings of inadequacy. Those affected need more and more to prove themselves. Success produced a good feeling only for about four days. Then one of two things happened:

1. Jim began to feel guilt for his success because he knew he was not really that gifted. That made him feel that atonement was coming and at times he called his investment counselor in a near state of panic. "Was the market going to drop suddenly?" he would ask his bewildered counselor.

2. Or he would ask about his other investments. "Are they going down to the point where my profit on the good investment will be lost? Should we get out of the market for a time? Are there any other investments that look good? When should they move up? Are you really watching my investments?"

We must remember that when people don't trust themselves because of low self-esteem, they also don't trust their decisions, including their selection of people to serve them. Low self-esteem also causes dependent behavior, because when you don't trust yourself you need to overly rely on others. The poor counselor to a Jim is likely to get many calls from his client to verify his investment picture. Not only that: The counselor is in an impossible position. If he takes any risk (and everything involves *some* risk), then he may be questioned. If he doesn't, he will be questioned for not trying to make bigger and bigger profits. Decision making will be shifted to the counselor, but he will then be questioned with regularity.

Sounds like fun, doesn't it? What can the investment counselor do? Just recognize the problem, realize that you didn't create it, then do your best to protect yourself.

Case 2: Myra presents a classic reaction formation defense mechanism. Looking at Myra Dixon's model, we note again a very thick line for the defense mechanisms. In Myra's case this means not only low self-esteem but also profound fear of expressing emotion. Myra is somewhat aware of her inner rage just waiting to explode. She's a walking bomb! However, you can't easily tell that by looking at her because 90 percent of the time she's quiet, passive, and either superficially friendly or withdrawn.

Myra presents a classic reaction formation defense mechanism. How did she get like this? Her statements about her childhood were that "I hardly knew a day that I didn't get hit." She stated that both of her parents were alcoholics who often became violent with no warning. She could never therefore predict what behavior she might show that would lessen the beatings. Myra had two broken arms from her father and a facial scar from her mother. At age 15 she was removed from her home because the abuse was finally seen by someone who wanted it stopped. She was placed in a foster home but didn't know how to behave in a more typical family setting. She left her second home at age 17 and has been on her own ever since.

Myra did well in school once she was on her own. A bright woman, she had visions of getting ahead. She went into sales but had problems because of her temper. Then her creativity was discovered and she used graphic arts and other talents to get ahead. She became a master of deception; people meeting her for the first time thought she was very mellow—until they got on her "bad side."

That bad side showed itself whenever she felt someone had crossed her or taken advantage of her. Her low self-esteem told her that she was a "door mat that people liked to stamp on till I start stamping back." She could not stand to have people see any weakness because she was sure that she would then be abused. Though she was always overly friendly, Myra didn't let people get close. She used her smile to control other people, sometimes saying to herself, "If he only knew what I'm thinking."

Myra earned good money and that plus an inheritance soon gave her funds to invest. Her investment counselor saw her rigid powerful defensive structure and her seemingly gentle manner. He was unprepared for her explosion the first time he had advised an investment that didn't work out. He tried to explain but was never given a chance. He was wise enough to keep silent until Myra stopped berating him.

When he was able to get a word in, he talked to Myra about her investment philosophy. "Didn't you want a few investments that carried a little risk with the probability of good gain?"

Myra said, "Of course, but what you advised went down. In retrospect it was too risky."

Every time the investment advisor thought he was in sync with her, Myra exploded. Never knowing what to expect, he ultimately told Myra he just couldn't take the unforeseen explosions. If he sold some stock at a profit, Myra often became angry because it might have gone higher. If a stock did go higher, Myra might become angry because it took too long. Sometimes when the advisor couldn't reach her he couldn't get into a rising stock at the point where it was moving up. But if he didn't check in with Myra first, she would be even more angry if the stock went down.

Her advisor finally gave up and referred Myra to another advisor. That relationship failed too. Other advisors commented that Myra seemed like a really "sweet, easy going gal:" How could she be difficult to invest for? They soon found out and they gave up.

Myra found the perfect solution: She bought a computer and everything else required and began to do her own investing. However, like all of us she wasn't to know perfect success. She didn't have an advisor to scream at now—but at least one computer ended up on the trash heap!

Case 3: Finally, in the Bill Hill model, we see that the ego line is strong and continuous. It is just what it represents: a strong ego. We don't assume total ego strength because nothing is perfect. Strength is relative and everyone has areas of uncertainty and vulnerability.

The circle representing Bill's ego is not totally unbroken but the holes are tiny. With all that ego strength Bill does not need powerful defense mechanisms. Those defenses that he does have are reality based and used only when there is some external pressure. Even then Bill uses these defenses only for a short time. The prime example Bill recalls was when his wife Cathy needed surgery and Bill felt a need to deny the possibility that he might lose her.

Bill's childhood and adolescence give important clues to his personality. Bill was very close to both his parents but in different ways. He saw his mother as someone highly protective and easy to listen to. She worried somewhat and gave him directions as far as "staying safe," as she called it. She seldom became angry. When she did, she was able to talk it out with her son. Bill felt that most of the advice she gave him was good advice, and it was not offered in a demanding manner. Bill described her as having "a world of patience," and saw her as slow to ever see something negative about him.

Bill's dad was both similar and different. He was strikingly similar in that Bill felt important to dad just as he did to mother. His perception was that his parents had fun doing things with their children. They came to watch many of the children's activities, and they didn't become critical when some activity didn't go well.

Bill felt that his dad was a very open person who helped cultivate Bill's fantasy life. Bill recalled his dad saying that without imagination there could not be creativity. "You don't have to walk in someone else's footsteps, son, but know why you're going in another direction," Bill often heard his dad say. Dad was a great listener who seldom told others how he thought about anything. He encouraged his son to do his own thinking and "march to your own drummer."

Bill was an enigma to many who knew him. He was sociable but also liked his private time. People found him very direct and prone to make up his own mind. Yet he easily empathized with others. He quickly understood the position that people held but he seldom said whether he agreed. He often said that others should follow "what works for you."

Bill's friends described him as very secure, creative, and easygoing but able to say "no" when he felt the need. He was certainly not easily led. In fact Bill was seen as highly independent; many friends thought he would never marry because of that. When he did, he married a woman very much like himself.

With this background Bill's investment approach was predictable. He found an investment advisor who was very flexible. He made some conservative investments but also a few that were more daring. He set goals for himself, so he knew what profit he was seeking. As a rule he followed logical guidelines for his investments but he was well able to say "I was wrong" when he made a poor selection. He didn' tobsess on his failures, or on his successes. He didn't arbitrarily become angry at his advisor if things didn't go well. Although Bill can express his feelings, he has not been one to become overly guided by his emotions. Finally Bill has been willing to evaluate his own decisions so that he could tell someone just what his batting average is for all types of investments. That includes such things as type of stock, how conservative, how daring, and even tips from others.

People who know Bill well describe him as very open, direct, not argumentative but looking to select information from others. He is very diverse in his thinking but never impulsive and he relates well to others around him.

These are three personality types that help us see how the various ego types and their defenses work. It doesn't take a lot of thought to identify people we all know who fit these models. Before we become too condescending, though, let's realize that these are not pure types. There's a little of us in all of them, and of them in us.

How do we develop skill in identifying which model best fits people we know? First and foremost, learn to be a good *listener*; most people are not. Listen to what the person defends and to what produces the greatest emotional reaction. Note what is denied with any frequency; for example, the person who often says, "It's not that I don't trust your advice," is really saying he's worried because he doesn't trust your advice. Finally, look at behavior that seems atypical for this person. Inconsistencies usually show some concealed areas rich with conflict. Be quiet, look, and listen and you will see our models in much of human behavior.

Chapter IV
Mood Disorders

Our purpose with these next few chapters is not to become skilled diagnosticians. Instead we want to continue our approach, that is, to understand how our personalities affect investment performance. This chapter discusses our emotional life. For the sake of clarity we separate thinking and emotion, though in reality there is often a mixture. For example, a person can have a thought disorder and also show severe depression. If you really want to know about disorders, check out the most complete diagnostic manual, the American Psychiatric Association's *Diagnostic and Statistical Manual of Mental Disorders*, 4th edition (known as DSM-IV).

Mood disorders, which are very common, can wreak havoc in people's lives. It's not unusual for mood disorders to upset every area of a person's life, including relations with others.

Severe depressive disorder is a good place to start, because it's responsible for many psychiatric hospitalizations. Feelings of hopelessness, helplessness, and worthlessness abound. Sufferers often feel sad and empty. They may have difficulties with sleep, either too much or too little. They have markedly little interest in pleasure and with the onset of the depression they usually lose interest in activities they once enjoyed. Their personal appearance, perhaps once spotless, may now deteriorate. Weight gain or loss is common, as is fatigue. Some depressed persons become agitated; some become slowed. It is not at all uncommon for them to have problems concentrating. It's not surprising all these negative feeling can result in suicide.

We can easily see how this unhappy picture can affect investment. The very fact that some people have less interest in the world will limit their investment knowledge. Someone who feels worthless is likely to not care about anything—including investments. The severely depressed person, not trusting his judgment, will not want to make decisions. Often he may blame others for decisions he himself actually made.

A depressive disorder may last for years; when it does, it becomes harder for the lay person to diagnose because there is no before to contrast with the after. If, for example, you have known a person for two years who has been depressed for four, you may assume that "he's just that way."

How can you detect who is suffering from depression? If you review the symptoms we described, you'll have a good start. Be aware, though, that the same depressive disorder can cause opposite behavioral reactions, e.g., weight gain or loss. Take a good look at extremes of behavior.

As you will find over and over, change is most significant. I recall a lovely women in her late fifties who always greeted everyone with a smile. She was outgoing, talkative, a good listener, and skilled at getting people to talk to her. Then almost overnight the smile faded and so did her interest in others. One of her fellow workers who succeeded in getting her to talk learned that her daughter was very ill. Talking out her feelings helped some but it was only when her daughter's early diagnosis proved wrong that the depression went away. The beautiful smile returned.

We should always keep in mind that not all problems stem from childhood conflicts. Organic change, life stress, money problems, and many other current difficulties can cause depression. The key for recognition is change.

Not all depressive disorders are long term, but these brief episodes can at times be even more significant. After all, when something is always present we're more apt to recognize and adjust to it. Then, too, investments are often made very quickly; a short-term depression may without warning influence the decision-making process.

At the other extreme are those suffering from mania. A brief manic episode lasts for at least a week but may be longer. The usual symptom pattern poses a great threat to investment strategy. One symptom is increased feelings of omnipotence and infallibility. The person's energy level increases so that there is less need for sleep; there is often rapid speech and racing thoughts. The person is likely to be distractible, jumpy, overactive, pushing toward rapid and excessive work. She may become overinvolved in pleasurable activities (like shopping) to the point of danger. Decisions are impulsive and irrational. During these episodes many people become irritable when someone disagrees with them. Their feeling is that others do not recognize their genius; they may even accuse the other party of jealousy. Won't that be a fun person to advise!

Another disorder has features of both mania and depression. Once known as manic-depressive disorder, it's now called bipolar disorder. There are essentially three varieties of bipolar disorder: in one, where there are more manic phases, in another depression predominates, and in the third there is fluctuation. In some situations one cycle predominates for long periods; at the other extreme there can be what is called "rapid cycling," where the person may literally be depressed one minute and then climbing the walls the next.

In the investment context we're discussing, this disorder poses a great threat. One of my clients would buy a number of glamorous stocks when he was on a high. Later, when he would slip into his depressive cycle, he would order his broker to sell "everything that's down." There were times when he sold stocks that promptly moved higher. The fact that someone can go from high to low to high again makes it hard to read that person. As soon as the advisor adjusts to one strategy he has to cope with a major change. Besides, when depressed, the person as a rule becomes more dependent because he does not trust his judgment. When manic elation sets in, he trusts his judgment too much.

Two other mood disorders should be mentioned in passing. In cyclothymic disorder, there are mood swings but they are not as intense as in a major depression or bipolarity. The less intense emotional reaction often makes diagnosis difficult, but there is enough reaction to cause problems with investment approaches.

Dysthymic disorder presents itself with many symptoms similar to those of a severe (major) depressive disorder. (If a person has ever been diagnosed with manic episodes the diagnosis of dysthymic disorder is not made.) A major problem in diagnosing this disorder is that victims do not recognize the symptoms unless a trained person asks specific questions. It becomes so much a part of someone's life that they accept the symptoms as just part of their make-up. Dysthymic disorders, which can last several years, can be disruptive. After all, anything that attacks your self-esteem will have a destructive influence on your life!

The major thing to note with these last two disorders is that they are not likely to be detected by looking for change. They have become so much a part of the person's life that they seem natural. In that case you still need to note the symptoms and, with understanding, help the person adjust.

In many diagnostic manuals, anxiety disorders are listed separately from mood disorders. We have put them together because it makes more sense here. Anxiety is an emotion, and a very uncomfortable one, but so are depression and mania. Many who experience depression, feeling unable to cope, also become anxiety-ridden. Then, too, those who are anxious when they are with others may become depressed due to isolation.

What is anxiety? Most of us have experienced it at one time or another; the symptoms are certainly like those of being fearful. For example, among the criteria for panic attacks are fears of dying, of going crazy, and of losing control. Many have reported bodily sensations like sweating, rapid heartbeat, and shortness of breath. It is as if the person is under attack. Perhaps the main differentiation is that with anxiety the source of the threat is often unknown.

The problems created by anxiety are numerous. Whenever we are frightened our scope narrows. If we are alert for threats, we don't have time to see the bigger picture. When your heart is pounding you don't look at your investments calmly. And when fearful, people doubt their abilities to cope with a situation. They consistently expect the worst.

So what are they going to do with their investments? Well, the first thing we would expect would be constant fear that things will not turn out well. They will be on the phone immediately with any mild drop in the value of their investments. If their investment goes up, though, all should be well, right? For a time that might be the case, but soon their fears take over again. "Maybe things have gone too well," they say. "Let's get out now while we still have a profit."

As long as fear dominates our thinking, behaving rationally is unlikely. The tendency is to see threat all around, to run from imaginary fears, and thereby to miss really good investments.

For the sake of clarity we mention a variety of anxiety disorder, the panic attack. The onset of this disorder is abrupt. The fear reaches its high as a rule in 10 to 15 minutes. One common variety is agoraphobia, the fear of being in a situation or place that produces such discomfort that the place is hard to get out of. The bodily sensations, like choking, are very upsetting.

This is one form of disorder that does not seem to affect investment functioning much except that the victim may feel that he must get away. He will not have confidence in anything being safe and will feel he can't adequately cope. Withdrawal is common.

Then there is the post-traumatic stress disorder (PTSD), defined from experiences of military personnel during the Vietnam war. The essence of the disorder is that a most unusual and frightening trauma experienced under threat of death or serious injury is re-experienced over and over. Persons with PTSD often withdraw because they are so fearful and feel severely unable to cope.

As far as PTSD having an impact on investments I think it not very likely. We may all feel traumatized by the stock market at times but that doesn't meet the requirement for this disorder. A PTSD victim who experiences "flashbacks" is likely to want to get away and pull himself together. He won't be giving or receiving much investment information.

We are all aware that the seasons and holidays can have a major impact on our emotional lives. When the days grow short and the temperature is cold, some people literally become withdrawn. Still others will say, "That's when I catch up with my reading." Summer may produce so much pleasure that we escape to the golf course. Holidays can stimulate happiness, sadness, companionship, or loneliness. To make your best investment record, you should know how these periods affect you.

There is one more emotion that should be mentioned because it can do so much damage. That is guilt. We won't offer any final definition of what it is; there are too many already. Suffice it to say that it is a feeling of wrongdoing or inadequacy. It probably has much in common with anxiety in that often tests that measure anxiety also produce high scores on guilt feelings. One myth must immediately be dispelled: that we feel guilt only when we do something that our cultural group feels is wrong.

Take being successful. Who could ever feel guilt over that? Yet I have actually encountered it many times in my work as a sports psychologist. I recall a wonderful golfer, Betty. She had a nice college career and seemed headed for professional success. But suddenly, on the brink of success, she began to fall apart. She often commented that she didn't deserve success and her fine game deteriorated.

When Betty came for help, it was striking how often she spoke about her father and *his* life. She was encouraged to tell more. It turned out that her father had once hoped for a career as a competitive golfer. He had failed. He wanted to travel but never had the money. Betty's father wanted to work outside; he never could. Betty did both as part of her golf career.

In an unguarded moment, Betty talked about how guiltridden she felt doing all the things her dad never could. With a few visits she learned and overcame her self-defeating approach and became successful. As it turned out, her dad was so joyful that Betty didn't defeat herself any more.

Just like anxiety or depression guilt feelings can cause irrational doubts that take away our success. These feelings can cause us to run from the world and refuse to keep up with what is happening. At the other extreme, manic feelings can cause us to make impulsive decisions.

Knowing yourself is vital. Recognizing how your moods influence your decisions will greatly help. Take into consideration what your moods do to your investment approach and then note how they affect your clients—and how their moods affect you.

It would seem incomplete to leave this chapter without providing one case history of a person afflicted with a mood disorder. Because the one selected goes back a long way, it illustrates differences in treatment programs through the years.

Case: As far as we know when Sam Woods's mother was pregnant with him, his delivery was unremarkable. There was only one comment family members remembered. Shortly after delivery Sam's mother said that Sam "looks bored." That comment came back to haunt her when Sam began to have problems.

But that was down the road. Sam's early development was all quite normal. He was slightly slow starting to walk, but once he learned he walked a great deal. His mother again offered a comment that people always seemed to remember. She said, "He walks so fast that I think he wants to get away from me."

Mrs. Woods did state that she felt somewhat insecure about being a mother because it took her so long to become one. Sam, as it turned out, would be her last as well as first born child. From her comments it sounded as if she were pleased because "one is about all I can handle."

Her friends could not fathom these comments because they saw Sam as not at all oppositional and not at all demanding. If anything he was on the quiet side. Sam enjoyed his many toys that could be played with only one person, even when they were intended to be used by two or more. When electrical games came along, Sam was by himself for hours.

Mrs. Woods thought she heard Sam talking to someone else on numerous occasions. She assumed he was using imaginary playmates, as she knew he was alone. However, she never inquired, and Sam never offered. Mrs. Woods often stated that boys need to have some time to themselves. "As long as he isn't making a fuss up in his room I don't check up on him," she observed.

Sam gave a number of signs that he was a bright little boy. He used some big words when talking with his father and he learned some reading skills even before starting school. He also became adept at playing electrical games. Sam often showed skill at talking about many of the places the family had visited in the summer. People were often surprised at some of Sam's comments because he was not one to volunteer much conversationally.

Mr. Woods was also on the quiet side; many of their friends commented that Sam and his father were very similar. Both enjoyed doing things by themselves and could do that for hours at a time. Neither had much to say, but when they did talk they showed their intelligence. Mr. Woods was an auto mechanic and Sam showed interest in his work. It was clear that father preferred working with objects rather than people and Sam seemed headed in the same direction. Neither father nor son liked to ask others for advice or help. In fact, Mr. Woods had nearly died with a ruptured appendix because he hadn't wanted to disclose his pain.

It used to drive Mrs. Woods wild the way that Sam and his father would spend time together and not talk. "How can you do that?" she asked. "We didn't have anything to talk about," Sam replied.

There was another significant trait that Mrs. Woods failed to recognize. Because she could not read Sam, she could not tell how he felt. As a rule mothers are able to recognize the different moods of their children, but not in the Woods's case. Mrs. Woods felt again the similarity to his father. "It's like they only have one mood," she said.

On occasion Sam left the house and his cherished room to go outside, but he still stayed by himself even when there were neighborhood boys that he could have done something with. One or two boys came over to the Woods's house to play with Sam, who was in the backyard. The visitors tried to get a game of some kind started. Sam just kept playing by himself and when asked said only one person at a time could play.

The years passed without much that was highly eventful. When Sam entered grade school, each school report mentioned Sam's lack of involvement with other children. The teachers all liked Sam because they felt he was easy to teach, perhaps because Sam never asked any questions, never raised his hand, never had to be told anything twice, always had the correct answer when called upon. One teacher commented, "If all my students were like him, teaching would be a dream."

In fifth grade Sam's grade school started a wrestling team with a coach who had placed in national competitions. He was a low-key, highly supportive person that nearly everyone loved. Coach Glenn was the sort of dynamic leader whose teaching inspired dedication. Coach Glenn first met Sam in one of the gym classes and the two showed a fine rapport.

Sam went out for wrestling entirely on his own. His mother was pleased because it was one of the first things she had seen Sam do with other people. She was also pleased to see Sam make a decision on his own. Sam's father didn't say much of anything to Sam or his mother. He did tell Sam that he looked forward to being able to see him wrestle. Sam made some excuses about not being ready yet to show what he could do. It didn't matter to his father—he just said he would wait until Sam said it was okay to come.

Sam's wrestling career went along well. He learned new moves rapidly and skillfully applied them in his matches. He seldom showed any emotion and his coach felt this worked to his advantage. His opponent could not tell when Sam was tired or hurting. The coach liked Sam's discipline.

When Sam lost a match and was given constructive criticism, he tended to withdraw and pout. Coach Glenn tried to reach Sam but that was increasingly difficult. Then, in an effort to reach Sam, he sat near him on the bench. He put his arm around Sam's shoulders and tried to get him to show some emotional response. His motive was to help Sam see that the criticism was part of learning.

Sam didn't react favorably, however; he looked right at his coach and then got up and walked out. Coach Glenn was sure that he would come and talk to him after the wrestling meet. However, when the team returned to the locker room Sam was nowhere in sight. Sam didn't show up for school the next day and he didn't come to practice. Coach Glenn was against chasing after him because his philosophy was that young men had to take responsibility for their own actions. However, coach had to put a team together. If Sam was not going to wrestle, coach had to know and so he called.

Sam refused to talk to his coach and his parents were divided on how to handle the situation. His mother felt that Sam should talk to his coach. His father said it was up to Sam to make that decision. So Sam did not. He asked his father to turn in his wrestling uniform. When Mr. Woods did, he avoided any questions Coach Glenn had.

Sam had nothing to say when any of his classmates made comments, whether they supported what he did or supported the coach. Whatever was said produced no reaction in Sam.

The school counselor was concerned. He invited Sam's parents to meet with him. Mr. Woods said he couldn't come, he was just too busy at his work. Mrs. Woods said she would like a meeting. At first the counselor suggested she wait until Mr. Woods could come in. When that looked as if it would never happen, Counselor Matt Blair invited Mrs. Woods to meet with him.

Matt was the sort of man who never wasted any time getting to basic issues. He observed Mrs. Woods' tension but that didn't slow him down.

"I asked you to come and meet with me because I am very concerned about your son Sam," he began.

"But he's back in school again, so he must be okay," Mrs. Woods protested.

Matt recognized a communication problem. He had sent a signal that something was wrong with her son. In her mind that implied that there was something wrong with her as a mother. That was more than she could handle, at least at this time. As Matt looked at her across the table, he had the feeling that she was shrinking. Of course she wasn't, but she was sinking into her chair. A second glance told Matt that there were small tears falling down her checks.

Matt addressed what he felt was her concern: "I think most of us as parents feel blame whenever there appear to be problems with one of our children. In point of fact there are many things that cause problems. You, I'm sure, have been a very good mother."

Her tears increased for a few seconds and then Mrs. Woods smiled and thanked Matt for the kind words. Matt waited and then Mrs. Woods began talking again. She spoke of some concerns she had always had about her son. She was invited to tell Matt what her concerns were. She said she didn't know.

Matt directed her to try to describe what it was like to be with Sam. One very key question that Matt asked was how she felt being with Sam. What were her feelings?

That hit a nerve. Knowing how we feel when we are with a person tells us something of what that person is feeling also. Mrs. Woods' head droopped a little for a few seconds. Then she looked up at Matt and answered his question. "My feelings were that I was shut out, that I couldn't share with him, and couldn't even reach him. My own son." Understandably the tears came heavily now.

Matt gave her some time to pull herself together before coming to the point. He assured her that he understood her feelings, thinking how painful they must be to a mother. Then he cautiously mentioned some of the things he saw that concerned him about Sam: "Mrs. Woods, what concerns me is that I have never seen Sam smile or for that matter, laugh."

Mrs. Woods thought for a while and then agreed. She wondered why that had not occurred to her; while she never claimed to be an expert, it didn't seem right that she had failed to recognize his unhappiness. She asked Matt what he would recommend. He replied carefully. He stated that he would like to have Mrs. Woods talk to her husband about the meeting. Then if the Woodses agreed, he would like to refer the family to a clinical psychologist. Mrs. Woods agreed and accepted the card Matt handed her. It was a doctor that Matt felt was very good.

Mrs. Woods was worried but felt some relief because there might be help for Sam. However, she felt very down when her husband refused to consider any such move. He insisted that Sam didn'thave any problems other than being a typical young boy. Mr. Woods saw Sam as a "tough kid who doesn't have to gush with flowery emotions all the time." Mrs. Woods said that Sam didn't seem happy and didn't relate emotionally. He always seemed the same as far as what he showed.

Mrs. Woods could see that she and her husband had totally different impressions about what was going on with Sam. To her he was very unhappy, while her husband felt that he was normal because he had behaved similarly as a young person. Mrs. Woods felt at an impasse but held onto the card Matt gave her. She planned to go see Dr. Jones by herself one day.

Sam didn't go back to wrestling but he began raising his grade point average. He was quiet but didn't get into any trouble. He didn'thave many friends and he seemed more comfortable with others who were quiet and not very social.

Toward the end of sixth grade some of his classmates began teasing Sam and Sam showed signs of running away. Once he was cornered by a bully and without warming Sam exploded. The bully was startled and then showed fear himself. He was then ridiculed by some of the classmates who had been teasing Sam. For a time this took some pressure off Sam. He became a kind of hero who could be so powerful that even a verbal outburst could chase a bully away.

Some of his classmates approached Sam to try to be friendly, but admiration only goes so far. Sam never showed any friendly emotion back; he was as distant as usual. He had started to exhibit a little nervous laughter that didn't reflect any depth. There was still the feeling that he had only fake emotions.

There was another change, too, but this started during the summer. Sam had always been very neat about his appearance. In fact it had seemed that he became upset when he wasn't neat. Now that all changed. He looked as if he had slept in his clothes and at times he did. What was most striking was that he just didn't care.

The summer went fairly well for everyone but Mrs. Woods. She didn't feel she could help Sam because she couldn't reach him or her husband. There was no one to talk to and she showed signs of depression. She felt blocked and helpless and she still blamed herself for many of the problems she saw.

When school started in the fall it looked like more of the same. Coach Glenn approached Sam to try to get him to wrestle again. They were standing in the hall and Sam let out a scream that stopped everyone in their tracks. Coach was a gentle man and he didn't know what he might have done. He was embarrassed and wanted to help but didn't know how. While everyone was wondering what happened, Sam just left the school. He went home and went up to his room. He shut off the lights and lay down on his bed.

When Mrs. Woods heard about the problem, she went up to his room to look for him. She heard him mumbling to himself but she could not make out what he was saying. His posture was rigid and he didn't respond to her voice. She could not get him to talk to her about what had happened.

Mrs. Woods then made a couple of calls. Her first was to Mr. Woods. She described what had taken place at school. Then she described how he was behaving at this time. She felt Sam as well as they needed help. Mr. Woods agreed. Her second call was to Dr. Jones. He was pleasant over the phone and offered to stop by in the early evening to see Sam. He felt Sam would be more natural in his own home.

When Dr. Jones arrived Sam was behaving somewhat differently. He was not talking to himself but was instead lying in a very rigid posture. His muscles seemed so rigid it was as if they were frozen together.

Dr. Jones tried to talk to Sam but he never responded. In fact he acted as if he couldn't hear anything. Dr. Jones tried a few more times and then motioned Sam's parents to go outside with him.

As soon as they were seated and as relaxed as possible, Dr. Jones began trying to understand what had happened. He asked if there had been any similar kinds of behavior. Mr. Woods said no but his wife said she was not so sure. She described Sam's emotional expression or lack of it.

"All right," Dr. Jones started, "so he had what is called 'flat affect'. That means a narrow range of emotion." He paused, "Then he didn't appear happy or excited in a joyful way. Maybe it was difficult to know what he liked because he always seemed the same."

Dr. Jones then went on to state that flat affect is one clear sign of a mood disorder. So is the tendency to be so withdrawn. He then explained what was happening now. Sam was in a catatonic state, a state of extreme withdrawal and marked rigidity of the muscles, again a sign of a severe mood disorder.

Dr. Jones asked the parents to give him some idea when these symptoms were first manifested. Mother felt approximately around birth and dad more recently. Dr. Jones wondered if there had been any delusions like false beliefs or hearing voices. Both parents were sure there had not.

Then it was the parents' turn to ask questions. They wanted to know what caused this, what kind of disorder it was, and could it be cured. Mrs. Woods wondered about what she felt was the withdrawal and lack of emotional expression.

Dr. Jones took the questions one by one. He said there didn'tat this point seem evidence of a thought disorder but you can't be sure. It looked like a mood disorder of the schizophrenia type. What were the signs? Well, first the flat affect, the withdrawal, and then the catatonic state.

What causes this disorder? We used to blame the parents, especially the mother. Current thinking is that there is a lot more to it, probably some disorder of the brain. How curable is this disorder? Dr. Jones said it's hard to say but chances now are much better. He said that medication now available had been highly beneficial in many cases. There are also many who like some form of therapy.

Sam had to drop out of school for a few months but his medication worked very well. He was back in school the second quarter and able to handle his academic subjects. He didn't go back to wrestling, however. Sam had some additional problems before things got better. At one point he displayed inappropriate affect; an emotion that doesn't fit the current situation. As an example, he would be laughing when something depressing had happened.

During junior high and regular high school Sam continued to show a great deal of superficiality in his affect, but he did build some friendships. Though he still preferred keeping to himself, those close to him saw periods where he did enjoy social activities. For example, Sam enjoyed watching his school's athletic teams. Once in a while he took a girl with him but he still was distant emotionally. He also went to his senior prom but he didn't dance much. Sam still was very self-conscious about activities requiring movements of the body.

During his last year of high school Sam began to express some interest in an occupation. He talked of earning money and wanted to be productive. He knew that although he felt better around people he would probably never be basically a "people person." Because he mainly liked working with things, he began looking for that kind of job.

Sam's dad showed him how to repair small appliances. From that Sam went to bicycles and lawn mowers. Some of the time he made good money and he did enjoy the work.

Sam had a relapse shortly after graduating from high school and had to again be admitted to a mental hospital. When Sam suffered a breakdown, it always seemed to involve the emotions with no thought disorder. What usually took place was superficial affect. But Sam consistently responded favorably to treatment. He didn't need to be in a hospital for long.

Although it always seemed that the medication brought Sam out of his psychosis, it was the talking that helped him develop insight. He began to identify those things that set off his disorder. Sam realized that arguments were upsetting to him and he usually avoided them.

Sam realized that it took him longer than most to get to know people. He accepted that and allowed himself to sit back and observe before allowing closeness. Sam also learned how to tune people out when he found they were irritating or overly critical. In fact, at one point Sam put together a list of people he deemed important. Those were people whose opinion he sought. He jokingly said that if someone's name wasn't on that list he didn't care about his opinion.

As Sam's repair skills improved, so did his referrals. He got to the point where he needed to have someone handle his accounts. He approached his mother and she accepted. She had become less critical and her relationship with her son developed nicely. Now the two were able to work together. She eventually helped Sam increase his clientele by good advertising. Mrs. Woods thought about all the two of them accomplished. She didn't feel so shut out now.

The years rolled by and one day Sam realized that he was in his mid-twenties. He felt well established in his career now, making a surprisingly large income. And he loved it. Sam also found something else that he loved. She was a nurse named Jo. They seemed to have much in common and Jo was a good complement to Sam. Where Sam was brash and quick to withdraw, Jo was slow to lose her cool. She seemed to have endless patience. Sam confided to his mother that he had "found the one for me." When his mother met her she liked her right away. She was sure it would be a good marriage for Sam. She agreed with Sam's idea of telling Jo all about his health history.

Sam did tell her. To his delight she wasn't at all concerned. It turned out that Jo was rather well-to-do, having inherited an abundant trust from an uncle. She hoped that Sam would agree to their investing their money together. Sam wanted to think about that because he felt there was too much going on right now.

Sam arrived at adulthood after having much turmoil. His story is typical of others I have seen with this disorder. What is he like and what can we expect? That of course is variable, but Sam's life can be described very well because many of us knew him over the years.

Sam was a bright person; once he learned how to trust his doctors he made excellent progress. He learned, what he called "some important warning signals." That is, he saw behavioral patterns or feelings that told him when he was on the verge of "stressing-out," causing a short-term breakdown or a bad decision. This could happen in any area of his life. When he felt tension building up, he learned to see it and get away from people.

Jo also learned to recognize Sam's signs and she would then give him some distance. She knew when to bring up a business question and when to postpone it. She recognized when they were at an impasse and she too would pull back and engage herself in her own activities. She also could determine when she had to make a decision on her own.

Sam's emotional life still showed ups and downs. He always had a narrower emotional range than the average person. Happy or excited for him was what most people called just their day-to-day emotional state.

It took Jo a while to learn to interpret Sam's happy moods. In the beginning she thought he was only lukewarm on something when he was actually very enthused. His whole range of emotion was toward the low end. But his affect was not so bland and he had no more temper explosions. Sam still used withdrawal as a last resort when he was agitated. He never did have another catatonic state but he sometimes talked to himself.

Sam developed a keen sense of humor and many people found him pleasant in social situations. He and Jo appeared to have a strong marriage and became astute at sharing duties. She always was the one with a good business mind. Sam recognized that and supported Jo in that endeavor.

That leaves us with one very important relationship to delve into: investment advisor and Sam. Does the mood disorder affect Sam's investment approach? Indeed yes. His advisor, Ed, had known Sam in high school but he had to learn to recognize Sam's moods. One trait that took some adjusting to was Sam's lack of enthusiasm. Ed called Sam one day, for example, to tell him that a particular stock had doubled. Should we sell? Sam just said, "Sure"—no jubilation or enthusiasm.

Ed even repeated his statement and emphasized that it was a *profit*.

"Oh, that's nice," Sam said, very casually. Ed had to learn that this would probably be the extent of Sam's excitement.

When the investments went down, though, Sam quickly became very nervous. Consequently Ed could make only very conservative investments for Sam, though he could make more potentially big gainers for Jo.

Additionally, Ed could keep Jo appraised of how things were going, but not Sam. In short order Sam learned that he couldn't get very involved with investments because the tension was too much for him. Ed never shared any of his investment concerns with Sam.

Sam also didn't like change. His attitude was that if a stock is high, stay with it. If it's low, maybe you should get out. Sam was never comfortable with the idea that an investment can move quickly: "If it can go up quickly, it can also go down quickly."

Ed learned, too, that it helped Sam to be told that things were going well, provided they were. If investments were generally down, Ed could calm Sam by first telling him about those that were up. If none were up, Ed could still find something positive to mention to Sam. But the positive had to be presented first. Otherwise Sam would tune you out.

Together for a long time now, Sam, Ed, and Jo have been quite successful. There have been a few miscommunications, but everyone has these. When Sam was encouraged to write Ed notes on investment ideas and directives, that improved communication. Jo's investments have progressed more than Sam's, but Sam doesn't mind. He prefers his approach for him, and he is probably correct.

Now let's see what a thought disorder does to our investment approach.

Chapter V
Thought Disorders

There is a persistent belief that it's simple to tell when someone has a thought disorder. In fact that does not have to be the case; a thought disorder can be well concealed. Before we begin our inquiry into this area, though, we need to answer the question, What is a thought disorder?

Generally a thought disorder is what many people refer to when they say someone is "crazy" or a "lunatic" (a term that comes from the outdated notion that mental illness is caused by action of the moon). Another term that has fallen out of usage is "he's gone haywire," from the notion that when mentally ill, people "went all over the place" as haywire does when a bale of hay is freed from the wire. Thus the concept was presented that a thought disorder equates to very uncontrolled behavior. There have also been some who used the term "schizophrenic" when people were changeable from one minute to the next. I have seen an article describing a football team as schizophrenic because it played great ball the first half and very poorly the second half. That is not the correct usage of the term.

The classical signs of a thought disorder are delusions, hallucinations, or both. A delusion is a false belief; the person experiencing it is not amenable to logical examination. The most common delusions are of persecution and of grandeur. A hallucination is a sensory experience without an external stimulus. It can occur with any sense, but hearing voices is most common.

Is it easy to spot a thought disorder in another person? The answer is an emphatic "no." Just think of the times a team of psychiatrists and psychologists has tried to determine whether someone is competent, "sane," or "psychologically fit."

Sometimes a case history helps us attain better understanding.

Case: I was once involved in a custody case that seemed to develop overnight. A couple who seemed to have the ideal marriage were suddenly embroiled in a court action. There were claims, counter-claims, and dozens of accusations.

One accusation made by the husband, Bob, had dangerous legal implications. Bob accused Betty of having a very close relationship with their stockbroker. Some of the statements Bob made seemed quite plausible. Their broker had recently been divorced and he seemed to spend a good deal of time talking to Betty. Bob claimed that Betty had influenced the broker's investment strategies and that as a result Bob lost money while Betty gained.

In the custody investigation complete histories were taken, as is usually the case. Both were interesting. Betty was somewhat of a rebel; she often said she marched to a different tune than others. She had her own unique clothing style and, unlike other young women, wore no jewelry. She was light on makeup in an era when women used a large amount. She wore her hair very short, again in contrast to others of her day.

Betty's political ideas were very different from those around her. Born and reared in a conservative Republican town, she had long been a liberal and a Democrat. She didn't offer her opinions but when challenged she could aggressively defend her position. She was big on women's rights and tried to convince every girl who would listen to get all the schooling she could. It goes without saying that she believed women should have their own careers.

Taking her own advice, Betty had attended school part-time, graduating from college and earning many credit hours toward a law degree. Then she joined a law firm as a legal assistant, pursuing sexual discrimination cases. Her job was investigator and she soon had an excellent reputation.

Betty had never gotten into legal trouble, though her picture had appeared in the college paper for leading protests. She had never been a drug user but did drink some, though never to the point that it could be called a problem. Married at age 31, Betty and Bob had several children.

Bob was a study in contrast. He was ultraconservative and exceedingly conforming. Very popular with everyone, he had been a skilled athlete all through school. He was known as a hard-driving guy who always played all-out. A keen competitor, he had a knack of winning games in the last moments of play. In fact, he was known in high school as the "comeback kid," because he won so many games with late heroics. But Bob never changed the play, i.e., he never improvised. If the coach sent a play in to the huddle, that was the play Bob used.

Bob joined the high school debate team as a sophomore and at first looked very skilled there, too. However, here Bob encountered problems because he was so predictable. The opposition knew what he was going to say before he said it. Bob quit debate as a junior, saying, "If you can't be great, why do it?" He had been elected junior class president so he was rather busy.

Bob encouraged smooth social interaction. He always seemed interested in the person with whom he was talking. He never took a controversial position and usually acted as if he agreed with the person talking to him. Bob was never overtly angry; people remarked that it was amazing how much he put up with without becoming angry.

So there we have Bob the conformist, the go-along guy, and Betty, the individualist who can be assertive in doing things her way. Bob felt sure that he would win custody of the children because he never made waves and was universally liked.

The custody evaluation showed Betty to be pretty much the way she presented herself. She was calm and logical, socially oriented but also secure and comfortable about having her own ideas. The big shock came from the custody evaluation of Bob. He began his evaluation by stating that all this was a waste of time and money. Then when questions were raised about his self-identity, he erupted. He said that he was "too much for Betty to handle so she turned to that twit of a broker we've been using."

Then Bob began talking about how he didn't really need anyone because he was better than others. He knew more than his stock broker, his tax attorney, his doctor. According to him, there was no one around him who had any degree of competency compared to him. In an unguarded moment Bob said, "Sometimes in the dark I hear them talking about me." Then he denied that statement. Bob had enough self-awareness to know what he could reveal about himself without altering his public image. He had developed an ability to create whatever public image he desired.

So what went wrong? Probably it started with marital problems. He couldn't get emotionally close and that began to distress Betty. Then he feared her accomplishments and independence, apparently feeling she was slipping away. Then Bob became overly jealous of the advancement of one of his previously closest friends. Increasingly, whenever he didn't reach some goal he blamed others, always saying they were jealous. He often felt sabotaged.

The final straw that made his disturbance noticeable was the investigation that revealed his low self-esteem. In the end it became clear that he felt very inadequate but had hidden that fact for years. When his defenses crumbled, a full paranoid disorder came into view.

With treatment Bob did improve and was able to admit that he had, off and on, heard voices of people "plotting against me." This man who had many achievements had hidden his thought disorder for a long time. Many famous people have done the same thing. What this should illustrate is that when people have a mental disorder, they aren't necessarily incapacitated. They can, for example, do good work on Monday and then become illogical and destructive with their work on Wednesday.

It's helpful to remember that while emotions may alter our behavior, a thought disorder may change our behavior and thinking. A well-known emotional disorder that involves a thought disorder is schizophrenia. Though two prime signs are delusions and hallucinations, it's not unusual to also see grossly disorganized behavior or speech and flat affect. Flat affect is best described as acting like someone very bored and unable to show any emotional fluctuation.

The investment problems thought disorders create are quite obvious. Anyone who is disorganized is going to have problems establishing a logical plan of attack. Goals are likely to change from one moment to the next—if in fact the person can set any goals. The delusions are likely to be a problem because the client doesn't respond to what is happening. I knew of one person, for example, who claimed that the stock market "crashed—they put up phony numbers to hide the collapse from us." That same person said he saw a religious figure telling him not to listen to his investment counselor! It may be impossible at times to communicate with a client so afflicted.

An important disorder to understand is delusional disorder. The delusions in this disturbance are of not bizarre, which means they do occur in real life. For example, where there are marital problems one mate may actually follow the other. It's this quality of reality that separates the delusional disorders from the schizophrenic type of delusion.

Again an example from my clinical practice comes to mind. Let's call this couple Dave and Rita. Though they were a strikingly attractive couple, Rita never saw herself that way. She was very attached to Dave, but Dave was very independent and emotionally controlled. The couple had an excellent investment advisor and each had a separate investment account. As he became more and more affluent Dave spent more and more time at his advisor's office. He could afford to because he had his own insurance agency with a solid staff.

Rita began to worry that she might lose Dave once he became financially independent. Trouble became observable when Rita began calling the advisor to be sure that Dave was actually where he said he was. There were times when Rita interrupted an important call being made by the advisor. Then she began to state that their mutual advisor preferred Dave and was working against her. In fairness to her, it isn't fun to be caught between spouses, so Rita may have been accurate in her feelings about their advisor, that he was irritated with her.

Rita told her best friend that, "I just know when Dave gets rich he'll leave me." Her friend tried to convince her that Dave was very much in love with her and would not leave her. In fact, if they had abundant funds, think of all the fun they could have traveling! Rita couldn't be convinced. She had heard too many stories about how success makes a person look for someone new. "Men are especially that way," she said, with detectable anger in her voice.

Then a confrontation took place. Rita had the feeling that Dave was putting money aside, hiding it. She tried to learn something from their advisor but got no information. There was a call from a travel agent who also seemed secretive. Again no information was forthcoming.

Rita decided it was time for more direct action. One night after dinner she told Dave she just had to talk to him. "I feel something is going on and that I'm probably losing you. Am I right?" Rita asked.

Dave smiled. "You're partly right. I have had a great year with our investments and your account has also done well. So here's my anniversary gift to you." With that Dave handed an envelope to Rita. Inside were tickets and accommodation arrangements for Europe. Just what they had always dreamed of!

Rita didn't know what to say, so she told Dave she loved him and was happy beyond words. Psychological problems don't have to end badly. Making profits with your investments doesn't have to make life worse. Certainly in this case the delusional disorder was brief. You may be sure Rita never had another one!

The final disorder to be mentioned under this section is called brief psychotic disorder. The symptoms are the same as for a schizophrenic disorder. The difference is that with a brief psychotic disorder the symptoms last at least one day but less than a month. Recognizing something that comes and goes rapidly may be difficult. From a psychological viewpoint the investor may not be talking to the same person from one day or month to the next.

Looking back at the various disorders, we can see how destructive they may be to investment performance. The disorders may be substance (drug) induced or caused by a medical condition. The onset can be quick or slow. Duration can be long or short. The person with whom you shared so many investment dreams today may literally be a stranger tomorrow.

You can minimize the damage if you become an observer who knows what to watch for and when to take constructive action.

Knowing the signs of a thought disorder is useful, but there is nothing like seeing the real thing. The following case history gives a clear example.

Case: Robert Peters was born in a rural area near a large southern city. His ancestors had been farmers all the way back to the Civil War. They had once been very wealthy but the war, followed by lowered demand for farm products, cut deeply into their financial position. Several generations experienced poverty-like conditions. They had to work outside jobs, but they did hold onto their land.

The Peters family somehow remained very close both to one another and to their ancestors. Robert, for example, heard so much about his great-great-grandfather that he felt like he knew him. Calling themselves The Peters Clan was very typical of how they saw each other. Thus there existed a feeling of knowing one another, when in fact they did not. Yet many were the times that Maria Peters, Robert's mother, likened some trait or behavior of Robert's to an ancestor who had been dead over 70 years.

Perhaps that type of atmosphere encouraged a superstitious approach to life. Magic was a hobby of Robert's dad, Bob. Bob loved to put on magic shows at charity events, birthdays, and holidays. Bob had a mystic air about his performances; there were times when he acted a little grandiose. He would freely tell anyone within range of his voice that "You have to have a little of the devil in you to be a gifted magician."

Bob had gone through a period where he said he could move objects by concentration on the path he wanted them to follow. He could be very aggressive. Probably he had by suggestion convinced some that there was movement. None of the more critical people ever saw anything move.

Maria also had a very superstitious bent. She felt that the moon had certain curative powers. She loved talking about her ancestors, who also went back to the Civil War, and some of their achievements. Maria believed that her great-grandmother had actually been brought back to life. She had a written account from her great-grandmother that she would bring out for "doubting Thomases."

All the current family members were very close to one another and, at least in spirit, to all of their ancestors. Bob in particular enjoyed bragging that "We were all, on both sides, God-fearing, hard-working, honest people. And loyal—we haven't had a divorce in our family for over 80 years."

When Robert was born he was said to resemble a great-grandfather, based on a very dim photo. A child often "inherits" traits because his family keeps telling him he is a duplicate. So it was with Robert. These are some of the traits credited to him from his great-grandfather:

1. Shrewd, able to really cut a wonderful deal. He knows how to sell.

2. Aggressive, he can win any argument and no one takes advantage of him.

3. A "man's man," which meant that he would be admired by men.

4. But his aunt added, "Oh, I think with that gleam in his eye, he'll be a ladies man, too."

5. Bob saw his son as being a very successful person who will "make some contributions." Bob added that he could just tell his son would be a very bright young man.

6. Mother saw him as becoming very warm and kind to people. She pointed out that unlike most newborn babies, he didn't cry very much. That, she felt, indicated that he was secure into himself but also that he didn't want to ask a lot of other people. She felt that he was a "giver" and hers was the first concern registered. Mother saw all the world divided into "givers and takers"; she was concerned that others would take advantage of his goodness. Could this be where Robert's suspicious side got started?

7. Asked to describe what he thought Robert would be like, Uncle Ned said, "I don't know where all of you get all that stuff. I think we just got to wait and see how he turns out."

From all that could be seen, Robert developed very rapidly. He walked and talked early. He didn't utter a first word, it was a first two words: "mamma - dada." Even before he was able to walk he could get around. In fact he got into everything. His mother was not at all happy about that because she was meticulous about her home. She yelled at Robert while Bob yelled at her to stop "because you'll scare our child."

At age three Robert had an imaginary friend he would talk to anywhere he happened to be. Some who didn't know him well gave him strange looks and shook their heads. His mother worried about this but his father said very little. Both parents hoped this was just a passing game for Robert.

The imaginary friend was still around at age four and now Robert began to blame things on "Marvin." For example, Robert spilled some sugar on the table trying to get a snack. He knew he wasn't supposed to be up there helping himself, but he did it anyway. When his mother confronted him, he insisted that he hadn't done it.

"Really," exclaimed his mother, "and who came in and did that?" "Marvin, and he didn't mean to do it. Don't be mad at him." His mother wasn't mad at Robert but she was more concerned. She began to feel that Robert had a major problem. She talked to her husband and he too was worried. No one had a clear idea where to go or how to handle this behavior. Bob hoped that when Robert started school he would spontaneously give up his friend. Maria had a similar hope but she was not as optimistic. However, she said, in kindergarten they had a psychologist who might talk with Robert.

Robert started kindergarten that fall and seemed happy to be there. He knew he was a quick learner and, like most bright children, he enjoyed showing off. A few days after Robert started school, his father's father suddenly died. At the family gathering there was a lot of conversation about family ancestors again. Many of their superstitions were discussed, often relating that to death and what happens after death.

Robert was very hurt by the loss of his grandfather. They had been exceedingly close and in fact Robert had been with him a few days before he died. At one point he asked his mother if his grandfather would be coming alive again. She looked perplexed and finally came up with the best answer she could find: "Well, in a way, son, yes; we'll all come back to life one day. That's what the Bible says." Robert smiled and left the room, mumbling that he hoped pappy would be back soon.

The following week Robert returned to school and he told some of his friends about his grandfather coming back. Some of them laughed at him; some even said his mother had lied to him. That produced a great deal of anger but he didn't hit anyone. Instead he went off by himself and cried. Two days later his friend Marvin was back.

The school psychologist, Dr. Greeley, called to ask Robert's mother if he could talk with her. She was pleased because she had long had some concerns. Now she had more because Marvin was back. She hoped to get some answers.

However, from her point of view the meeting didn'tgo well. She asked many questions that weren't answered. For example, she asked if it was normal for a five-year-old to have a make-believe friend. Dr. Greeley asked what she thought and she did give an opinion. Dr. Greeley reflected her feelings and opinions back to her. He pointed out a second time that she felt Robert's behavior was not normal.

Whenever there was a pause Dr. Greeley asked about her relationship with her husband. She answered that they had a good relationship. Then Dr. Greeley said that he had talked with Robert and he wondered how his father related to him. Mrs. Peters asked what impressions Dr. Greeley had gotten but again the question was always directed back to mother. That was true with every question asked.

Whenever Dr. Greeley did respond, it was to tell Mrs. Peters what children need or to ask her opinion and feelings. He never stated whether Robert's needs were being met or what might be wrong. Mrs. Peters came away from that meeting hating the phrase, "What do you think?." When Dr. Greeley asked her if she wanted another meeting she couldn't resist saying, "what do you think?"

None of this helped Robert, and that was her major concern. Her family doctor had tried medication and that had slowed Robert down a little, but Marvin was still there. Some friends had suggested various doctors but Mrs. Peters decided to wait.

Robert continued to grow and to enjoy many of his school experiences. Robert had wisely given up talking to Marvin, though his mother believed he still talked to him when he was alone. In second grade some of his classmates began teasing Robert about being "odd" or "queer," but by and large school seemed a positive experience, largely because he was so bright and liked to learn.

No one was sure how it got started but Robert began to become obsessed with "things being hurt." He saw a dog running wild one day and asked his parents who it belonged to. His father said, "No one owns the dog because he has no collar." That started a long series of questions about where the dog would get food and who might look after him. "Will he die?" Robert asked his father.

A few weeks later Robert saw a beautiful monarch butterfly smashed on the car windshield. He went through a long discussion about the butterfly: Did it have a family? What would happen to the sons of the dead butterfly? This, along with other comments specifically referring to his grandfather, suggested that he was still hurt by his grandfather's death. But it seemed impossible to get him to talk about any of his feelings.

Robert's parents found that they had to be very careful about anything they said around him. In fact that very comment was made by Bob, and Robert heard it. For many days after that Robert would not listen to anything his dad said. If his mother tried to protect him when it seemed his feelings were hurt, Robert would withdraw. He never wanted to feel overprotected, but at the same time he didn't respond well to criticism.

This was clearly exemplified in fifth grade when he was exhibiting a project meant to illustrate how a piece of metal could be bent in two opposite directions depending on the heat applied. When some of his classmates made fun of it, Robert just packed it up and left the classroom. Though he didn't show any emotion, he refused to talk to anyone.

In sixth grade things took a bad turn for Robert both at home and at school. His dad had a heart attack with no warning at all. One of the paramedics who came to their home made a comment on how bad Bob looked. This suggested to Robert that his dad was going to die. He started screaming that "This is unfair, my dad is too young, we need him." Robert did calm down some when the family doctor told them that Bob was not going to die. For a short time Robert relaxed, but then he began saying that the doctors were lying to the family. He seemed all of a sudden to become more suspicious of people.

Then he developed a crush on one of his teachers. At first she seemed to recognize his need for support as well as some protection from more aggressive boys. Thinking she could help, Miss Lynn spent extra time with Robert. There were times when she criticized some of his classmates for picking on Robert. In the short term that was good for Robert but not in the long run. Because it made him seem like a mama's boy, it eventually brought more teasing.

Then two simultaneous occurrences hurt Robert. First Miss Lynn's protection exposed him to ridicule. Then the principal told Miss Lynn not to spend so much time with Robert: "You have other students who need help, too, and you're being criticized for neglecting them."

That upset Miss Lynn, particularly because this was her first full-time teaching assignment. She therefore over-corrected and left Robert unprotected. Now the other youngsters really began picking on him.

The final blow came with a girl that he found attractive and enjoyed talking to. He followed her wherever he could. Robert thought she really liked him and maybe she did. Perhaps she became tired of his being around her all the time. Whatever it was, she poked fun at Robert. "I can't hardly even go to the john but what he follows me," she said to a couple of girls. They quoted this to others, who all laughed at Robert.

When Robert heard this, it was all he could take. He was seen by other students talking to himself outside the gym. The next thing anyone knew he had climbed to the top of the roof and he began yelling for everyone to stand back. Several teachers tried to maintain communication and to persuade him to come down. For about 30 minutes there was a complete standoff. Then the principal went outside on the roof near where Robert was standing. Robert waved him not to come closer or for sure he would jump. The principal said he understood but added, "Robert, this will be sort of hard on your mother, won't it? Your dad is ill, now this with you." Robert started crying and backed away from the edge of the roof. The principal quietly suggested they get down and Robert tearfully agreed.

The next day Robert was taken to a psychiatrist, Dr. Wells. Robert liked him. Dr. Wells had a casual, relaxed approach and Robert didn't seem to feel pressured or judged. He even liked Dr. Wells's sense of humor.

Robert admitted for the first time that he had been hearing voices. "Can you recognize to whom the voice belongs?" Dr. Wells asked. Robert could not.

"Did the voice tell you to jump?"

"Well, not exactly. The voice said that it was because of me that all those bad things happened. It said I would be better off dead," Robert added.

Dr. Wells realized that for some reason Robert felt terribly guilt-ridden. He scheduled regular visits to try to find what had caused all this turmoil, but he also felt that Robert needed some immediate help and so he prescribed medication. The medication worked extremely well. Robert reported that he was no longer hearing voices (having hallucinations).

Bob did recover from his heart attack and he did build a deeper relationship with his son. Father and son got to the point where they not only could talk together but enjoyed it. Talking and sharing became fun. However, Bob realized that there were some things that his son would not feel comfortable talking to him about. He therefore encouraged Robert to see Dr. Wells whenever he felt the need. That, however, didn't work out. Dr. Wells moved his practice several hundred miles away to be near his very ill mother. As fate would have it, he was away for three and a half years. In the long run that had quite an impact upon Robert.

As far as anyone knew, Robert wasn't having any more severe thought disorder problems. He had limited social skills. He therefore had few male friends and was even more awkward with girls—he had no relationships with them. In eighth grade there were many mixed parties but Robert seldom went. Dancing was popular but Robert never learned to dance.

Robert moved into high school with an excellent grade point average and he enjoyed his studies. He had no idea what occupation he would like to pursue but he liked learning. He had become a very good-looking young man, well-groomed with a winning smile. Girls often approached Robert and his tendency to refuse them made him even more appealing to many of them. They saw him as hard to get. He also had a reputation for being "a man of few words" and that too was appealing.

One girl, Mary Jean, did appeal to Robert. She was petite, quiet, never pushy, and easy to talk to. She knew how to dance very well and enjoyed showing Robert a few steps. She came to his house on a number of occasions to talk, study, and dance. Robert's parents liked her.

Things seemed to be going better for Robert so he didn't pursue any type of treatment. He had even discontinued his medication, using it only when he felt nervous. His school grades in high school had improved each year and Robert was close to the top of his class. He now had a game plan for a career: He wanted to be a stock broker. His plan was to get a graduate business degree, an MBA. He was sure he could make it academically.

Mary Jean had her mind set on a nursing career. She didn't want a long school career but she was very interested in helping people. Several times she had looked at Robert and said that what she really wanted was to get married and take care of her own children.

In Robert's life things almost always seemed to go wrong just when things looked like they were going well. The first blow, and a major one, was the loss of Mary Jean. Unexpectedly her father had been given a huge promotion in both finances and responsibility. The trouble was that he had to move to the west coast. No one seemed to recognize it at the time but now Robert had lost the two people, other than his family, with whom he felt the greatest rapport, Dr. Wells and Mary Jean. Robert didn't know what to do to relieve the terrible unhappiness and restlessness he felt.

Meanwhile, his mother, going into Robert's room to put away some clothes, was struck by an odd design on his dresser. She realized it was some sort of symbol that had significance for someone practicing superstitious rites. She had never seen anything like that with him but she now wondered if he were trying to deal with his losses with superstitious thinking because he somehow remembered what was said when he was a child. "Could there be a genetic tie there?" she asked herself. Then she decided there couldn't. But whatever caused this behavior seemed to be adding to her son's problems. She wondered how she was going to bring this up to Robert.

She didn't get the chance, however: Her husband, Bob, called and she went running. His tone said clearly that something was very wrong. She yelled to him and he told her where he was. There was one unoccupied room in the basement where Robert used to go to be by himself. Maria felt a chill go down her spine and she had what she called a premonition.

When she entered the semi-darkened room she saw Robert sitting next to his father. Robert was swatting at various portions of his chest; in a moment she knew why. He was yelling for his father to "get these little bugs off me." Periodically he would come up with a weird chant: "Here they go an' away we go." He was disheveled and jumpy. It was impossible to talk to him for long. Maria sat next to Robert for a few minutes but didn't attempt to speak to him. She patted his shoulder and just waited. After about five minutes she decided to try and communicate. "Robert, do you think we should go upstairs and get some of your medication?"

Robert looked at her and went silent for a few minutes. Then he turned to her and spoke.

"No, mom, it will have been poisoned," he said.

Both Bob and Maria assured Robert that they would not have allowed anyone to get near the medicine. Somehow Robert agreed to try the medication to see if that helped. He had developed enough insight to be aware of how badly he felt. He did go upstairs and take his medication.

Robert calmed down and became more reasonable. However, he said that whatever the reality, he was convinced that someone was sabotaging his life. He felt that other people had been jealous of him for some reason. They had come and kidnapped Dr. Wells and then they forced Mary Jean's father to leave the area.

What was striking was the fact that Robert could rationally understand that no one was out to wreck his life, but he still *felt* like someone was. He couldn't understand why that feeling persisted, but that was his delusion. When he was experiencing his delusion, his associations became very loose. For example, he said that Mary Jean had very pretty blue eyes and that made him sad "because blue is what people are when they are sad."

Robert went to another psychiatrist in town, the one who had replaced Dr. Wells. He didn't find him as easy to talk to. Dr. Royce was more formal and did a lot of interpreting of what meaning lay behind Robert's statements. Robert never had liked people to tell him what he felt or what his statements meant.

However, Dr. Royce was pleasant and he tried to understand Robert's critical comments. When Robert found out one day that Dr. Royce shared a common interest with him, namely investing, the two got along rather well. The new medications also helped remove the delusional thinking.

Robert seemed to improve. During his college days he was free of any thought disorder, with one brief exception. In his sophomore year he had gone through a fraternity initiation with quite a bit of drinking. There was a good deal of talk about sexual relationships and questions about which male was the outstanding one in this group. Robert had a one-day relapse where he was not able to trust anyone. No one made much of this because there was so much drinking going on.

Robert continued his psychiatric treatment, but it was on and off. Sometimes it's hard to see when you have a problem, especially when it doesn't seem to cause other problems. Robert couldn't see the little nuances of his paranoid suspiciousness and his occasional inability to make decisions. He was pleased with his collegiate academic performance and he was sure he would be successful.

Finally, through a friend he secured a position with an investment house. It was of course on a trial basis because the managers felt Robert had much to learn before actually guiding investments. Then, too, the investment house was small with not many openings for new personnel. Robert was able to join this group only because they were friendly with his father.

Robert immediately had difficulties with his investment decisions. His tendency was to go entirely on what he called a hunch and not follow the accepted rules of the trade. When the investment went sour Robert blamed the "rich people who dominated the investment field."

Robert also had problems with those people who came to the agency for service. If they gave him a difficult time he tended to make sarcastic comments to them. If he didn't think that they had a good investment strategy, he abruptly criticized their plan. He also tended to be very short with the women who came in.

Every so often some of Robert's faulty logic would show itself. He couldn't handle the sharp ups and downs of investment cycles. To Robert, if the market was moving up he expected it to continue. If you asked him about this philosophy of no change, he would respond with. "Oh sure, it'll reverse, just not now."

Because Robert continued to live at home, his expenses were minimal. He had few social friends and no special girl friend. He and Mary Jean had corresponded for a few years and then Robert stopped writing back. She felt that he must have found someone else, and so she stopped writing.

After six months at the investment house Robert began to have his own investment style, one directly related to his thought disorder. Granted his mental health was better, but he still couldn't get away from problems that distorted his thinking. One example was his inability to trust anyone completely. He believed that everyone was out to make themselves look good and others to look bad. He always referred to everything as a "dog-eat-dog world." This affected his investment ability because he wouldn't ask peers to critique his investment programs.

He said the same about books and articles and refused the aid of usually respected sources. He said often that one problem with the world is that no one wants to make his own decisions and then stand by them. That was another shortcoming because Robert stood by his investments forever. He never wanted to sell a stock that was down because that made him "a loser." Lypic was a stock that Robert bought (with his own money, thank God) at 20. He watched it go to a value of one dollar.

Not trusting meant that the world operated by no logic at all, so Robert stayed with only highly conservative investments. Also, if an approach worked once, he used that approach over and over, even when it no longer worked.

He also had a pronounced tendency to stay with the same type of stock regardless of the world situation. For example, as soon as Robert made a profit with some oil stocks, he began to buy oil stocks almost exclusively. He could not be guided by multiple variables because he couldn't process divergent bits of information. Finally it was recognized by everyone that Robert not only didn't trust others, he didn't trust himself. But he couldn't admit that even to himself.

However, no life should have rain falling into it all the time. One bright day the sun came out for Robert. He had pulled himself back together again and was feeling a little more optimistic about his life. When the phone rang, he immediately recognized the caller's voice: "Hi, Robert, it's Mary Jean, how are you?"

The two of them talked for over an hour and then decided to go out for dinner. Being together was just like old times. The relationship built up from there. Mary Jean had changed her mind about her career choice. She had decided to become an investment advisor.

Robert's good fortune continued when Dr. Wells moved back into the area five months later. Robert went to see him and then decided on more psychotherapy to go with the medication. Dr. Wells requested psychological testing in order to help define underlying motivation. As many had suspected, a faulty self-concept was at the root of Robert's problems. Dr. Wells was able to help correct that.

Business became an interesting portion of his and for that matter Mary Jean's life. They not only married, they became business partners. Sharing activities can greatly strengthen a good relationship. Mary Jean acted as a stabilizing factor in Robert's life and Robert added spontaneity to her business approach.

Things went well after that and this couple became successful on a number of fronts. Robert was able to accept that he needed to recognize the signs of flareups of his thought disorder, but to my knowledge it never emerged again. Credit should go to Mary Jean and Dr. Wells—in that order!

Chapter VI
Cognitive Disorders

In order to talk rationally about cognitive disorders we must understand what "cognitive" means. Some sources state that cognitive refers to the mental processes involved in "knowing." These are the processes used in comprehension, memory, reasoning, and judgment. Cognitive functioning is often referred to as intellectual functioning, or intelligence.

Cognitive processes are contrasted with emotional functioning. We thus contrast intellect and emotion, but we have already mentioned that the two are often intertwined. When some people become highly emotional, they seem to lose all reason.

It seems very workable to define intelligence as the ability to learn and then the ability to use what we have learned appropriately. For example, early in grade school we might have learned that 12 x 4 = 48. Later in our lives we are presented with an arithmetic story problem: If you purchased four books that cost $12 each, how much would you have to spend? To solve this, we had to apply our multiplication tables. We might even take this problem a step further by now asking how much money we would get back if we gave the clerk a $100 bill. Now we have added subtraction to the process. The mental processes involved in this arithmetic problem were memory and reasoning. We also had to comprehend what the task involved.

All of these various processes come together in problem-solving. But what would happen if one of these processes is impaired? Let's take actual case histories.

Case 1: Mary Ann walked and talked early and always earned very high grades in school. She was double-promoted in seventh grade. Her high school record was even more impressive. Mary Ann joined the debate team and placed in state at the end of her sophomore year. She was always able to see the main point in her debate strategy. She had a very strong memory for fine detail.

Mary Ann continued to get very high grades throughout her high school years. Very popular, she was also elected senior class president. Understandably she was awarded a scholarship to a small liberal arts college.

College proved to be more of the same. Mary Ann had even more success in debate and also maintained a high overall grade average. She became very interested in law and accounting. She began to feel that she wanted a professional career despite the fact that her father talked against it.

After an internal struggle Mary Ann decided to do her own thing. In graduate school she continued her outstanding academic career. She had an excellent background in accounting but it was law that finally won out. She started what seemed a promising career dealing with civil rights violations. She was very respected by others—colleagues, clients, and those who just knew her socially.

Mary Ann commanded a big salary and was not one to spend lavishly. She had paid back her parents for their investment in her education. That was her way of telling her father she liked the success she had earned. She had no serious romantic attachments and consistently put money into investments. As she did that, she developed an increased interest in investing. She had one stockbroker, Bob, with whom she had great rapport. The two never had been at odds on anything and Bob never made an investment without talking to Mary Ann first.

Then a few things began to happen that must be regarded as unusual, to say the least. Mary Ann had always been impeccably well-oriented and sensitive to the world. She was big on current events. But one day after her thirtieth birthday she was in Bob's office and wrote three checks with different dates. Bob didn't think much of it, figuring that she was still hung over after her birthday celebration. He did think it odd that she would confuse the date when it was the day after such an important date, but nothing further was said.

In the next few months Mary Ann developed a tendency to talk to Bob at 10:00 am and then call at 4:00 pm and not recall the earlier conversation. Once she called Bob at 9:00 am and asked him to buy a particular "hot stock" immediately. She was sure this one would go up rapidly. Then at 12:30 pm she called again and seemed not to remember her earlier call. At first Bob thought she was pulling his leg but he soon found out she was very serious.

This was followed by three social incidents in which times were set and then forgotten by Mary Ann. On one of these occasions Mary Ann had forgotten to pick up her boyfriend in order to join other couples.

When Mary Ann missed her parents' anniversary, there were many hurt feelings.

Mary Ann's father began to talk about emotional problems. He said that his daughter should be thinking of marriage and a family, not running after "the almighty buck." He was sure that if she would just settle down and have a "normal woman's life," things would get back to normal. When someone asked about her memory her father rejected that concern: "She can remember things she did as a young child. How could she be having memory problems?"

Forgetting social events can have a terrible effect on someone. You feel embarrassed and often believe that people are making fun of you. Mary Ann believed that people were feeling sorry for her. That she couldn't tolerate!

The situation seemed to get worse and worse. Now there were times when Bob and Mary Ann had arguments. Mary Ann didn't feel there was anything wrong with her memory, but Bob was telling her that she didn't accurately recall previous conversations.

There was one change that Mary Ann did seem to recognize. She had always learned mainly by seeing and not all that much by hearing. She remembered her early days in high school when she had taken classes where teaching was mainly by lecture. She had been forced to record the lecture and then have it typed so she could learn by seeing. Now there was an intensification of that situation to the point where she could now *only* learn by seeing. However, her judgment was sound and her stock selections were as good as ever.

There came a time when Mary Ann was pushed by all of her close friends to go see her family doctor. She made an appointment and he listened to what she described. Then he referred her to a psychologist. She wondered if he thought she was losing her mind. He insisted this was not the case.

The psychologist gave Mary Ann an intelligence test and then went over it with her. Her performance was not consistent. Her knowledge of word meanings was extremely strong; this ability tends to hold up well with age. Her visual abilities were excellent. Tests of judgment were strong. Long-term memory was superior. But short-term memory was very weak. The psychologist read off some numbers (like 8-1-7-5-) and asked Mary Ann to repeat them. She was well below average with that ability. So, too, was she when writing unfamiliar symbols in random order.

The conclusion was that Mary Ann had a disorder that was affecting her short-term memory. She could still call forth old memory, she could reason, and she could think abstractly. Mary Ann was told that she had a very early onset of Alzheimer's, a form of dementia. The bad news was that there's no actual treatment. The good news was that it had a slow onset. Mary Ann had to recognize her deficit and learn to adjust to it.

Just imagine the potential here for investment problems. Supposing Mary Ann had a wonderful stock that she forgot to call Bob to buy. The stock rapidly goes up and Mary Ann thinks that she did put a buy order in. Can you see the potential for big problems?

Case 2: Gray presented a different sort of cognitive disorder. He had a significant impairment of short-term memory but there was also some long-term memory loss. That meant that pieces of information acquired a year earlier couldn't be recalled. Gary's disorder had begun at age 66, and it included a loss of executive functioning, which includes abstraction, organizing, planning, and sequencing.

The first loss that Gary showed was short-term memory. The difficulty in recognizing this was that Gary had been known to have a poor memory from age 10 on. His mother often commented that if she gave Gary a list with over three things to buy he would forget at least one. When someone has always been weak at something, people around him adjust and don't easily see any additional loss.

Gary began to present concrete rather than abstract thinking. For example, if asked about a proverb such as "a stitch in time saves nine" he would say "if you don't stitch something, it could break more." The abstract answer is that "if you let something go, it will require more work later." The problem is that most of our society's rules are abstract. As a result, it was very difficult for Gary to act in accord with general procedures. Leap Year was a concept he could never grasp: How could a year leap?

As far as investments were concerned, Gary couldn't balance a number of categories that are commonly used to help predict stock movement. His advisor found it very difficult to explain his investment strategy. As Gary's dementia advanced, he quickly presented signs of aphasia. This meant that he often couldn't understand language that once he could. At first, this was somewhat difficult to recognize because Gary was a member of a minority and people were used to having difficulty understanding him.

Soon Gary's dementia began to notably affect his cognitive functioning. He increasingly lost interest in contact with people, partly because he couldn't communicate with them. He was retired, so there was no standard by which to judge vocational adjustment. His advisor, though, was very aware of the loss and how difficult it was to work with Gary.

Gary's cognitive losses continued. Concern grew that he could no longer be responsible for his own well-being. Eventually he was provided with a guardian—right after Gary went to a new investment house and asked the first broker he saw to look at his portfolio and then sell everything. (The funny thing is that soon after the stock market did drop substantially.)

Of all the types of dementia Alzheimer's is clearly the best known. There are two varieties, late onset, after age 65, and early onset, before. The disorder may not initially be noted because the onset is gradual but the cognitive loss is continuing. Alzheimer's can combine with other disorders to further complicate the picture. For example, there can be depression with the Alzheimer's. In my clinical practice I have noted many persons who became depressed because they recognized that there was something wrong.

Case 3: I will never forget the first patient I ever diagnosed as suffering from this disease. One of the diagnostic approaches is to present the patient with a design on a 4 x 6 card and ask that it be drawn on a sheet of typing paper. This woman was very conscientious; she clearly wanted to do this task perfectly. She asked about five times, touching first the card, then the paper, whether she had the right idea. She would repeat to herself, "Draw this design on this card onto this white paper."

Then she would pause and end by drawing the design on the 4 x 6 card. That ruins the design card because it adds to what belongs on that card. The next person would draw the original design plus what the woman had drawn.

My patient seemed to know immediately what she had done for she started to cry. Over and over again she berated herself for not being able to do this correctly. She asked me why she couldn't get it right and apologized for "ruining your card."

Well, of course, she was reassured that she had done the best she could and not to worry. But it was clear that a connection was missing in her functioning. She could comprehend what the task was supposed to be but that one instance of short-term memory loss caused her to fail the task.

As things turned out she was rather typical of the early-onset Alzheimer's patient. She displayed an early sign, not being able to remember how to get back home. Several times police officers saw her wandering in a confused state and took her home. She was very fortunate that she lived in a small town where everyone knew everyone. She was lucky, too, that she had always enjoyed walking and that she could walk from her house to the shopping center. As time went on she gave up driving and went shopping only with women friends or with her husband.

This illness forced her into a dependency that she didn't like. I later found out that the woman had once been a very astute business person. She had done most of the hiring and the ordering of materials for her company. She had come from a large family where people had to look after many of their own needs, so she had become very mature and self-sufficient. Her cultural background was one of "if you have a problem, learn to work it out on your own." Now she had come to a point where she had to rely upon others. Understandably her depression began to grow.

As fate would have it, she remembered me as "the man with those cards that I couldn't draw." She told her husband that she needed to talk to someone about what was happening to her. She decided that she wanted to see me because she remembered that I didn't yell at her for "ruining" my cards.

We set an appointment and she came early with her husband. For the next 40 minutes I listened as she talked about all the things she couldn't do. She spoke about what a good mind she had had. She even spoke about following the stock market and often making her own selections. Now she couldn't even remember how to get to her broker's office.

After she had ventilated some of her frustration, I directed the conversation to those things she could do because she seemed to hate relying on others and because she was feeling worthless. It took her a while to mention things that she still enjoyed. Like most people, she tended to drift back to what she couldn't do.

Then I began to hear how much she liked doing things with children. She spoke about her family and it was clear she was able to establish a great rapport with children. I asked about her interest in spending time at a day care center and for the first time in a while I saw that beautiful smile again. We were soon able to arrange things so that my client could spend some time at this center. She wasn't actually paid, although she did get lunch there. She said that she had forgotten how good peanut butter and jelly taste!

For the sake of clarity and without being demeaning we should note that her activities were safe. She didn't cook because forgetfulness there could be a problem, but she was well oriented to listening, reading, playing, and loving children. And the children simply loved her. They had not found many adults who showed such interest in them. The staff enjoyed her, too.

Life is often a matter of making accommodations and compromises. This client had to give up some of the things that were pleasant to her. Shopping had to be done with others, as did travel. She had loved making investments and now that wasn't feasible. But even there we were able to make some accommodations. Her stock broker agreed to meet with her and her husband once or twice a month to tell her what investments he had made and why. She didn't always remember but she felt active in the decision making. From what I heard she made a very good adjustment and I didn't need to see her again.

We know that Alzheimer's is a disease related to changes in the brain. We have seen what those changes can do to change a life because of memory loss. Other kinds of cognitive loss can also be very disruptive to normal functioning.

Case 4: I was called in as a consultant when a man seemed to undergo a major personality change. He had always been very quiet; some even described him as passive. He had never been one to make waves and was always able to hold back his emotions until he could resolve any conflict. Then he began slowly to change. His first confrontation took place with, of all people, his financial advisor. There had suddenly been some disagreement about investments. His advisor mentioned that he had called about them and got an okay.

That brought a screaming retort, "I don't care, I can change my mind, too," and off George went. Next there was a screaming match with his wife, also about investments. George was convinced that his advisor was not doing what had been agreed upon. His wife had disagreed. George walked away, saying he was thinking of suing his advisor. Then he turned to his wife and added that he would sue her if she defended the advisor.

What mainly surprised everyone was not George's attitude but the intensity of his anger. There were many who had a ready explanation. They knew something of George's background. He was very dominated by a father who never praised him for anything he did. His mother tended to be overprotective, probably to make up for the harsh father.

Because George had always done what his father wanted, he chose a college and a career that dad liked, selling real estate. Some felt that George might have been even more successful had he only been more aggressive, but by adulthood that was just not in George's character. George was a reasonably good golfer and joined one of the better country clubs. Though his passive nature kept him from being competitive, he probably could have won his club championship had he been more competitive.

As his explosions became more severe, the theories among his friends increased: domination by dad, smothering by mother; desire to be more aggressive, feels he can't; can dominate advisor because George is a big investor; feels he can now dominate his wife; wants more money for feelings of power—all adds up to explosions.

On the surface it sounded somewhat logical but life can be a fooler. In this case fate entered in. George became frightened when he lost much of the feeling in his right hand. A glass of water he had been holding just dropped out of his hand. He made an appointment with his doctor, who ran some tests of George's circulation. Nothing showed up. Now came the question of whether there was an emotional disorder. He was pushed into making an appointment with a psychiatrist. After a number of hours exploring his childhood, the doctor decided there were no major symptoms of emotional disturbance.

The psychiatrist referred George for psychological testing to see if anything showed up there. The testing did find some important signs of disturbance: Abstract ability was very weak and reasoning ability was poor. There were definite signs of impairment of George's brain. The problem was organic, not emotional.

George's primary doctor next ordered some additional tests. There were clear signs of a tumor and surgery was suggested. George lost his temper but underwent surgery, with an excellent result. The tumor was benign and was removed completely. After George healed, his personality returned to its previous placid state. In this case the emotional and personality change had an entirely organic cause.

Another disease, Pick's, is also a pre-senile degenerative brain disease that is classified with the dementias. With it there's usually some intellectual deterioration but also major signs of loss of social adjustment. Persons with this disorder often find it very difficult to regulate their emotions.

Case 5: I recall a patient, Tom, living in a nursing home who was diagnosed with Pick's disorder. He was referred for psychological testing each year for the three years that I visited this nursing home. The problems were always the same, namely that he just couldn't get along with people. He had gone through five roommates and he couldn't find another one to agree to be with him.

Tom never came to any group programs and never joined in any activities at the home. He was not highly unpleasant but he seldom went out of his way to talk to any other resident. I decided to ask him why not and his simple reply was, "They don't like me, why should I like them?"

So I decided to ask the other residents what they didn't like about Tom. It was fascinating because every person I talked to, male or female, said the same things. They said that Tom didn't say nice things to people. He said whatever he wanted to say, regardless of its impact on the other person. Several told me about a woman, well liked, who had decided that she was going to lose weight. She worked hard with exercise and restraint with food. To most of the residents she did seem to lose weight. The few who disagreed didn't say anything.

But Tom sure did. He said in loud tones that he felt she still sagged in many places and had "just as much fat as ever." Imagine how that went over! One of the residents asked Tom why he didn't just keep his mouth shut if he thought she didn't look good.

Tom said, "I don't know—it just seems to come out."

That is quite true of those who have Pick's disease. They often find it most difficult to be diplomatic and to adjust socially. There are those who feel that this disease affects the frontal lobes of the brain, impairing executive skills like planning and organizing. While Pick's is a form of dementia, it has some similarity to Alzheimer's, especially regarding social skills.

It's generally accepted that cognitive disorders of the dementia variety start slowly but then progress, i.e., cognitive abilities continue to decline. My clinical experience tells me something very different.

Case 6: Jerry was from a very well-to-do family. As a youngster he seemed to have an ideal adjustment. He was an excellent student but showed intense anger when he received any grade lower than an A plus. He joked that he could stand something less than perfection but "not much less." He was strong in math and a constant reader. His general fund of knowledge was extensive. He had a fine sense of humor, was a good conversationalist, and generally seemed to know where he was going. His father had been active in the stock market and Jerry wanted to follow in dad's footsteps.

Looking at the family from the outside they seemed ideal. Jerry and his father did everything together fishing, scuba diving, watching sports, playing catch by themselves. They also spent hour after hour talking about the stock market. Jerry's dad even taught his son how to trade stocks and predict those that had a good chance of going up.

Jerry was close to his mother, too, and they shared a great deal. Jerry said in later years that he came to his mother whenever he had a dating problem. Jerry's mother came to many of his athletic events and she yelled as loudly for him as any of the fathers did for their sons. Jerry was an only child as his mother had been unable to conceive again.

Jerry graduated near the very top of his high school class and went away to college knowing he would be successful. Jerry missed his parents but he said, "Right now I feel as if I'm on top of the world." He even spoke to his dad about the possibility of his dad going into the investment business with him. The world looked rosy.

All of a sudden Jerry's world turned upside down. His teachers called his father to say that there was something wrong with Jerry. He couldn't function in his classes. He couldn't follow directions and they wondered if he were really trying. It was common knowledge that Jerry often found it difficult to get out of bed in the mornings. He missed a number of classes as a result, and that he had never done before.

Jerry's parents were as confused as anyone because of the sudden reversal in his behavior. Back home their family doctor had a long session with Jerry and concluded that he was very ill. He gave him a Mental Status Examination, which tells how sensitive the person is to the world around him. The patient is asked, for example, to give the date, to remember some numbers given in a series, to explain proverbs, to give his address and perhaps his phone number.

Jerry had always been very involved with the world around him but his doctor quickly learned that he couldn't name his state senators or the vice-president of the United States. He didn't know the name of his state governor but oddly gave the name of the governor of a neighboring state. This confused his doctor until Jerry's father recalled that the family had visited that state right before school started. Jerry had greatly enjoyed that visit and had talked about going back again. Could Jerry possibly be living in the past?

Jerry had become sullen and quiet and didn't communicate any longer with his family. Sometimes he appeared in a daze. Often his sentences didn't make sense. His conversation was clipped and he became irritated quickly when someone couldn't understand what he was saying.

Jerry also changed emotionally. He had always been a warm, outgoing person who empathized with others. Now he seemed cold and always in a hurry to get away from people. His mother said that it was as if Jerry didn't want to spend any more time with people than he had to.

Something else was most unusual for Jerry. He had always been a very empathetic person who knew the likes and dislikes of everyone close to him. He was known to be a very skilled giftgiver, something you can't do without being empathetic with the recipient. Jerry's mother had a birthday during this time and with all Jerry's problems, she didn't expect a gift from him. To her surprise she received not one but two gifts from her son. Both were perfume of a variety that she greatly disliked.

There was another important change in Jerry's behavior. Jerry had always been highly organized and reliable. If Jerry said he would meet you at 12:00 he would arrive with the last chime of the clock. Now he was showing not just poor organization but disorganization. He couldn't plan well. He couldn't place things in a logical sequence. This showed up when he was helping with dinner. Jerry first cooked some part of the dinner that cooks quickly and then planned what takes a long time to cook. By the time the slow item was done the fast item was cold.

Some things began to make sense only when these symptoms had gone on for nearly a year. Jerry just "hung around" places and as far as anyone could tell didn't have any game plan. When it was also noticed that Jerry was very concrete, the pattern began to make sense. Jerry's executive functioning seemed impaired, as evidenced by problems with abstraction, organizing, planning, and sequencing.

Memory loss and impaired executive functioning are two signs of dementia. Was what his doctors thought was an emotional disorder really an organic disorder? It was hard to believe with someone who seemed so healthy and was so young.

Jerry was called back to talk to his doctor, and after a long delay the facts started to fit together. For a number of reasons Jerry had never felt a desire to use any kind of illicit drug. He had felt happy most of the time, he could express his emotions freely, and he could talk to his parents. Granted he was somewhat serious-minded but he could have fun, and he was very achievement-oriented.

When he entered college, like many others he began to feel some insecurities. He decided to take a little time off and hit the party circuit. At the second of these parties some fellow students began to tease him about not being a drinker. At first it had no impact but after a while it began to get on his nerves. "Okay, give me a beer," he had said to the guy pushing him.

Jerry drank some of the beer and made a comment like "So what's the big deal?"

The pusher didn't stop there. He poured another drink and chided Jerry to drink that one. Jerry did and soon he began to have a major reaction. There were drugs in this drink. Jerry felt like he was flying—or at least that he could fly.

There was something in his reaction to these drugs that seemed to have an appeal for Jerry. For the next three weeks he visited the pusher and continued to use the drink with the drugs. It would be difficult to say what changed, but something sure did. After three weeks Jerry abruptly swore off the use of substances. At that point he didn't even drink beer.

But it was too late. The drugs apparently had a long-range effect. The diagnosis was substance-induced persisting dementia.

This variety of dementia doesn't necessarily have a continual decline. In fact Jerry fortunately make a complete recovery. It took about a year before he was again doing well in school and other life areas. He ultimately said that his experiences had given him an idea about a future career, lecturing to young people about the potential for destroying your life by using drugs only *once*!

Delirium is another form of cognitive disorder that can affect a person's ability to function rationally. Dementia and delirium have some similarities but they are two distinct disorders. We spoke about dementia starting slowly. Delirium develops rapidly, usually over hours or a few days. It's a disorder that often fluctuates during the short term, such as a day.

Delirium is primarily a disorder of consciousness. The sufferer has problems focusing on the world around her and has difficulties in shifting attention from one thing to another. From this description you can see why the Mental Status Exam is useful. There's usually a weakening of memory but at the same time memory can come as well as go. The attention span also comes and goes, again making diagnosis difficult.

It's obvious that this disorder can have a great impact on any investment program. When someone has a condition that makes her behavior variable, it becomes hard to diagnose and harder to allow for. If that disorder also affects contact with the world, the investor is in trouble. It's, after all, the world condition that primarily affects our investments. You can conclude that any time an investor who was very aware of world events begins to lose track of time, the date, where she lives or world events, she may be in deep trouble.

There's another classification of disorder that can affect cognitive functioning, though not to the extent of a full-blown dementia or delirium. That is an amnestic disorder, a memory loss that involves either an inability to recall prior learned information, to recall new learning, or both. The first type is referred to as "remote memory." With this type of loss a person cannot profit from what he has learned. At some point the memory loss is likely to create problems socially. To qualify as an amnestic disorder, the memory loss does not occur solely in the course of a dementia or delirium. This disorder can be transient (lasting a month or less) or chronic (more than a month).

Case 7: Amnestic disorder is one that I have seen in abundance in nursing homes. I recall one very lovely woman of advanced years to whom I administered psychological tests. She was very pleasant to work with and we found that she could reason well, was logical, and was able to think abstractly. She said that she felt lonely and added, "I wish I could go shopping once in a while."

I felt she could shop provided there was someone who would see that she didn't forget to get back on the bus. I also felt she could profit from some group work. Group interaction, I reasoned, might reduce some of her loneliness. She had excellent social skills and it was also likely that she could make a contribution to the adjustment of others. Elderly people often feel useless because they don't feel they can make worthwhile contributions. Sound mental health practices tells us that we all need to feel important.

Our lady wanted to know what I was going to recommend. When I told her she smiled, said she was glad I didn't think she was crazy, and would I call her guardian and tell him. I agreed and decided to call while our patient was with me. I reached him first try and relayed the information. He was pleased and said he would see that all the forms were completed. When I hung up the phone I saw a very happy lady.

The very next day when I arrived for work there was the same client wanting to know when I would call her guardian. I carefully reminded her of the conversation I had had with him while she was present. She said if I said so she would believe me but she didn't remember. Same thing the third day and by the fifth day she was asking when she got her turn with the tests. Others, she said, told her they were fun and she wanted a chance to "show how smart I am." Fortunately, her memory did improve to the extent that she was able to remember those who had seen her and those she met with in her groups.

We all know that there are people who have a way of forgetting things they want to forget. It's amazing how many people forgot why it was they wanted to see me. I had a broker friend who gave me an interesting example of what I call "classic strategic forgetting." He had a client who was very active in the stock market. He often called and asked my friend to make a quick buy of a stock that he was sure was going to go way up. However, when the stock went rapidly down, he couldn't remember telling his broker to buy.

This is a selective memory loss. Those with a true cognitive loss are another story. Among the many causes, one that is always suspect is heavy drinking. We can't always recognize the drinker but alcohol breath is a good indicator. Other causes can be the aging process, health problems (such as circulatory), and drug reactions.

As far as investment is concerned, we need to be sure that cognitive functioning is lucid enough that decisions are consistent with the person's investment approach. I recall one situation where a client for years checked every investment decision made by his broker. Then all of a sudden he didn't call and didn't come in. When his broker called him, he said he would be in the next day, but he never showed up. Again his broker called, this time saying he had a great investment prospect. Again there was a promise that went unfulfilled when the client didn't show up. Great investments came and went but no client.

One day the client came in unexpectedly wanting to know why there had not been any new investments. He didn't remember any of the broker's calls. Nor did he have any explanation as to why he had not maintained contact. The broker noticed some memory gaps and even some confusion. He prevailed upon his client to see his family doctor.

The medical examination answered some questions. Since the problem was circulation to the brain, the client was soon restored to normal cognitive functioning. Now if only those investments will be as successful!

There are a number of situations that can be very challenging to the investment advisor. Three such conditions are of early life derivation.

The first of these is mental retardation, a diagnosis based upon a number of factors. There must be a intellectual examination establishing an IQ of 70 or below. There must also be impairment in current adaptive functioning, meaning that the person cannot meet standards expected for the person's age in self-care, interpersonal skills, ability to communicate, home living, and self-direction. Onset must be before the person is 18 years old. Along with this we have now established that an individual may have a reading, math, or writing disorder.

For you as a broker probably two things are most significant in dealing with someone who has mental retardation. One is to try to establish communication at whatever level the client functions. Don't talk down to the client but also try to avoid complicated wording. Another part to this is to try to find out how the client communicates best. Does he understand better when you write it out? Is hearing better? Does he do better when you use an example? Or when you tell an illustrative story? Do you have more success when you smile or when you're serious? I wouldn't recommend that you start by asking the client if he has any questions. That often puts people on the spot because they may feel that their question is probably "dumb."

As you talk you may develop a keen idea of what is on the client's mind. Then you can ask, "Is this what you're wondering about?" If the client says "no," don't assume that's true. He may just not be ready to raise a question.

The other thing is to be sure that you communicate with the client's guardian. That doesn't mean communicate as you legally must but rather in a way that builds good rapport. The client's guardian could be very helpful to you in the future, and with good communication you may better understand the goals of the client through the guardian.

Another disorder that usually has at least roots in childhood is called attention deficit disorder (ADD). This has only been recognized recently. It essentially means that an individual has a short attention span and can't focus on most things for very long. People with this disorder usually had a very difficult time in school and were often accused of not paying attention. They usually don't like activities that require long-term concentration. They will generally be bored if you don't let them shift tasks.

There are obviously a whole series of implications here for school but we're talking about investments. Whatever you have to say, say it quickly while you have the client's interest. Secondly, don't try to explain much of anything when the client is off on another topic.

You may also wish to plan beforehand what you're going to say so you can boil it down. You need to make your part interesting to the client and you should try to be simple and brief. When the client drifts off, let him go for a minute and then bring him back.

A related disorder is attention deficit/hyperactivity disorder (ADHD). This, too, is a relatively new psychological diagnosis—not that such behavior is new, because teachers complained for years. Some muttered, "I have to scrape him off the walls." This is generally a disorder observable in some of its components before age seven. Some of the more notable signs are inability to await a turn, blurting out responses before anyone has asked for them, interrupting others, and great difficulty sitting still. Typically there's impairment in ability to focus on one task or topic at a time, and inability to follow through on an activity. Sometimes, as the following case history illustrates, people with ADHD can become extremely impulsive and do things not in their best interests.

Case 8: Holly came from a family that didn't believe in doctors or medication. During her school years she was apparently regarded as very hyperactive and distractible. Holly recalled that her fifth grade teacher had moved Holly's desk into a corner so she was blocked in. That seemed to help provide an external control that Holly needed. However, when Holly's parents objected, the practice stopped.

When Holly entered the sixth grade she, like many children, was given a psychological test. Most of the faculty were extremely shocked at how bright Holly was shown to be. Then they realized that the surprise was simply because she couldn't apply herself. Again her parents refused medication.

Holly was only able to scrape by in high school because by now the material was too complex for her to handle with her inner distractions. Since school was becoming increasingly unpleasant for her, Holly dropped out at the end of her last year. She decided to get a job and earn a little money.

Holly was an attractive girl who spoke well when there was pressure to do so. She was tidy about her appearance and showed a high energy level. You never got to know just how high until you knew Holly better.

She was quickly placed as a receptionist with a small legal firm. The boss who did the hiring said Holly was hired because of her inviting smile and general attractiveness. She didn't have many responsibilities with that position. She answered the phone, greeted people who walked in, asked who they wanted, and directed them to the right person.

That should not have been all that complicated as there weren't that many places where someone could be directed. But Holly continued to make errors. Finally, the office manager decided that she would have the visitor wait at the front of the office until someone came to take them to the right office. That way all Holly had to do was push a button and all buttons had names right on them.

Well, that too worked for a little while, until Holly either forget to buzz someone or got the wrong person. On one occasion Holly pushed the wrong button, realized it, pushed another and ultimately had four attorneys all coming to meet the same person.

Holly had been perceived as hyper by everyone in her office but now it was observed that she became even more jumpy when criticized. Holly also seemed to be becoming increasingly irritable. She knew something was wrong but she didn't know how to correct it. She usually felt that the blame lay with the office manager and some of the other staff. Sometimes Holly became angry because she felt everyone was expecting too much of her.

The problem peaked during Holly's fourth week as a receptionist. She had forgotten to tell one of her bosses that he had gotten an important call while he had been on another call. She told the second caller that he would have to call back or that she could have her boss call him back. There was a pause at the other end of the line and Holly couldn't accept the quietness. "You're not somewhere that you would be embarrassed if he called are you?" Holly said. Of course it was meant as a joke, but the caller didn't think it funny. "Just take my name and have him call me," the caller said with an icy tone. Fortunately Holly didn't respond to that—but she forgot to tell her boss about the call until much later.

Other people in the office began to complain and mentioned things Holly had done to decrease work efficiency. All the personnel felt that she was often rude, especially when someone asked something of her. Sometimes she responded in a sarcastic manner. Twice she knocked half-full coffee cups over on her desk. This was done in anger but again it showed how impulsive she could be, and it surely didn't look good to clients. Then there was the day it rained: Holly had a new hair style and had not brought her umbrella. Came time to leave, it was still pouring, and Holly impulsively took someone else's umbrella. When she arrived for work the next day she returned the umbrella. She couldn't understand why people were angry with her: "I did bring it back, didn't I? It's not like I stole it."

The straw that did the proverbial took place when Holly locked everyone out of the conference room just before a conference was to get started. Two of the four attorneys were on vacation and the third was on a case in a nearby city. Holly had wanted a set of her own keys for that room and she was going to get a key made from the office manager. No one was sure what happened to those keys but Holly maintained that they were never given to her. She therefore borrowed the fourth attorney's keys and then locked them in the conference room.

Of course it was possible to get the door unlocked once they were able to secure a key from one of the others. But this didn't remove the anger and frustration. Holly was let go.

That turned out best in the long run for Holly. Someone at the firm told her about a group of doctors that treated ADHD. Holly had never heard of that and her feelings were hurt. "I ain't got no bug like that on me," she exclaimed. But she did seek help.

She learned that with ADD you have to get actively focused on something, while with ADHD you must be slowed down. She began to understand her impulsiveness and she learned how medication could help.

It took Holly about a month to get stabilized and then what a wonderful difference! She began to notice things about people that she never had before. She began to use her high intelligence and she was able to take more interest in things. The next job she secured was one that she enjoyed and did well at. She looked back at her past life and now began to realize what had been going wrong. She found that people responded to her in a different manner.

Holly married soon thereafter and in short order she had several children. She found that she enjoyed family life even when her second child was suspected of having ADHD. "Why shouldn't she? She's my kid," Holly said. But Holly was very happy that she knew what to do to help her.

Holly was not an investor in anything, but just imagine what might have been if she were. Her impulsive behavior would place her in great jeopardy. She wouldn't have been able to read about investments and she couldn't have listened to her advisor or absorbed the advice he gave her. Maybe they would have had fights over what she was advised to do. She would have found some way to get things twisted.

Cognitive functioning is being able to understand what's going on in the world, whether it be current events or investment news. We are flooded every day with more information to process. That points up a disparity as our population gets older. Older people process information more slowly on the whole—at a time when decisions must be made quicker and when there's more information to consider.

Cognitive disorders are likely to increase in numbers because there are more and more older people. We all need to learn how to communicate with them and what their special problems are likely to be. Many of the elderly have found that what they thought was an adequate retirement program is not. They may well decide that they need a different investment program.

Another important area of interaction is also more and more challenging. That is working with the increasing number of Americans who come from another culture, creating a challenge not only to communicate but also to understand what they want. Will they have dramatically different goals? Will they look to retirement or focus more on happy times today? Some cultures encourage more aggressive business dealings and more risk-taking than others do.

And consider the role of women from one culture to the next. Some cultures strongly encourage women to look up to the male. There's a tendency to feel that primary decisions should be the role of the man. What will happen when a particular client relates dependently to her investment advisor? Will he feel uncomfortable after having dealt with more independent American women? Will he seek to disavow that much responsibility? It will take some real interpersonal intercultural skills to resolve that kind of conflict.

All these factors suggest that the world of investment will not be a dull place. But isn't that what we want and expect—that the road to riches through investments is open to all?

Chapter VII
Personality Disorders

If you ever have a desire to know someone well, pay attention to this chapter. Understanding people will come more from comprehension of personality disorders than from anything else. What is referred to as a "clinical disorder" (e.g., depression, anxiety disorder, manic behavior) can change rather abruptly, particularly given all the medications now available, but personality disorders are more constant. They also have a great impact upon the individual.

What is now called a *personality disorder* used to be called a character disorder. Character was considered the basic unit of the personality.

Character is like the skeleton of the personality. Someone who has a skeleton made up of weak and deformed bones, as we all know, would be susceptible to injuries. Lifting heavy objects might cause broken bones; joints might not accommodate the demands of quick movements. Fatigue might curtail physical activity after only short periods of exertion. Physical stress will take a heavier toll on someone with an impaired skeleton than on someone with a strong, well-formed skeleton.

The same is true with a personality disorder. These disorders are like a predisposition toward some forms of behavior. There's a general loss of flexibility to the extent that behavioral patterns must be repeated even though they impair a person's ability to reach goals.

A number of characteristics must exist for the diagnosis of personality disorder. We have already mentioned inflexibility in patterns of behavior. The disorder shows a pervasiveness along a broad range of interpersonal and personal situations. There's very significant distress and impairment in social and occupational functioning. There's a persistent pattern of deviation from the person's cultural background in such areas as cognition, impulse control, interpersonal relating, and affective life.

To further elaborate the last four criteria, *cognition* refers to how we see others and events and *affective expression* refers to how appropriate

93

our emotional responses are, their changeability, and their intensity. For a diagnosis of personality disorder these behaviors must have endured for a long time, perhaps going back to adolescence or very early adulthood.

This may be a very suitable description of what is required to support this diagnosis, but our goal is to understand how behavior affects the world of investments. To better understand human behavior, we must realize that most conflicts, disorders, and personality characteristics are a matter of degree. But what of the people who have not reached the level of disturbance required for a diagnosis of personality disorder? Can we learn anything to help us with them?

I would say yes. Let me remind you of the skeleton analogy. We all have a basic personality that gives us predilections toward certain behavioral patterns. These might be called *behavioral constellations* when they are not so severe as to indicate a personality disorder.

I also refer to milder expressions of these characteristics simply as *personality traits*. We are talking a matter of degree. In other words, a pervasive pattern that is a personality disorder in less pronounced degrees would be a personality trait.

The more pronounced the personality trait, the more rigid the behavior and the more it follows the dominant trait or traits. People are often confused about behavioral predilections. We have two thoughts to offer: If one trait predominates, identify that trait and you'll be able to predict behavior quite well. Second, the less one trait dominates, the more difficult prediction is. Because emotionally healthy people have more behavioral options open to them, their behavior is therefore less stereotyped.

In this chapter, I first present the personality disorders and then give a case example to illustrate the behavioral patterns—the illustration may be of a personality trait rather than a disorder.

We start with *dependent personality disorder* for a number of reasons, a major one being that after working with people for 30 years I have come to feel that problems with dependency are very often behind peoples' problems. Here are the key signs of this disorder:

1. Hates to make decisions without excessive advice and reassurance from key people.
2. Cannot readily assume responsibility for main life areas.
3. Fears he can't take care of himself; feels helpless when left to his own resources.
4. Has trouble undertaking new projects or experiences.
5. Constantly seeks support and even nurturance from others.

6. At times does unpleasant things just to attain support from others.

7. Has major problems differing with others.

Now let's see how these patterns take shape in peoples' lives.

Case 1: Joe applied for counseling saying that he felt he should be "doing better in my marriage." What was striking was that he seemed to avoid any reference as to what about *himself* bothered him. Everything was in terms of what someone else wanted from him.

He was told that therapy or counseling cannot make a person over in the image of another. "What do you want to change about yourself," he was asked. "What bothers you in life?"

Those who knew Joe could have suggested many things. Joe's problems on the golf course were fabled. He had a good swing and could hit the ball well. The trouble was that he didn't trust his own judgment, so he tried to rely on the judgment of his caddie. When the caddie diplomatically refused to make the decision, Joe became anxious and angry. If the caddie made a wrong selection, Joe was furious. Joe soon exhausted the selection of caddies.

What had prompted Joe to seek professional help was marital conflict. Everyone knew, for example, that Joe was always late to social events. People just assumed that Betty, who always looked lovely, was slow getting ready. One day Betty became irritated at always having to take the blame. She revealed that Joe was the slow one because he could never make up his own mind about what to wear. Betty had to pass on everything he put on.

Some people who saw Joe's inability to make decisions wondered how he had been so successful in business. Those who knew him well knew the answer: Joe had inherited not only a successful company but a wonderful staff as well. Joe relied on them—and in that his decision was very sound.

What gradually ate away at Betty were the constant demands Joe made on her. She had to reassure Joe that he didn't look older, that his gray hair was becoming, that he was still strong, and, most often, that she still cared about him as much as she had when they were first married.

Joe also became increasingly jealous. Betty was in business, so of course she had business meetings. Joe began to ask who she was with and what they talked about. Sometimes he would try to direct Betty against meeting with someone he seemed to dislike.

More severe problems began when Betty started a new career with a dress shop that she bought with her own money. Perhaps she thought that having dressed Joe all these years gave her the skills needed to dress her customers. Betty was instantly successful and Joe was very jealous of her success. He began to push harder and harder for her to sell the business. When she refused, Joe gave her an ultimatum: him or the dress shop. She chose the shop. He came for help. Like many with strong dependency, Joe had become upset when his support system was threatened.

Like many of the other personality types we will review, Joe has a problem with self-image. It's very difficult to feel confident when at the same time you feel the need for constant help because you don't trust your own judgment. Joe also has much periodic anger: Being that dependent makes you feel helpless. You need the support but hate feeling that much under the control of someone else. That's when the dependent person will push against his support figures to try to gain power and control. This is often called *hostile-dependent* behavior. People have been heard to say in therapy, "I hate my wife because I need her so much."

Joe's severe problems were also affecting his investment program. He had selected a respected advisor on whom he relied totally. However, when short-term results weren't totally positive, he was quick to question. Sometimes Joe seemed to enjoy a degree of failure so he could point out that others had inadequacies, too! Joe loved to tell his advisor about his own ideas but he never wanted to follow through on them. Since he hated any kind of change, his investment approach was rigid.

Another problem that caused investment difficulty was Joe's tendency to find different people, concepts, and ideas to depend on. That meant that a particular strategy worked out with his advisor could be abandoned because someone new in his life foresaw catastrophe. Or Joe wanted to pull out money currently invested for some new project. Joe was inconsistent in many ways, as in differing with his advisor: He had to be assured that his advisor was not angry at him because of a difference of opinion.

Joe presents a severe case of a pattern often seen in our society. When people are in a situation where they *must* make a decision, they do. Joe reached a crisis and though he couldn't change his personality, he did alter his behavior. A marital compromise was reached: the partners each had some portion of their lives where they made their own decisions.

Joe's advisor left him for a time and came back only when Joe insisted he would change. Some rules were established. There would be a time limit on calls and meetings. Joe could discuss investment approaches but he had to make more decisions and offer more ideas. His advisor would explain why he suggested something, decisions would be mutual, and both would accept responsibility.

Next we have the *avoidant personality*, a disorder characterized by marked social inhibition and extreme sensitivity to criticism. Again, there's evidence of very low self-esteem. The person with avoidant personality:

1. Has deep concern about being rejected or criticized when interacting socially.

2. Feels uncomfortable in new social situations and becomes very inhibited because he feels so inadequate.

3. Stays away from jobs that require much social contact out of fear of rejection.

4. Avoids intimacy in relationships.

5. Won't get involved with people unless certain ahead of time of being accepted.

6. Perceives himself as socially awkward and unappealing to others.

7. Finds it very difficult to make a commitment to anything risky.

Case 2: Bev was a strikingly attractive young woman of 26 who would blush and become embarrassed when her looks were praised. She simply couldn't accept praise: Bev often commented that people who came to know her would see her as "just an ordinary blond.

Although she was attractive, she never seemed able to attract young men and then build something that lasted. There would be a few dates and then the couple broke things off. Men described Bev as cold; said that she seemed to become more withdrawn after a few dates.

Bev had been the same in school. She was actually very bright and often earned high grades, but as soon as she began to do well with one subject she was off to another. She was, for example, going to be a teacher but when she tried it she hated having to take charge of so many people who "question you all the time." Once when she was student teaching she had a conference with her supervisor. He felt Bev had done a good job but had some suggestions. After making a suggestion, he turned away from Bev for a moment. Next thing he knew she was gone. She didn't like the criticism and went home.

Bev tried a few other jobs but none gave her the privacy she wanted. She thought about forestry but decided there were too many males in the occupation. She got a job working in a lab. That appealed to her because she had very structured rules to work by and there was very little people contact. She tried it for a few months, things went well, and this became her career.

Bev did have an investment advisor, one she inherited from her father along with a moderate nest egg. The main problem for her advisor was that she wouldn't communicate with him at all regularly. At the start of their relationship the advisor had called to set up a meeting. "I want to be sure I'm following your investment philosophy," he said.

Bev assured him she would but she didn't come in. So he sent her some papers explaining his approach and asking her to sign and return one indicating she agreed. Bev sent back only those papers that gave her permission for investment.

Bev never involved herself in the investment process. She never complained; nor did she ever say "nice job," when an investment was successful. Her advisor stayed on out of respect for her father, but Bev never gave any suggestion or appraisal of his investment approach. Her advisor was once heard to remark, "I wonder if she even knows how successful we've been!"

Now for *paranoid personality disorder*, a category that will be familiar because we discussed paranoia earlier. There are, of course, some major differences in that here we are addressing something that is an ingrained part of the personality. If we were to consult an accepted diagnostic manual, we would again encounter the word "pervasive." The primary symptoms are widespread suspicion and distrust beginning by early adulthood. A person with this disorder:

1. Has a pronounced tendency to show unwarranted suspicion that people are taking advantage of her through deception and exploitation.

2. Is very hesitant to confide in anyone because of the baseless fear that somehow this information will be used against her, though often she cannot give a solid reason for any distrust. There's suspicion about future behavior even when a person has done nothing wrong in the past.

3. Distorts remarks heard to the point that others are seen as making threats when they are not. Neutral actions are falsely perceived as threatening.

4. Never forgives! Carries grudges over small things like jokes and being left out of some activity, convinced that others will never play fair and give adequate credit.

5. Has frequent unjustified suspicions about the fidelity of a loved one. (With this symptom a reality check is important: married partners can be very provocative with one another, so it may not be all paranoia.).

6. Tends to see attacks on her reputation, character, or competence where other people wouldn't see anything destructive.

Case 3: Pam's problems may have started early in her childhood. She was the last of eight children and friends of her mother always indicated that her mother was already very overburdened before she was born. Pam got very little attention from anyone in the family except for the sister seventh in the birth order who was three years older than Pam and gave her attention by constantly beating up on her. If Pam had a toy that her sister wanted, the sister just took it. Pam's mother reportedly did nothing to correct this situation.

Pam claimed that things became even worse for her as she got older, principally because her older sisters resented having to act as babysitters and academic tutors when Pam had school problems, which she often did.

Pam soon began to show significant behavioral problems. She started missing classes at school and was caught fighting with classmates. There were strong suggestions that she was using illicit drugs. Her parents were called to the police station because of curfew violation. When Pam was caught under the influence of alcohol, her parents had had enough.

Pam was sent to a girls' high school that resembled a military school. The girls had to be in their rooms at a certain time and couldn't wander over the campus after hours. The girls could go out to a movie only one day a week. There was no dating until the junior year. A girl could have family visitors on weekends only, though Pam's parents almost never visited anyway.

Pam was at first rebellious but then became acquainted with the athletic coach. Under "coach's" tutelage Pam soon discovered a talent and a love for athletics. She was an outstanding swimmer and softball player. Pam began to be more accepted. She claimed that it was the first time in her life she felt that way. As her athletic success brought her more and more attention, Pam recognized that she had to do something about social skills. She tried more and more to fit in with others students and even with the staff.

One problem immediately showed itself. Some of her peers were jealous of all the attention Pam was suddenly receiving. Pam responded at first with humility and even tried to use humor to disarm her critics.

However, that became more and more difficult because her success brought her more adulation from coaches and teachers. Her peers then claimed she was just being modest to curry more attention from the coaches. Pam was not adept at fighting back verbally; she was vulnerable when others used verbal approaches to ridicule her.

Things stayed pretty much in balance until Pam hurt her shoulder playing softball. She lost velocity with her pitches and power at the plate. Some claimed that she wasn't hurt, just seeking more attention and excuses for increasing failures.

Pam was amazed at how quickly people could turn on her. Suddenly she wasn't invited to parties or asked to join groups. She began to see rejection and criticism everywhere. Even when people joked with her she saw it as ridicule. Because Pam couldn't accept any constructive criticism, corrective measures were impossible.

With her social isolation Pam had plenty of time to study. As her grades continued to improve, athletics fell into the background. She repeatedly said, "You've got to do it for yourself: You can't count on others," and indeed she followed that rule and had an excellent college record.

After graduation she found a job very suited to her talents. She was recruited by a firm that acquired businesses that were doing badly, reorganized them, fired a lot of employees, and got them to start producing again. Pam fitted right into that mold: it was her job to do the firing and to warn others that if they didn't improve they would be out. Pam became very successful.

However, her personal life didn't go as smoothly. Pam was twice married and divorced. She never trusted her husbands and was convinced they were unfaithful. She lost several very close female friends because she was convinced they were out to steal something from her—her business position or a boy friend.

Pam's distrust was damaging her investment programs, too. She found an excellent advisor and the two had worked very well together, at least while she was married when she had a husband to complain about and to be suspicious of. She often complained to her advisor about her husbands; while he never took sides, she felt he supported her.

With her second divorce Pam shifted her suspicions to her advisor. If he sold at a high, Pam said he didn't want her to have a maximum profit and become more independent. If it was a loss, the criticism was that he wasn't watching her investments. If he called to ask her advice, Pam said he didn't want to take responsibility for his investment. If he didn't call, Pam said he didn't value her opinion.

Somehow the two decided without a major fight that they couldn't work together. It was an amiable separation but Pam has one area of hard feelings. Her former advisor now handles the account of one of Pam's few close friends and what angers Pam is that he's doing a great job!

Histrionic personality disorder is one that we will quickly recognize, because people with this personality or trait readily stand out in crowds. They have to, or they will be very unhappy. A person with this disorder:

1. Must be the center of attention.
2. Is often seductive.
3. Has shallow but quick shifting emotions, and therefore lacks depth.
4. Uses physical appearance to attract attention.
5. Is easily influenced by others.
6. Uses dramatic language but language that lacks detail.

Case 4: Henry always had a way of being the center of attention. His humor usually ridiculed someone else while calling attention to something he's good at. For example, Henry, who had a very extensive wardrobe, loved to comment to those who didn't, "It's nice that you don't care that much about how you look."

Henry's wardrobe changed every time there was a new trend. He had no style that was his because he changed so rapidly. Then he let everyone know when he had something new. But then, Henry did that with everything he owned, car, golf clubs, or furniture.

Henry has always had a pronounced tendency to let other people know he was special and therefore not easily satisfied. He often commented that he was too talented to accept what others settled for. He would never settle for a casual moderate-priced restaurant, for example; it had to be the most elegant one around.

There was a similar pattern to his relationships with women. Henry dated many women. He was always convinced that each of them cared deeply about him. He claimed that nearly all had wanted to marry him but he was still looking for that "special girl."

Henry was exceedingly demanding of women. They, like him, had to stand out in a crowd, although there was a rub there: They couldn't divert attention away from Henry. But they had to be physically attractive and dress to show off their looks. His women had to be on the quiet side, again so they wouldn't take attention from Henry. Some of his women were known to be less than geniuses. They were allowed to have their own ideas—as long as they were the same as Henry's. Henry was also big on loyalty—not he to his women but they to him. When he went to a party or a dinner he could flirt but his date dare not.

People who had known Henry for a long time said that his behavior had not changed since high school. He was always dramatic and highly excitable. He had spent nearly a year in high school drama class but ultimately decided to drop his "acting career." He felt that others were jealous of him and worked to reduce his parts and "emotional expression."

He did have excellent athletic ability in that he was fast, quick, and strong. He was very well coordinated and learned quickly. He had a good arm and wanted to play quarterback. He had visions of roaring crowds, of winning football games in the last few minutes, and of exciting headlines.

His coach had other ideas. He found Henry difficult to coach; he never hesitated to change the play his coach had sent in. The coach objected to Henry throwing long pass after long pass—most of which were intercepted—so Henry was switched to a defensive back. His self-involvement created problems there, too, because Henry tried to intercept all the time. As a result he neglected defense and gave up touchdowns. When criticized he quit the team.

Henry next met the first person in his life that he truly idealized, Walter. The two decided to attend the same college and then start a business together. Both earned good grades in business and accounting and the four years went by uneventfully. In their senior year both were interviewed by a small but successful insurance agency. Offered jobs they both decided that for the short-term would fit their needs.

The main work for both Henry and Walter was to sell various types of insurance. Both men found early indications that they were successful salesmen, but Henry became colossal. He found that he could make most people like him because he "always tells them what they want to hear." His own emotional life was so shallow that Henry could seem sincere when in fact he was acting.

As the little company began to grow, Henry and Walter began to invest in it. The original owner began to have misgivings about his two outstanding salesmen. He saw situations where insurance policies were sold that really weren't needed. A verbal confrontation ensued. Henry and Walter offered a buyout, their boss decided it was time to retire, and he took their offer.

The new owners went on as before. They also made some successful investments. As the income began to swell Henry increased his spending on things designed to call attention to himself. He first started with new clothes and then went to a more extravagant car. He also lavished gifts on the women in his life. Walter told him he was wasting his money on the gifts; the women didn't really care that deeply about him. That made Henry very angry. He was convinced that every woman he dated was intimately tied to him, but apparently Walter was correct because none of the women stayed around very long.

It was Henry's investment approach that brought on disaster, though of course his extravagant spending helped. Henry had concluded that his problem was not overspending but under earning. As is typical of the histrionic personally, Henry was highly suggestible. His dramatically shifting but shallow moods attracted others who were excitable and impulsive.

"I should be worth a lot more than I'm currently getting," Henry said over and over. "There's a lot to be made out there but you need good advice to get it." At this point Henry started taking advice from the gambler types. "Life's a gamble and if you don't take a chance you won't ever win" became Henry's model.

With his flighty approach to people he went from one advisor to another. He had no overall plan. Sometimes he bought a stock and then impulsively sold it on a slight down trend. Next time in the same situation he bought more. When it went down he bought still more.

The same thing happened with those who gave him advice. Once he heard a man he had never seen before mention a stock during a golf game. "The guy is a great golfer so he must be the winner type," Henry decided. His former long-time advisor pointed out there was a major problem. "Henry, you take advice from everyone. One time you make what was supposed to be a long-term investment and then you sell three days later. Then you make a short-term investment long-term. I can't bring you success that way."

"All right," Henry said, "then quit." And he did!

As you may readily guess, it didn't take Henry long to run through friends, business advisors, acquaintances—and money. Suddenly Henry was the center of attention but it wasn't the type anyone wants. People were trying to collect money Henry owed them.

Leaving Henry to his troubles, let's consider the *narcissistic personality disorder*, easily recognized from Greek mythology. It reflects a pervasive neediness for admiration, inability to empathize with others, and grandiosity. This personality is the self-centered type on a grand scale, characterized by:

1. Preoccupation with fantasies of extreme success, power, and brilliance..

2. Grandiose feelings of self-importance, with a desire for others to immediately recognize him as superior even when he lacks the achievements necessary to earn those accolades.

3. A feeling that people owe him a great deal.

4. Use of others to selfishly gratify his needs.

5. Envy of others.

6. Failure to identify with the needs of others.

This disorder often looks a lot like histrionic disorder to most people, because none of us enjoy people who are all into themselves.

Though I have not counseled anyone with this disorder, I have been told about several investment advisors that have had narcissistic people as clients. Here is a good example.

Case 5: One of the first major problems presented by Nancy was her search for the perfect advisor; one who would quickly make her "fabulously wealthy." That was about all she ever thought of. She felt that she was owed all these riches because she did so much for others. She often called her advisor yelling because her investments hadn't gone up enough. On one call she made one very telling comment: "Your other clients may be happy with those puny profits but I'll tell you, Buster, I expect and deserve more out of life."

She called her advisor at any hour of the day or night whenever there was a notable activity with investments. And she was never satisfied.

What ended the relationship was when Nancy called her advisor at home at night. It didn't matter that he was home comforting his wife after a difficult delivery of their first child. When her advisor told Nancy that, there was a quick reply: "Don't you realize that those are my investments we're talking about?" That was the last time they worked together!

Our next problem, borderline personality disorder, is very serious because of the numerous areas of disturbance. There's again a pervasive behavioral pattern of instability of relationships with others, confused self-image, unstable affect, and pronounced impulsivity. These people have major problems adjusting. Borderline personality disorder is characterized by:

1. Desperate attempts to deal with abandonment, which can be real or imaginary.

2. Severely unstable interpersonal relationships with a tendency to fluctuate between extremes of idealizing someone and then treating that person as worthless.

3. No clear, established, stable self-concept, which lack makes the individual inconsistent.

4. Impulsive, self-damaging behavior like overspending, gambling, or substance abuse.

5. Threats of self-destructive behavior.

6. Intense emotional instability, with brief intense dysphoria, irritability, or anxiety.

7. Chronic feelings of emptiness related to the lack of self-image.

8. Inappropriate and intense anger, and difficulty controlling the anger.

9. Short-lived and stress-related paranoid ideation.

We can see why investing with such persons is difficult.

Case 6: We have no information about Brad's childhood or adolescence, with one exception. Brad several times stated that he was always in trouble. He used drugs, had physical fights, and was a reckless driver. He had four significant car accidents by age 18.

As a young adult Brad was in and out of relationships, twice married and divorced, with each divorce costing him considerably. He came from a wealthy family and his father was generous in paying his bills. With his second divorce, though, he warned Brad about future "quickie marriages and divorces." Brad promised to be more careful. He let it be known that he would "never get married again."

While playing golf he heard a mutual friend talk about his stock broker and how he could make "big killings in the market." Brad wanted to meet him. When he did, he immediately decided that the broker was a genius. He shifted all his investment funds to this "genius."

At first the investments turned out rather well. Brad realized substantial gains. He began seeing himself as powerful, a big winner, and a great judge of character. He often took personal credit for investment successes. When friends doubted his investment abilities, Brad became more and more agitated and desperate to prove himself. He would show them who could make money!

Now his ego was at stake. He wanted everyone to see "what a powerhouse guy I am." So, with four friends in tow, he went to a gambling casino. The more he lost, the more he gambled. After losing several large wagers in a row, he became enraged. At first he didn't want anyone to see how much he hurt. He maintained he could afford it but his anger turned into rage. He yelled that "the tables are fixed," and claimed that he was being cheated. When one of the security guards tried to restrain him, Brad threw a punch. Then he was escorted to jail.

Now with the gambling losses, the drinking, and the legal costs, money did become an issue. He called his broker to say that he needed cash but he was told everything was invested in stocks. "Who told you to do that?" he asked his broker. "You did," was the reply.

All of a sudden the broker that he idolized became the target of his rage. He knew he could have won back what he lost if he had the funds to back his wagers. Suddenly Brad began to feel that everyone was against him and had deserted him. He was all alone, and he felt empty, helpless, and suddenly worthless. He was afraid to go anywhere for fear he would hurt someone because he couldn't control himself.

After one of his tirades, the broker decided to let Brad do his own investing. When Brad finally had a breakdown his investments were handled by his father. Whatever happened to Brad, I don't know.

Antisocial personality disorder presents a challenge, as can be seen from the basic definition: This is a pervasive behavioral pattern of violation of the rights of others. Persons with this disorder are so reckless that they may place others in jeopardy. They seldom plan ahead. They are irresponsible and often irritable, engaging in physical fights.

A major sign of this disorder is the tendency to engage in unlawful behavior. These people, often gifted manipulator, are prone to con people. They generally don't empathize with others, even people that they have harmed.

I have never seen at first hand the investment behavior of someone with this disorder but I have diagnosed a number inmates at correctional facilities with this disorder, noting some similarities in behavior. These people have not been able, generally speaking, to see cause-and-effect relationships. They think of what is happening now but not of what this portends for the future. The ones I have seen don't seem to feel rewarded when they do something that pleases another person; thus making someone feel happy had no appeal. Often they wanted to win by harming someone else. Finally, they often showed sudden destructive behavior like fighting—sudden, internally provoked rage that outsiders couldn't see coming. Often the antisocial person didn't expect it either, or so they said.

Clearly investing with those who have this disorder might be very difficult. An advisor who didn't take care might find herself advising someone who wanted wealth but didn't care how he got it. That can lead to serious problems!

Schizoid personality disorder is marked by emotional distance in social relationships. These people generally prefer solitary activities, seem not to be interested in or moved by praise, and show no desire for close relationships. The signs are of an emotional rather than a thought disturbance.

I knew one such person, an excellent accountant. He loved to comment that "emotions get you in trouble and I don't have that problem." He never did seem to become emotionally close. If you knew him as an accountant but not socially, you would probably feel there was nothing wrong with him. He was certainly not one to hurt others.

Similarly, the person with schizotypal personality disorder has no interest in having close friends. Social anxiety is often present, as are feelings of suspicion of others. However, it's the thought disturbance that is clearly notable. There are odd beliefs and thought patterns, peculiar superstitions, often unusual perceptions, and many bizarre fantasies.

I knew one man professionally who had this disorder. He was an amateur investor and gambler who charged for his opinion on wagers or with the stock market. He claimed there was a balance in nature that allowed prediction. He loved to talk about his "discovery," which he just knew would one day create riches.

His first example to me involved expected frequencies with coins. "Now, Dr. Gunn," Sal began, "what percent of the time does heads come up on a coin?" He always brought you into one of his concepts as if he were laying a trap.

Before I answered I felt like counting my fingers. "Fifty percent of the time," I said, with hesitation.

"Of course," Sal shot back. "So out of one hundred throws there should be fifty heads and fifty tails," he said as if making a monumental proclamation. He went on. "I've studied this situation for years and discovered it with coins. If you throw coins ninety times and you have fifty heads and forty tails you'll find that tails will come up nearly ten times out of ten with the next ten throws."

I didn't know whether to laugh or act amazed. It took me a few minutes to decide. "Are you saying that the coins know about these frequencies and where they are in that frequency?" I asked.

"You bet I am and I'd put money on it," Sal said with great excitement. "One day what I've found will make us rich."

"Not me," I said, "I don't have the temperament for this kind of investment. Do you use that approach with the stock market, too?"

"Yes, and it's working right now. My stocks are nearly all up."

Sal didn't mention that the whole market was up and had been for some time. I didn't mention it either.

This little example of his thinking can well illustrate what might happen with investments. An advisor who thought this way probably wouldn't last long. But what do you do if you have a client whose mind works that way? Probably you'll lose your client when you set limits, but maybe that's a blessing. If you go along with such an illogical approach there may be legal action.

Finally we have obsessive-compulsive personality disorder. This has become well known as people make reference to compulsive people. We used to believe that it was a great asset to be so thorough; in fact many people felt guilt-ridden if they didn't keep a scrupulously clean house. Now we aren't so sure.

The traits of this disorder are perfectionism, preoccupation with details, order, miserly spending habits, rigidity, inability to delegate, and excessive dedication to work. As you read through the list, you can see that many of them involve a judgment call. If you needed brain surgery, would you want your doctor to be extremely dedicated to his work? At what point does highly dedicated become excessive?

We could say that excessive devotion to work means more devotion than is *necessary*, but you almost need to have that call made by someone in the same profession or occupation.

Many decades ago I saw an investment banker who fit these descriptions.

Case 7: Obie came to see me first because of marital problems. He said his wife had complaints but since he didn't, he wasn't sure if there was a marital problem or not. He said he didn't feel depressed or anxious.

Obie was eventually able to talk about some of the things that made his life difficult. Gradually we got around to his work. That seemed the most important area of his life and it was a major reason why his wife was so unhappy. She felt that he was so dedicated to work that he had little time for anything else, including his family.

As Obie spoke about his work it became clear that his compulsive behavior handicapped him. So, too, did his tendency to obsess on a single idea. He realized he couldn't switch his approach very easily. He had low levels of adaptation. There were times when he was literally paralyzed by his compulsive approach. For practical reasons change was in order, but he was hung up on not wanting to let go of his rigidity.

"I enjoy being successful," he said at one point.

"Do you really," I asked in a challenging way. "What reward or satisfaction do you find when you do something well?"

Obie looked shocked. "I never thought of that, but I just realized I never celebrate anything I do well." "So there's no reward?" I reflected. His facial expression provided the answer.

In the weeks to come we looked at the interplay of his work and personality. These are some of the problems that Obie was able to define:

1. He lacked flexibility because his approach was so rigid.

2. He did study his investments and in a sense his thoroughness could be an asset, but he took so long studying that opportunities often passed him by.

3. In a down market he was so analytical that he couldn't react quickly.

4. He was fine with a market that moved up slowly and waited for him to make up his mind.

5. In a market moving up quickly he had the same problem as in a market rushing down.

6. Thus he usually couldn't move with any rapidity.

7. He also couldn't easily adjust to something new or different.

8. He couldn't readily use new information from other sources.

9. Having limited contact with others, he couldn't obtain a variety of sources of information.

10. His tendency to obsess on his failures narrowed his scope.

11. He didn't adjust well whenever the investment world changed.

12. He was not a good listener because he clung so rigidly to his own ideas that he didn't process what others were saying.

13. He had problems with interpersonal relationships because he rigidly pushed his ideas, which seldom seemed to change. Then he became irritated when others "couldn't follow his logic."

14. Without being aware of it he had emotional downs that affected his work—it's hard to live without rewards and without intimacy.

Obie gradually moved into a more rewarding life. I never knew just how far he might have gone because just when he began to become a sociable, enjoyable, and relaxed person, he succumbed to illness. I missed him, so I guess he did learn to be more emotionally giving.

These disorders affect many of us. They are important not primarily as disorders but rather in the smaller version: traits. There are few persons who would have all the characteristics that make up a disorder.

To me the significant factor is the smaller version. Someone may be dependent enough to affect his behavior but not to the extent of a disorder. Yet the trait of dependency may do many things to our investment picture. Recognizing traits should help both client and advisor.

One word of advice: When you think of people, try to look at what is and not make judgments. Judgments turn people off and that won't help them or you. Try to remember there's a little bit of us in everyone, and vice versa.

Chapter VIII
How To Be Aware of a
Client's Psychological
State

Now that we've talked about the ingredients that shape personalities, we have to put them all together. It's one thing to say this is what a mood disorder is; it's another when you want to apply all this information to a real person. It's easier to describe a mood disorder than to diagnose a person as having one. In real life you don't get perfect matches.

When we speak about a psychological state, we're referring to the condition of a person at a specific time. It's like saying, "My boss is angry." We all recognize that someone's psychological state can change from one time frame to the next. But even that's significant because it immediately says, "This person is not consistent." However, we also assume enough stability that predictions can be made about a behavioral pattern.

One very common error is to make two assumptions: (1) We judge people by how they interact with us, and (2) we weight someone's personality heavily by how they interact with us the first time we meet. It's as if that first experience becomes indelibly ingrained in our minds.

There are problems with both approaches, the second, for instance, because all of us have good days and bad ones. Someone who has had a wonderful day where everything has just gone great is sure to be optimistic, floating on air. It wouldn't be fair to expect that kind of reaction constantly. Let's make one of our first rules, "Don't be inflexible in your opinions of others."

The first assumption is one of my pet peeves: assuming that how someone interacts with you is how they interact everywhere. An acquaintance, Don, was upset because he had been referred to as "aloof." Clearly the description was most inaccurate. He asked me one day if I saw him that way. I couldn't stop laughing (not the best way for a shrink to respond to someone's discomfort. I rationalized that he wasn't a patient!). "Don," I began when I got control of my laughter, "you're one of the most outgoing persons I've known. Why the question?"

His story was that a fellow golf club member had asked him for a golf game and perhaps dinner later. He had said no several times and then came the "aloof" label.

"So you got classified because you didn't want to join one person for a social activity. Knowing you, you had a good reason."

"I felt I did," Don said. "Golf with those guys is an all-day event. They gamble quite a bit and then the drinking goes on later. Sometimes they start card games after that. I don't like gambling and I want to get home to my family. I just don't enjoy this guy and his friends, but I don't want to be nasty either."

This illustrates how we classify people according to how they interact with us. People who have performed psychological services are quick to recognize that they can get rapport with some and not others. If we're going to classify someone, we must do it across a broader spectrum.

Most of us believe that our psychological state will sooner or later affect our business transactions, so that tells us we must learn to recognize our own state quickly and accurately, as well as the state of the client. How long and how well we have known him is a complicating factor.

First, let's look at the situation where the investor has not known the advisor. Often these are clients referred by someone who has known and probably worked with the advisor for some time. Usually when a person refers a friend to an advisor it's because the advisor has had outstanding success.

Case 1: George referred Fred to Bill, saying that Bill was a "great" advisor. George went on to say that Bill had made him a bundle of money, quickly. Fred went running to Bill ready to make his fortune. Of course Bill doesn't know what George said to Fred, and unfortunately he never asked Fred about his goals. Bill gave Fred some advice, Fred jumped on it because he was so in awe of Bill, and after a month, though there are profits they aren't what Fred anticipated.

Fred showed his unhappiness when he finally confronted Bill. "Why is it you made George a fortune, $70,000, and you can't do that for me?" Fred wanted to know.

Bill was confused. First, it wasn't $70,000, it was $50,000. Second, George had more money than Fred and there was no worry that he might have to pull money out of his investments because he needed money to live on. Third, George wanted a long-term investment: it just happened that there was a quick profit.

Ethics didn't allow Bill to tell Fred about someone else's investments. That's confidential. What he could do was explain in general terms that you must compare market conditions over time. When George invested, everything was going up. When Fred invested, most signs were indicating a down market.

Fred got into such an emotional state that it was difficult to reason with him. In the end Bill lost a customer who for nearly a year made negative comments about Bill as an advisor.

What psychological factors contributed to this? Bill didn't really know Fred and consequently he had neither background nor behavioral patterns to work with. What Bill should have noticed were the grandiose comments Fred made when he met with Bill. There were warnings like: "George says you're a genius." "I've heard you're quick with the profits." "George says you made him a bundle." "I'm already sure, just meeting you, that you'll do great for me."

These kinds of comments tell us that these people have unreasonable expectations. They want a miracle worker, a parent, and a magician with a crystal ball, all rolled into one. With that psychological state a client will never really be satisfied. Make a big gain in January and she'll expect the same in February. Had Bill seen the excessive idolization, he would have been in a position to correct this situation.

The psychological state of someone you haven't known well is difficult to evaluate, but there are some things that can guide you. For instance,

1. *Appearance.* You can tell a great deal from how someone looks. Appearance shows whether people take pride in themselves.

2. *Energy.* The energy level, as we discussed earlier, can be significant. If it's too high, you may have a manic or hyperactive person to deal with, someone who makes decisions too quickly. Could this person become notably demanding? Is this a person who wants sudden profits and gets jumpy when asked to wait? If energy level is too low, this person may hate making quick decisions or changes. Does this person think slowly? Could this person be depressed? To help estimate energy level, note how the person walks or gestures, the speed, aggressive versus slow and awkward.

3. *Greeting.* If you shake hands, is the handshake strong or like a dead noodle? Some persons grab your hand like they want to crush it. Others have wet palms, often due to great inner tension.

4. *Talk.* Is the speech clear? Is there a heavy accent that could limit communication? Is the pace rapid or slow? Note how often you need to ask for repetitions because the words flew by too rapidly. If the speech is slow, you may find yourself completing sentences. The volume will tell you about aggressiveness and passivity, depression, low self-esteem. If communication is poor, you want to be very sure you understand that client's investment strategy.

5. *Initial mood.* What is the predominant mood at first meeting? Does the client seem shy? Shyness as a personality trait's often misunderstood. We think that shy people are always quiet and passive. That is not necessarily true. Someone who initially holds back may become very angry when he feels he has been taken advantage of. What other emotions does the person show? Does he smile a lot, is he bubbly and outgoing? Does she respond to your emotion? Do you have a sense that here is a happy person? A warm person?

6. *Reactions.* What does this person respond to? Does she seem to like humor? Is he the serious type? Does he like casual conversation? Is she almost always business-oriented?

7. *Mannerisms.* Does this person become defensive easily? Is it often? Does she try to let others know that she's very knowledgeable about investments? Does she seem open or notably guarded?

8. *Social Interaction.* Does the client appear highly aggressive and independent? This may seem like a good behavioral pattern but it can have major drawbacks. An advisor is there to advise; if you have someone who resists advice, you'll find it difficult to work with that person. All of us need some help at times. If a person just wants to have someone make his investments, not consult, you need to know that at the beginning. And you need an understanding that if the investments fail, you know who chose them. If your client is a person who wants an advisor to make all the decisions, that needs to be recognized. Does that seem what she wants? Does the client follow one approach and recognize that she does that? If not, there may be some conflict as to which role each of you plays. Then the question becomes, is she consistent? Does the client become argumentative? Does she seem to want to push her own ideas? How does the client approach investments?

9. *Investment Approach.* Does he have his own ideas for the most part? Does he get new investment ideas from his advisor? Does he often seek tips from other people?

10. *Reasoning.* How does the client seem to express his ideas? Is he easy to follow? Is he logical? Does he draw conclusions that are widely different from those that others would draw?

11. *Awareness.* Does the client seem well oriented to what's going on in the world around her? Or does she show little interest in current events?

12. *Interactions.* How does the client react to others? Does he interrupt them? Is he sarcastic? Is he friendly and supportive people? Does he seem to enjoy communicating with others? Does he generally appear very sociable? Or is he more the solitary type?

13. *Family.* What do you know of her family? Is she married? Divorced? Have a family? Children living at home? This last may seem at the moment very insignificant, but if a client-advisor relationship develops, it could become important. What if she was married, then is divorced and the financial resources are split. Now the advisor may suddenly have another client. Sometimes important tax decisions are based on family structure and overall income.

14. *Your Role.* How does the client like to be treated? Does he essentially want a "yes man"? Does he like someone to play the devil's advocate? Does he just want straightforward investment information? Does he like to use you as a sounding board?

Putting together information from these 14 categories, you'll have a good start in knowing your client.

When you first meet a new client, there's no reference point because you don't know him. There are some important questions you want answered in order to be the best advisor you can be:

1. What does your client want? That means type of investments, income goals, financial gains.

2. How does the client wish to be treated by an advisor?

3. What is his general health, especially mentally and emotionally. Does he have any significant psychological problems?

On the other hand, if you have a non-going professional relationship with your client, you'll want different kinds of information. You can know your client better because you have seen a wider sample of behavior in a variety of situations. If you have only seen a client on days of positive investment returns, you have no idea about the client's response to losses.

With an ongoing relationship an investment advisor will want to understand the client's psychological state even better. Now an important ingredient is added: change. It won't help to "know" that a client's psychological state is of calmness if he's currently raving over a loss.

Ours is a world of change and people change as well. Sometimes the change brings growth and greater success, but change can also bring disaster. To be successful we need a yardstick for change. Is it constructive or destructive change?

Case 2: Jerry was a young man whom I had known only socially. I had never seen him professionally, but I had been down wind of his golf clubs being fired through the air. He once came forward to our golf group to apologize and he said, "It helps me ventilate my anger—did you ever try that with your clients?"

"No, Jerry," I said, "my office is a little small to throw golf clubs." He laughed and went back to his group. His temper explosions were legendary. He never hit people but he yelled at them, berating them at times. His financial advisor often mentioned the problems he had with Jerry.

Six months later, his advisor asked me if I had ever seen a spontaneous change for the better in someone. He said that all of a sudden Jerry seemed very pleasant, diplomatic, and sociable. He was now easy to discuss different ideas with. "Now, when we disagree I can give advice and Jerry doesn't fly off the handle."

No one knew why for another month. Then we had an opportunity to meet Jerry's new wife. Seeing them together it was obvious that she had a wonderfully positive impact on Jerry's disposition. In the brief time of their marriage she had transformed Jerry into a rational, calm person who could express his feelings comfortably.

It's nice to realize that some change can be for the better. Perhaps we should all be encouraged to remember that positive things do happen. But some changes that look positive are not, at least in their totality.

A friend, talking to me about Jerry's personality change, told me about another man who had a temper like Jerry's. Because he always went south for the winter, many of his friends hadn't seen him for a number of months. When they did, they were surprised as to how mild he had become. Then they were told that his personality change had been caused by a stroke.

With some of these thoughts in mind let's look at some ways to identify changes from past behavior in the client's psychological state:

1. What is the client's energy level? Is it higher or lower? Has the behavior become more variable? This is an important area because it can pick up physical as well as emotional problems.

2. Is there a change in enthusiasm? There can be two sides to this question. A person who has become very compulsive about something may seem enthusiastic, but enthusiasm means a more joyful countenance. Very few people who are despondent or greatly discouraged show any enthusiasm.

3. Is the client optimistic about his future? Does he have goals? One key sign of depression is a loss of positive attitude, which can also be a symptom of organic impairment, such as dementia.

4. How does your client interact with his or her spouse? This is a question that cannot be asked directly but it's important. Severe marital problems are likely to carry over into every area of life. Very severe problems could lead to divorce, and that will nearly always affect finances. It might also be important to consider how the spouse feels about the investment advisor. If the feelings are negative, that, too, can become a formidable problem.

5. How does your client communicate with you? Is it less often than it used to be? Is it now over the phone rather than in person? Or does he constantly come in to see you? If so, why? Does he seem more worried about investments than he used to be?

6. How does your client interact with you? Do you see him as confused after the loss of a loved one? Does he appear to lack direction now that a loved one is ill? Do you get the feeling that he wants something but can't recognize what it's? Does he seem very lonely?

7. What do you know about your client's health? It's not a good idea to ask directly because he may feel it's not your business, but I've found that if I say to people, "How's everything going?" they'll often expand on that. Watching a client, you may see him taking a new pill, which means a health change. Some information may be forthcoming from appearance. He may have had a weight or color change, and even posture can give impressions. If there seems a problem, watch for other changes in your interaction.

8. How direct is your client in dealing with you? Does he look down or otherwise away from you? What sort of eye contact do you have with him? When people look away, it's usually because they have something important on their minds. Often the client is unhappy about something and doesn't know how to tell you about it.

9. Have you noted a change of interest with your client? Does he seem less interested in the world? Is he more critical than he used to be? Does he refuse to go out of his way for socialization now?

10. Are there any signs of alcohol or drug use, signs like dimmed consciousness, confusion, memory loss, change of appearance, and speech not as clear as it once was?

In identifying the client's psychological state, it's useful to be familiar with the personality disorders. Usually you'll conclude that there's no full-blown personality disorder, but you may see traits of one. These are important to help you identify basic personality. For example, in reading about a dependent personality disorder you may think of a client who has some of those traits but not intensely enough for an actual disorder. This is important because personality traits don't readily change. You have therefore identified basic characteristics that are likely to govern the person's behavior over time.

Let's begin with communication and thinking. Working with someone in the investment arena usually gives us important data here.

(1) Oral communication gives us a great deal of information. Someone who is angry will usually show it in tone of voice. Psychologists have found that people with the same emotion may respond at opposite extremes. For example, someone who's angry will either speak sharply or be withdrawn and quiet. The voice tone will not be moderate.

So you may ask yourself what you see with your client, especially compared to previous behavior. Is he short with his responses? Does he raise his voice? Does he glare at you but refuse to say much. If the answer to any of these questions is yes, you have someone who is angry but not ready to talk. If the voice is loud and demanding, you have someone who probably will talk to you once he has ventilated some anger.

What about someone who talks a great deal at length? In fact, you almost can't stop her? Once she gets the floor no can get a word in edgewise. She may interrupt if you try to make comments. She seldom asks a direct opinion. She may ask a question as if she were going to listen to you, then ignore your answer. For example she may say, "What do you think about high tech stocks—are they still a good buy?" When you're ready to reply, she adds a comment that tells us something: "I sure hope they are, because I've still got a lot of them. I think they should be okay." Notice that she didn't really need your opinion.

This person doesn't communicate in order to obtain information. She wants someone to reduce her anxiety over some transaction. She wants support, someone to listen to her, and to ventilate her anxiety. Her emotional state? She's afraid and not sure where to go to get out of what she feels is a bad investment. This is probably a person who can be easily influenced.

(2) A person's orientation or lack thereof can provide important information, especially as part of the aging process, but be careful. A friend called me to say that he felt his uncle was becoming senile—because the uncle didn't know his state senators, the governor, or much else about current events. I thought that a little odd because I knew the uncle was bright. Uncle's wife saved the day when she said that her husband didn't read anything but the sports section. We tried some questions about football and he was right on top of things.

Someone else mentioned having a friend who seemed not at all aware of our culture. It turned out that he was from another country but no one realized that because he spoke such wonderful English. One really needs to have more than one piece of information.

But change is still a very good indicator that something significant is happening. A friend of mine suddenly began to lose track of where he was or where he was trying to go. He couldn't remember his phone number or address. A number of times he couldn't find where he had parked his car. Yet he had no trouble playing bridge and he could follow complex movie scenes. He did have trouble remembering what day and date it was. Once, for example, he got up, dressed himself, and started to go to his car. His wife asked where he was going. The answer: "Well, to work, of course!" There were two things wrong with that: It was Sunday and he was retired.

Fortunately his family and financial advisor recognized the problem and were able to work around it diplomatically. Had they pursued some of his investment ideas, he would have lost a great deal. Eventually his dementia was diagnosed and measures were set up to make life better for him. He needed a lot of structure and there were many situations he could no longer handle, but by finding new activities he was able to escape boredom.

(3) What about alertness? Is that a part of the client's psychological makeup?

Case 3: Ted had a client, Larry, who was an absolute joy to work with. He was bright, verbal, and caught on quickly to subtle rules of investing. He was the type of thoughtful person who would buy you a gift on your birthday or anniversary. He remembered little facts about people, and knew how to focus on their needs. He was a wonderful salesman, the kind who knew what people were looking for without asking.

Larry's wife, Cathy, was cut from the same mold. She liked doing things for others. Many were made happier having received some of her baked foods. She was particularly gifted with desserts, but her main dishes were also delicious.

The couple seemed free of any major problems and everyone felt they were a joy to be around. They were always together and shared a great deal. They had reared two very well adjusted and highly productive children.

Cathy developed problems first, mainly stemming from her long-term high blood pressure. She began to lose awareness of people around her. As a matter of fact, she often couldn't recognize things related to her husband. He failed to comprehend what was happening and began to be irritated. She couldn't understand. It seemed to most people that suddenly Cathy was not that alert to people and events any more.

Meanwhile, Larry began to have problems of his own. His advisor realized that increasingly explanations about investment weren't so readily followed. When there was conversation about world events, Larry seemed confused. He began to lose interest in his investments, in friends, and in the world in general.

Ultimately a daughter took her parents to a medical center. Larry was found to have a circulatory problem, mainly to the brain. Vascular surgery produced a major improvement, although it took a few months before he was fully recovered. Unfortunately, there was no major cure for Cathy and she became increasingly withdrawn, but not from her husband. She seemed to recognize his loving care.

(4) Memory changes also give abundant information about a client's psychological state. How can they be determined? Mainly by contrasting what the client was like in the past with what he's like now. You can note whether there seems a major difference between long- and short-term memory. Short-term memory refers to recent events (e.g., within a week); it seems to go first. Long-term memory relates to important events in our background.

Memory loss can be caused by several factors. Organic change, including general aging, can play a big part. Substance abuse can cause memory loss, but so can depression. If the cause is emotional, you may be able to differentiate by asking yourself, Does my client seem sad? Does he have low energy and seem to avoid pleasures he once liked?

Whatever causes the memory loss it's a problem that will create investment difficulties. I talked with one advisor who showed me a list that he made up for a client. It listed in very simple language the strategies that were to be followed. The client kept a copy to refresh his memory.

(5) Loss of cognitive functioning is usually noticeable if the client has changed over the years. It's always harder to see change if you haven't known the client long.

The client's psychological state can be known by how well he understands what he's doing with his investments and life in general. Is this client one who makes many foolish purchases? Does he waste time? Does he reason very poorly? I recall one stock broker who had major problems dealing with a particular client's logic. Say he owned a stock that had recently dropped in value. After it had gone down a number of points he bought into it further. His rationale was that buying as it dropped meant that the stock didn't have so far to go up to make a profit. The trouble was since he didn't look at any other variables, his stocks usually found a way to go down more!

(6) This category is probably the most subjective of all those offered in this chapter. It's offered because it's important to at least get advisors thinking in these terms. The question is: Do you feel that your client is consistently having more difficulty understanding something explained to him? If you do sense a problem with comprehension, try to identify where your impression comes from

Now let's look at the emotional side of our lives:

(1) *Anxiety* is a good starting point. It can be one of the most helpful emotions in revealing important personality characteristics. Watching the level of anxiety rise and fall tips us to what's important to the anxious person.

Watch several people in an argument. When you see one person talking more rapidly and audibly, you can be sure that the antagonist has struck home. The loud one's ego has been hit; he has the dim feeling that his argument is weak. An old friend once sent me the notes a politician made preparing for an important speech. In the margin he had written the following: "Talk aggressively and forcefully because this argument is weak."

Anxiety can also be expressed by physical activity. Most of us recognize the stereotype of the husband pacing back and forth waiting for his wife to deliver. Watch some football coaches on the side lines and see if their pacing and overall physical activity don't correlate with what happens in the game.

Speech content is also very revealing. You may find the anxious person going over the same topic over and over. You might see "selective memory," so that some occurrences are blanked out. One broker told me about a client: "He clearly remembers the times I thought a stock would go up and it didn't. However, if I caution him about an investment and he goes right ahead, he can't remember my warning when the stock goes down."

Noting evidence of anxiety is important because it will tip you to some basic beliefs. For example, when an ultraconservative person buys a stock that has a higher risk factor, he's likely to exhibit increased anxiety. Anxiety's companion, guilt feelings, may also be seen under those conditions. Comments like, "It serves me right for taking the risk," can be very revealing. People tend to remember their failures longer than their successes, so experiences like this will become an important part of their makeup.

(2) A *panic reaction* is a severe form of anxiety. If one of your clients experiences this, it will probably be after some kind of loss. We say "some kind" because what's a disaster to one may be a mild temporary market drop to another. I don't believe most clients will panic about their investments. However, a colleague tells me that he did see that with one investor who had sold part of his holdings only to see the stock go dramatically higher. He was a person with very low self-esteem who felt that he had lost the only chance he would ever have for that big killing.

Signs of panic include many physiological ones like rapid breathing, increased heart rate, and sweating. In all probability the client will soon tell you what has upset him. Unfortunately, there's a good chance that if this happens once around investments, it will happen again unless the client seeks help.

(3) The psychological state of *discouragement* is usually easy to spot, although it's by no means always easy to spot the cause.. One investor was recently very discouraged even though his investments had increased in value. In talking to him his advisor learned that he had a big anniversary coming up and had wanted to take his wife to Italy to celebrate. He had hoped the gains would be even bigger.

Signs to identify discouragement may or may not be oral complaints; some people prefer to hold such feelings in. But there will almost always be a listlessness, a lack of faith in the future, and for that matter in oneself. Often there's a failure to set goals as well as reduced goal-directed behavior. Often there's some withdrawal, but you may also see the opposite: Feeling discouraged and unable to tackle problems on his own, a person may become overly dependent on someone he trusts.

(4) The state of *depression* is not always easy to recognize, especially if the person is quiet and also depression-prone. Most of us don't notice people's behavior unless something changes. Only if the depressed person was a "life-of-the-party" type before are you likely to recognize the change.

There are a few signs that give some hint of depression: Is the person much more quiet? Does he seem unhappy? Does he no longer enjoy many of the things that he once enjoyed? Is he less interested in relating to others? Remember, too, that memory loss can be caused by depression.

The person who is happy and depression-free loves new activities, learning, socializing, and pursuing interests that have been fun in the past. When you see a person who doesn't seem to care and is not involved, look for depression as a cause.

(5) The psychological state of a person who is *well-adjusted* is nearly always easy to recognize. The person will be pleasant to be around, constructive to others, warm, wanting to try new things, and taking responsibility for his own failures. The main characteristics of such a person will be the desire and ability to get involved. He won't see the world as threatening but he also will not underrate challenges. This will be the profile of someone we call a winner.

(6) Recognizing *anger* is not always easy.

Case: I still recall an adolescent, John, who fooled quite a few people. He was referred to me by two previous therapists because they couldn't get anywhere with him.

He had originally been referred to a mental health clinic because he was doing poorly in school although he was very bright. He was described as rather friendly and he had never had any trouble with the law. He actually showed very few problems other than low grades. His parents had been a little suspicious that he used drugs but several screenings failed to show any signs of that.

When I met with John, he certainly seemed pleasant. Something about his manner suggested that, if anything, he was a little too nice. I began to note that there was never anything that he said he disliked. For example, he wanted to get better grades and didn't know why he couldn't do better. No, nothing bothered him about school itself.

I decided that I needed to get underneath his defenses to see how he handled his feelings. I started asking him about situations where he should have felt some anger. One such scenario was his mother tending to complain about his low grades. How did he feel about that?

" Well, it's okay," John said, "I don't blame her. I know I could do better."

"Does her nagging make it easier or harder for you to do better in school?"

He answered immediately, without thinking, "Harder." That suggested that John was handling anger in a passive, secretive manner. Passive, because he likely punished others by not doing well at something, like school grades. Secretive, because his anger was expressed in a covert manner.

I became suspicious when I read about vandalism in the town where John lived. To make a long story short we ultimately got a confession from John of about 50 acts of vandalism, ranging from smashing car windows to shooting out other windows—homes, businesses, even expensive street lights—with a pellet gun. He had also started a few prairie fires in the fall. John might have continued to get away with these acts had it not been for some unlucky (for him) breaks. But his over-accepting and seemingly compliant manner said early that something was wrong. It was his concealed anger that was missing from his manner.

Most people are more direct in expressing anger. Clues to the state of anger are tone of voice, sharp gestures (such as finger pointing), and of course the content of what is said. Raising one's voice usually shows either anger or anxiety; it ought not to be difficult to determine which is primary.

People can express anger in many ways, however. Look at the person who goes behind your back and says things that are known to be untrue.

One thing to look for, if necessary, is how this person reacts emotionally to incidents that would cause nearly everyone to be angry. Does she under-react when told someone has just hit her car in the parking lot? If so, you may have a person who shows you very little of her psychological state.

The central theme of this book is that psychological factors greatly influence investment practices. In addition, one's psychological state can change; when it does, it can have a major impact on investment approach. If that change is not recognized, it can cause major problems. If the original psychological state is not understood, it can also have a major impact.

People are not always able to understand what they are saying, feeling, and desiring. Yet some of these people expect the investment advisor to understand them. If you can't be sure where the client is psychologically, you may have problems. If you can, you'll surely be far ahead of the game.

To try to help you become a more sensitive observer, we have created the following checklist. This is only to help you as an investment advisor to think in psychological terms. Many of us have used such a rating scale without being aware that we were doing that. An example is the person who has been shoveling snow from the driveway. He sees how much more there still is to be removed and says to himself, "If I do one more shovel-load, I'm going to collapse." And he may be right!

Here's how the checklist works. We have listed various topics. There are two circles presented for each topic: the left one records a greater amount and the right one a lesser amount. You can place an "X" near whichever circle represents your assessment of that trait. If you place your mark within a circle you'll have signified the maximum or minimum degree of that trait.

Let's look at the client's level of anger. We decide he has a lot. Then the answer would look like this:

	STRONG		**WEAK**
Anger	O	X	O

That can be done for all the traits if you wish, but if you're only interested in a few, just do those. Still, we suggest doing them all.

If you want to know how much change has taken place, estimate how you think your client was a half year, a year ago, or whatever time frame you wish.

	STRONG	**WEAK**
Anger	O	O
Sociable	O	O
Memory	O	O
Depression	O	O
Happy	O	O
Withdrawn	O	O
Trusting	O	O
Desire to communicate	O	O
Dissatisfaction	O	O
Cognitive loss	O	O
Quick on the uptake	O	O
Energy level	O	O
Withdrawn	O	O

Chapter IX
How Personality Shapes a Client's Investment Philosophy

Some think *confidence* is all a client needs. (1) He believes he only needs to pick good stocks, but (2) he has to know when to buy and sell them.

For a number of years now the magical words for achievement or success have been "think positive." If all you had to do was be confident in yourself and success was yours. While I have never doubted the value of confidence, that concept always seemed shallow to me. My work as a sports psychologist taught me there are many mental skills required to achieve what we want. I have seen many unsuccessful athletes just burning with confidence but they couldn't find success.

Case: One highly confident young golfer, Jack, went on a "high" every time he had a great game going. It just never occurred to him that he could do anything but hit wonderful shots. And indeed he did hit many! The trouble was that his judgment was very poor because of his emotional "high." This player had to learn how to lower his mood so he could think more logically.

Years after I saw Jack as a college player, he called me again to talk about a current problem. When we met, he told me that he had sold his very successful business and was now doing what he had always wanted to do. He was buying and selling stock. He felt that he had a special talent for that type of career. However, he wasn't doing very well.

"Oh sure," Jack said, "I make some profits but they aren't in keeping with all the studying I do. I read everything ahead of time, then pick a stock to buy. I have wonderful expectations but I've yet to hit anything big." Then Jack paused for a few moments and looked at me. It was easy to see that he was going to confront me on something. "Oh come on,

Doc," he said, "you're not going to tell me I'm too hyper again, are you? I take my medication regularly."

As a matter of fact I wasn't going to say that. Jack looked much more calm and even-tempered than he had before. But one thing didn't seem to have changed: Jack still didn't seem to know his feelings well. A person who has good access to his feelings allows for access to what's involved in their thinking and behavior.

I asked Jack to describe his selling and buying policies. He seemed to relish this. He described how he studied a number of stocks until he was sure he had some good ones. Then he studied some more, watched them a day or two, and if things looked right he made a purchase. Jack felt complete confidence in his selections.

Well, that certainly brought some questions to mind. Stocks don't all go straight up after we buy them. Sometimes they go down before they go up. What did Jack do if a stock went down right after he bought it? Jack had a quick answer: "My confidence level is so high that a little drop in the market is not going to deter me from my game plan." Indeed, looking over at him just bursting with confidence, I wondered about the other end of this continuum.

"Jack, what do you do if the stock you buy starts a rapid rise?"

Jack didn't hesitate: He insisted that once he set a goal, he stuck to it. So if he was convinced that a stock was going up 20 points, he waited for it to get there and he didn't consider selling. I waited a few moments and then Jack added, "Sometimes that stock goes way up to say where you thought it would, but now your confidence goes up with the stock value."

"So then you don't sell even at the higher price?"

"Right."

So now we had a clear picture of failure through over-confidence. You set a goal and if the stock turns out well, going up sharply, you don't sell. If it goes down, you don't sell because your confidence tells you it will come back.

I asked Jack to do both of us a favor: Check his records of purchases and sales. I wanted to see how often he hung on and rode a stock down from a previous high and how often confidence held him too long to a stock that had dropped. The next time we got together he told me he was absolutely horrified when he looked at his record. With all of his studying, he had made some excellent selections. Most of these did go up, but Jack held on too long. At the same time his confidence in stocks that initially dropped was very unrealistic.

The moral to this is that confidence, like almost everything else, has to be based on reality. No matter how confident you're , I would hope you wouldn't jump into deep water if you can't swim. Life is a game of readjustments and compromises with decision making.

Let's think about *the man who fears success.* This is a person with something to lose. How then can he make a gain?

Many would say, what could possibly cause anxiety when you've found success? But sometimes someone who seems to desperately want to be a winner is afraid to be a winner.

Case 1: A salesman once came to me for severe anxiety, which he said came on him out of the blue. Edgar said he was nearly to the point where he couldn't function. It took a number of sessions before we were able to get a clear idea of what led to all this anxiety. I had asked a very routine question: When have you ever had this type of anxiety before?

Edgar supplied a number of occasions. His first recollection was as a young child of about 10. After he had taken piano lessons for several years, his teacher had organized a recital.

Edgar had played very well; everyone he knew had told him how well he had done. Then his teacher had scheduled another recital, but this time a little more competitive. Edgar's teacher felt it might motivate the boys to work harder. He therefore said he would give a cash award for the best performance. Edgar was the immediate favorite. He remembers doing well and collecting the award. He also remembers that his teacher announced to everyone that while Edgar had performed well, there were a number of students who were catching up with him.

Edgar recalled that his parents, particularly his mother, kept emphasizing that to stay on top you have to keep working hard. He did continue to work hard but as time went on he lost some of his enthusiasm for the piano. One recital he recalled caused him a large amount of anxiety, again it was because everyone expected so much from him.

Edgar started playing football when he was in junior high school. He enjoyed the game, though he wasn't fast on his feet and was quite small. But although he lacked the physical attributes to be a good player, he was a very hard-driving young man. On those few occasions when he ran with the ball, he ran as hard as he could. On defense he tackled just as hard as he could. His teammates praised him for his "guts"; some said Edgar didn't care how big the guy was, he was still going to tackle him. Edgar was well liked by his teammates and his coaches, but his parents weren't very interested in his football games, or for that matter in any of his other athletic pursuits. His father voiced strong feelings that his son should stick to activities for which he had talent. Playing the piano could be an asset because you can always entertain important people. And people do become impressed, his dad would add.

Though his father was quick to say that his son was too small and slow to be an outstanding football player, none of this made a difference to Edgar. He kept playing football right into high school. Year after year Edgar heard people say he probably wouldn't make the team, but he always did. As a junior he even made the baseball team as an extra pitcher. The team had lost a large number of players through graduation, and two of the better pitchers had been sidelined with injuries. Edgar didn't get in many games but that never seemed to bother him. In fact, at the spring baseball banquet the coach joked that Edgar had the slowest fast ball he had ever seen: "His fast ball was so slow the hitters fell asleep waiting for it and were called out."

Edgar laughed harder at these jokes than anyone else. The whole thing was fun and he felt part of the team. The only person Edgar had any problems with was his dad. Edgar persistently heard his father say that Edgar was wasting his time.

Edgar started off his senior year by making the football team, but again only as a scrub. He didn't care because he was still having fun, but his dad objected. He told Edgar that he wasn't coming to any more games just to watch his son "ride the bench." Edgar quietly accepted that declaration and played on.

Edgar survived the winter season and now looked forward to his last year of baseball. The team had been even more decimated by graduations than in the previous year. They had nothing in the way of relief pitchers and Edgar decided to work for that opening because he didn't have much arm strength. He could at best pitch three innings before running out of gas.

Edgar worked very had in the spring practices and had his heart set that he would win one game before his baseball-playing days were over. In the very first game he had a wonderful chance to reach his goal. His team was ahead when the starting pitcher lost his control and started walking batters. Edgar was sent in and ended the inning, not on his own but two wonderful defensive plays. Edgar started the next inning with a three-run lead and was sure he would reach his goal right there. Everything, however, went wrong. He came out of the inning tied. Whatever hopes he had went out the window the next inning when he was so shaky he couldn't get the ball over the plate.

For the next couple of days Edgar was upset hearing that he "blew" the game. Mercifully his father had been out of town and never heard anything about his son's failure. Most of Edgar's teammates were supportive of him. Some noted that he had greatly improved as a pitcher in one year. The general consensus was that Edgar didn't have much talent but he did work very hard.

The third game was very much like the first and so was the sixth game. The coach noticed that when Edgar came into the game behind a few runs, he pitched better than when he came in with a lead. Edgar's coach tried to help by trying to get Edgar to relax but nothing worked. Edgar pitched very little after that and he never did get that win.

However, none of this seemed to Edgar to have any lasting impact on him. He graduated. He went to a small college and they are often in need of athletes to plug gaps, but whenever asked Edgar said no.

Edgar focused nearly all of his attention on school and a career. The more he looked around, the more he felt that he was interested in sales. He told several people that maybe he was interested because his dad had been a salesman all his life. Those who were on the scene felt that perhaps Edgar was still trying to get close to his father and gain his respect, but no one ever suggested that to Edgar.

Once Edgar was into his career as an insurance salesman, he did begin to get closer to his father. The two started playing golf together and Edgar enjoyed this even though he was not very good. He said at one time that nothing could be better than playing with your dad in beautiful surroundings. For the most part the two of them enjoyed one another's company. Edgar did the same thing, though, that he had in college: He set specific goals for himself. This was a "wish list," but not something that anyone thought could be achieved. Edgar wanted a round of golf in the 70s. "It would take a miracle," he often said.

One sunny day Edgar and his father, whom someone had labeled "Duff One," had a game with two golf pals, Jim and Tom. There was much laughter and teasing of one another but Jim pointed out at the conclusion of the seventh hole that Edgar was even par. The others were surprised and then shocked and unsure how they might keep Edgar relaxed. They decided not to call attention to what was happening. Edgar continued his fine play even with a three putt at the ninth which put him one over par for nine holes.

Without thinking about it, Edgar's three playing partners all congratulated him. But when they stopped for a hot dog after the ninth hole, Edgar later recalled, what kept running through his mind was, "Don't blow your chances for a great round."

Still later Edgar was able to recall that his father watched many golf events and was critical of anyone who lost after having a lead, labeling them "chokers." Edgar's recollection was that his father referred to the losers as "gutless."

As one could guess, Edgar played very poorly that second nine holes. His final score was 84, a good round but not what he wanted. Edgar said that his father often referred to that round, talking about what a shame it was to "lose it."

Edgar had good insight into what motivated him. He referred to nausea, trembling, and even sweating, all signs of severe anxiety. He found that what had taken place in high school baseball and on a golf course was happening many other places in his life.

As he made progress in his therapy, he came to describe his feelings with wonderful clarity. Edgar said that when he had reached a goal, it made him feel enraptured. He knew he deserved the success. At the same time he knew many people who lost something they had earned. Interestingly, Edgar didn't fear failure or get too upset when things didn't go well. He enjoyed sports until people began to expect more of him. Edgar said that what scared him was when he had something in his hands that he always wanted. Then he was vulnerable and full of anxiety.

As with so many others, Edgar's personality traits affected his investment approach, and his professional sales career. His anxiety often made him unappealing to clients and they went elsewhere. The problem with his investments was almost always at the high end. When he had the big profit in his hands, he showed heavy anxiety that he might lose what he so greatly desired. He couldn't make a decision, wanting one minute to sell and the next to hang in there a little longer. Edgar had to learn that when your dreams come true, that makes for pressure. If you're number one, as he once was, with his insurance company, there's always someone coming up that may take your place. Having something you want and losing it is painful, but that's life.

Edgar did well in therapy. He learned to set his own goals and not worry about what the other guy does. Then he did become a big winner everywhere!

Then there's *the gambler*, who (1) says he wants financial gain, but (2) really seeks risk. If he doesn't get it, he maligns his broker. The gambler is not an easy client. Just when you think you understand him, he goes off in his own direction once again. When the gambler does make a big gain, you may think joyfully that now he'll behave more rationally. He doesn't. In fact quite often he takes more and more risk, as if he had to lose faster because he had more to lose.

One thing you can count on is that the gambler will become angry and resistant toward anyone who tries to stop him. He seems to be compelled to take greater risk.

Case 2: A broker friend once asked me what he could do with a client who fitted this description. The broker had done well by his client, but no matter how much profit was made with the broker's guidance, the client always lost it. From the very beginning he chose stocks that were likely to drop in value.

Asking about the client's background I was told that he had gambled heavily for years. He had severe losses on the horses and apparently in Las Vegas as well. Knowing this, there seemed only a few ways to go: (1) Refer him to another broker, (2) try to get him to seek help, or (3) see if the account could be split so that one account would show what the broker could do and one would give the record of the gambler. That might bring reason to bear, though I doubted it.

The broker felt that he wanted to warn his client of the dangers of this type of trading. He felt sorry for him but he was frustrated. And the gambling became worse all the time.

The gambler's problems were solved in a very surprising manner. When his family had some major financial problems, his wife threatened divorce. Not wanting to lose her, the gambler finally put her in charge of their investments. Life for the broker became much happier.

The shifter is the type of client who shifts his problems from one life area to another, so that, for instance, marital rejection equates to "sell that miserable stock." This personality is not uncommon. People tend to hide their problems, largely to protect their self-esteem, as a story I got about third-hand shows.

Case 3: The Joneses had a rather rocky marriage. Mrs. Jones was the real power in the family, although both husband and wife tried to pretend otherwise. Though Mr. Jones was a very demanding man, he needed to lean on others for support, but he was very skilled at creating the appearance that others were seeking his advice. For example, he demanded that his investment advisor call him at 10:45 every morning. There was a reason: that was when most of his fellow workers were in the office. He wanted it to appear that his advisor couldn't completely function without him. In fact, it was Mr. Jones who had a problem making decisions and Mrs. Jones, who had no such problem, often became angry at her husband. She couldn't stand his passive approach and the couple often fought over that.

However, neither wanted it to be known that they had marital problems. She didn't want to be thought of as aggressive; he didn't want it known that he was not the one who ran the show. When the problems broke out, they both blamed their stock broker. Maybe at times they did fool themselves that they were really angry due to some stock transaction.

When Mrs. Jones took over handling their investment account, she quickly realized that shifting from one type of investment to another was not working, so she called a meeting with their advisor. It was agreed by all three that the broker would make the key decisions and he proved to be much more successful working that way. The morning calls were discontinued but Mr. Jones found a way out: He said the calls were no longer necessary because his broker had finally caught on to the "Jones approach," and investments were now on the upswing. Neither Mrs. Jones nor the broker ever said a word.

Another familiar client is *the person who feels the sky is falling.* There can be little planning in a state of panic, naturally.

By now we have plenty of evidence that some people always expect the worst. Once when there was a 90 point rise in the Dow, I heard an investor say, "Oh sure, but it'll go down tomorrow." In actuality the market had been up all week so we might expect some drop, but as a matter of fact it didn't go down the next day.

There does seem reason for appropriate caution. Blind optimism is likely to be burned from time to time. But if you always look for the dark side, the sun won't shine in your backyard, or on your investments.

The person with the magic key can also be hard to work with. This client is now a great expert who can't lose. Many people look for "a secret," but they're in trouble when they find it. Maybe because success usually takes time as well as hard work, many of us do seek an easy way out. We love to find short cuts to being a winner.

Case 4: Dave and Jean were such a couple. Jean's father had been an investment advisor for 40 years when he finally retired. Her mother had been a secretary with her husband's firm. They enjoyed being around investment activity. Dave's father was a train engineer who rode back and forth between the same two cities for decades. He often spoke to his son about finding something that would open doors, talking about a fellow employee who invested a "small part of his income and it made him rich." An exaggeration, maybe, but it got the point across to his son.

Dave went into the printing business with the idea that he was going to create something that he could market for a quick profit. He started some of the craze for bumper stickers, but his slogans never really caught on. He then made some warning signs for businesses but again found failure.

Their search for short cuts was evident in other portions of their lives as well. Jean, an avid golfer, had obtained a tip from a low handicap player. She was using this tip and scoring lower than she had in years. With Dave it was bowling but the same process.

Dave and Jean did have excellent communication; they thought a lot alike. Jean, too, kept searching for the magic key to riches. As they talked, both began to feel that maybe their destiny lay with the stock market. With genuine excitement they began to read everything they could find on stock market investing.

While Dave was doing all this searching, an idea popped into his mind. He was sure he had something. So did Jean when he told her. They decided to put this theory to the test. Looking through the financial section of the newspaper they made their initial selections. The next day they did a further appraisal, this time to see if they fit Dave's pattern for success. They did and the following day they bought eight stocks they felt should bring a profit.

They never asked any advice; they just relied upon their own judgment. They watched these stocks every day for a week. Sure enough, they were all above what Dave and Jean had paid for them. Dave and Jean were besides themselves with excitement. They wanted to tell all their friends, but felt it was too soon. They were so confident that they thought of writing a book about their discovery. Jean did write to a publishing house but never heard back. "Well, they lost something" Jean said to herself.

For the next week their investments continued to be quite profitable, and they told everyone who would listen. Some laughed but some asked if they could use their system. Dave was flattered and showed how his formula worked. Several of their friends asked brokers what they thought of this system. None were impressed because they noted that basic values of the stocks, like comparative earnings, weren't adequately considered.

By the end of the second week Dave and Jean had quite a following, though none of the more sophisticated investors. Some pointed out that when the whole market is going up, it's hard to pick a loser.

By the beginning of the third week Dave's magic key was opening no doors. All his stocks were now substantially down. People who rushed to him for advice now rushed to him to unload their anger. One recipient of advice was talking about a law suit for giving "horrible advice," but he decided against it. Before withdrawing the former friend said, "Dave, your stock advice is as lousy as your bowling and your wife's golf." Or at least that's what they told me!

The decision avoider has other problems. She says she only trusts the "expert"—but successful decisions were hers, while unsuccessful ones were her broker's.

Many people are afraid of making decisions; they seem to feel that nothing bad will happen if they just stand by and let fate make the decision. Making a profit on a good decision is a matter of timing. You cannot have good timing if you do nothing. Anyone who makes investments should ask himself whether he waits too long. Do his profits on paper melt away because of inaction? Do losses become more severe? If so, you might want to look at how often you've felt you should act but you don't.

The non-committer is a person with (1) no intimacy at home, and (2) a flighty investment approach. Not many people with these personality traits come to a psychologist for help. Usually they want to do it all on their own, though they will ask others for their opinions. There are two main problems often encountered when these people are investors.

First, they tend to have no loyalty to the investment program they have adopted. Sudden changes can disrupt any plan. If people don't make a commitment to a program, planning goes out the window.

The second problem has to do with the relationship with the broker or investment advisor. It's important to know your client and that usually cannot be done overnight. Communication should improve over time but it's difficult to get much unity and consistent understanding when there's frequent change.

The bandwagon client always tries to stay with the "trend," yet is usually a follower who is always a step behind. This person has plenty of enthusiasm but usually it's for what someone else has. He sees someone else's investment going up and he wants to get into the same thing in a hurry.

The trouble is that his timing may be far off. He pays no attention to the fact that he's not getting into the act from the beginning. When an investor is a step behind, that may well be the difference between a profit and a loss. It's also important to recognize that the bandwagon client is probably making a decision based mostly on emotion.

Another aspect of this approach can mean trouble for both investor and broker. Someone who is always chasing one or two investments will find it hard to keep the whole portfolio in balance. That can be a problem for the advisor, who is often the one expected to see to this balance. Whenever the overall plan is abandoned, there should be some dialogue. The bandwagoner doesn't allow time for that because he's in too much of a hurry to chase another stock.

The control freak claims he just wants good investments, but he constantly watches his broker. The control freak has dozens of statements about his motivation: "I just tell you what to do because I care about you: I don't want you to make a bad decision." Control freaks help build the practice of many psychologists, not because they come in but because they drive others into therapy.

I recall one such situation very clearly. What husband and wife wanted had always been very different. Sid wanted a homebody; Janet wanted a variety of activities outside the home. She liked her hair short, he insisted it be long. He liked to wear a beard, she didn't like that.

Surprisingly, it was a rather nice gesture by Sid that really blew the marital interaction. For years Sid had exercised great control over the way his wife dressed. An executive with a large company, he had sold her on the idea that how she dressed had a major impact on how he was perceived in his career. He maintained that his whole life was open to scrutiny.

Janet had gone along with that argument for quite some time but she had begun to rebel in other areas. She had decided, against Sid's wishes, to take some college classes, and she was increasingly giving thought to a career of her own.

On a few occasions Janet had gone out shopping or to class and had had problems with her car. Though an older model, it didn't have many miles on it. Janet only complained about the car's reliability (or lack of it). Sid had given the car to Janet when he bought a new one. Janet didn't expect to have a new car for quite some time. However, when she arrived home after shopping Saturday morning, there was a new car in the driveway. She wondered who might be visiting. Something prompted her to walk by the car and then she saw the ribbon. Sure enough there was a note attached; the note said, "Happy birthday, honey, Sid."

Janet was filled with rage. As she went into the house Sid was there, smiling and happy. His smile dissolved as soon as he saw Janet's face. He couldn't understand what had gone wrong. The car was well made; it had nearly all the extras. Sid kept telling Janet she was unable to appreciate nice things and all his efforts to please her. Janet's reaction was simply that Sid had never even given her the opportunity to choose her own car.

The controller may let you think he's giving you a lot of praise or favors, but he does this in order to be in control. This personality type might pose a liability threat. The danger with these people is that they look like they want to give a lot to others, but they can never let go.

The person who lives in a tunnel can only see whether a stock is going up or down, but never sees other important factors, such as earnings. There's a disorder recognized in psychology as "tunnel vision." The disorder, which restricts our field of vision, seems related to anxiety. Investors can have a similar problem. If visual perception is restricted, we may miss some very important determinants of stock movement. A good investor needs a broad vision, not a narrow one.

The home-run swinger wants to hang on for a new high—forgetting that home run hitters often strike out. This person poses a significant problem for himself. He could also be a problem for his advisor. It certainly feels good when you buy a stock at a low price and sell it at the very top. It's just very hard to do.

I recall making that statement to a casual acquaintance who sharply took issue with me. He said, "Well, whenever a stock sells at a high, someone had to have sold it so that stock was then sold at it's high. He went on to state that he was not happy unless he did sell at the high. "I don't like it when other people do better than I do," he said. My hunch is that he often felt unhappy, but from what he said I would classify him as a home-run swinger.

My curiosity got the better of me. I asked how he got along with his broker. "Which one?" he retorted. "I've had six in the last year!"

As the swinger talked on, I had two overwhelming urges. One was to get away from him. The other was to suggest that he relax a little and not be so pushy with people. It was clear from his comments that he often failed to sell anywhere near the top because he wanted that home run. I came away from that encounter feeling that this investor probably held some strike-out records, and then blamed his broker for not pushing him to sell.

"Call me when this market is over," is the cry of another type of client. "Sure I believe in planning, but not now," he usually adds.

There are many people whose moods vary with the stock market. In particular they get down as the market drops. They lose interest in doing very much. They may sit on their losses. It doesn't seem to occur to them that there may well be plenty of good investment moves or that inactivity doesn't help us become successful. Today may not be the time to buy or sell but it could be a perfect time to reset goals. Brokers who have clients like this may need to supply the spark needed to get them going again.

The tip person only knows he got a good investment if he heard about it socially. "The money is greener over at his place," he seems to think.

Sometimes we look at someone and immediately become convinced he's a big winner. He always seems to have the inside track. His car seems to go faster than everyone else's, he dresses better, he knows influential people. He's someone who can give hot tips.

My thought is that, if he had all this success, why is he still working? If you check him out, you may find that he's not the big success you think. I also believe we all need steady guidance and information. To be fair to your tipster, keep track of his tips and see what his batting average is. I knew one person who was given one tip that did very well. He passed that tip on to others. What was interesting is that he talked about that success for three years, during which time he had no other successful tips.

The person who played favorites loaded up on one type of stock—until he realized childhood memories were causing it.

Case 5: Butch looked very young. He was still fascinated by children's toys. He had invented a few and tried to get them marketed. He became known in his neighborhood as the "guy who fixes toys." Butch had two children and he was in his heyday when they played with toys. But some things change. His children stopped playing with toys. Butch didn't.

Butch was a key investor in the stock market, and his fascination with toys influenced his investment picture. He was prone to buy any company that made toys, bicycles, games, and amusement parks. Butch was not aware that he was investing that heavily in one area. What he was really doing was playing favorites, choosing out of a need related to childhood feelings, not because the stocks were likely to be a good investment. Once he realized this, he made better investments. This gave him more spendable income. He was then able to buy many children's toys, which he gave to charities. Children adored him.

The daily caller will call twice daily if his stock is down, saying, "The Dow is up. Why aren't my stocks?" Some investors become so nervous with changes in market conditions that they start with the phone calls. Some investors just call no matter what. Decisions generally should be made with planning and consideration. Unless those phone calls are part of a plan, they're not going to accomplish much.

There may be situations where a sale or purchase hinges on a specific criterion. Even so, wouldn't the broker be in the best situation to make that decision? To be in a position to make a determination, the investor will need access to very current information. It would be difficult for a broker to be able to disseminate all this information at the time of each client's call. The question is, do all these calls, every day, based only on a few economic indicators, really serve a purpose?

"My predictions are great," says another type of client, forgetting to add "as I remember them." Often, too, they're made too late.

Many people like to brag about their accomplishments; the pressure world of investing encourages this. How often have we heard someone say they almost won the lottery, having missed it by two numbers? With stocks, too, the bragging is likely to be about something that you "nearly" did. It goes something like, "If I had bought that stock when I knew I should, I'd be worth a bundle."

The proof is in the performance. Sometimes people with good intuitive judgment do well when there's no pressure. When it's the real thing, we tend to act by what we think is logical, though often it isn't. How many times did you as a youngster answer a test question without thinking, then think and finally change it? Later you found out your intuitive answer was correct. That can happen with investment decisions, too, and the investor must ask a major question: Is my intuition good but unavailable under pressure?

"Advisor, please tell me what to do," another client pleads. "You have the knowledge. The request is qualified: "Don't get me any bummers."

Many people hate making decisions about who should make decisions. They're saying that they don't trust their own judgment, and perhaps they shouldn't. It seems likely that as our population gets older, many clients will prefer to have the advisor make decisions for them, but some sort of understanding must be made at the beginning of the relationship. Watch to be sure that your client isn't saying, "You make the decision because I don't want to take the blame if the investment is unsuccessful." Naturally, you'll be blamed if it turns out poorly.

The me-too personality says, "I don't want much—just what your other clients get."

Perhaps because of my professional practice I've become suspicious of people who claim they don't want much. The phrase "I only want . . . " is just the beginning. It belies that they really want the sun and the earth (someone else can have the moon).

People need to settle their desires in reality. I may want my broker to make me profits of, say, $50,000 a year as I hear he does for one of his clients. But if I don't have the capital to generate such a gain, I had better realize that. Age can be a factor in what is a realistic profit expectation. Family size and composition can also have a major impact on investment strategies.

When a client begins to make major comparisons with other clients his ego may be acting up. Wanting to feel important, he feel that having what someone else has will do the trick.

If he feels that he deserves what some of his broker's other clients have, he may become irritable when he finds that isn't working that way. Rather than wait for trouble to show itself, it might be well to explain how different investment situations call for different goals and strategies.

"Of course I'm a person who listens," another client implies, failing to note that he only hears what he wants and what he hears won't change his mind.

All of us have some tendency to hear what we want and to forget what doesn't fit with what we want to believe. In the investment field this can cause disaster. That's one reason why the advisor needs to know if her messages are getting through.

I still remember many years ago after a lecture I gave at an investment house about the problems of hearing what you want to hear, one advisor, Glenn, talked about a problem he had with a client. Glenn had told the client that he doubted that a particular stock would reach $20 per share. The client later said he distinctly heard Glenn say, "I feel sure this stock will go well past $20." When the stock went to $17, Glenn recommended a sell. The client left a message that he didn't want to sell even though the stock had made a rapid rise. Glenn couldn't reach his client and was quite upset when the stock dropped like a bomb. When the communication problems came to light, everyone could see what had happened.

These are some of the types of people we have encountered in our travels. We hope this chapter will make working with these people easier. We do know they will provide excitement and challenge.

Now let's give the brokers their turn.

Chapter X
How Self-Knowledge
Can Help the Broker

As everything in the world becomes more and more complicated, specialized information is increasingly necessary. There seems no question about the need for professional guidance to assist us with our investments.

This brings up the old argument of "do it yourself," versus the "team approach." Since I don't like unnecessary arguments, it seems best to simply state the following: If you're going to do it all yourself, you'll need many different pieces of information.

The investment advisor is clearly one of the very first team members we all need. Money problems touch in all areas of our lives. A great illustration of this took place with a couple I was seeing for marital counseling. They had constant fights about expenditures. He was a person who enjoyed some risk taking, she hated it. He didn't mind being in debt with credit cards, she hated it.

I listened for a few weeks and never heard them complain of anything except money. What I kept hearing was that neither wanted undue risk and both felt they were on sound financial ground. They looked to me for answers. I didn't feel I had any. So I decided, after much soul-searching, to refer them to a financial advisor. They spent three sessions with this talented professional and then they called me to say thanks.

This is not to say that I don't believe in psychological help. I would never have written this book had that been the case. My feeling is that often everything is left to psychology, as if you only need a certain attitude to be successful.

Typical of this approach was a golf acquaintance who told me that he was going to get help with his putting. He said he was tired of high golf scores because of missed three-footers. He had found what he thought was the perfect teacher. This teacher used a mental approach: You can't putt well if you don't have a positive attitude.

Well, "three-putt Joe" went to his lesson on Tuesday. On Thursday I was to have a golf game with him. When he arrived I noticed he was quiet. His taciturn mood continued as he had one three-putt after another. I couldn't resist asking him if he had obtained any help from the lesson.

"Three-putt Joe" looked frustrated. "No, a positive attitude won't do me any good," he said. "My teacher said I got a lousy putting stroke—a positive attitude won't help." Actually, it often will, but the point is that technique is also very important. So is knowledge and skill. If you lack these a positive attitude is not going to do much for you. But I do maintain that understanding motivation and behavioral patterns is going to help increase an advisor's success potential. Knowing about your own personality helps both clients and advisors in their chosen roles.

How can the advisor learn more about his own functioning as well as his clients'? I believe that people who engage others in their professional work usually develop insight into people's motivations and behavioral patterns. For the advisor there's unrecognized psychological knowledge just waiting to be displayed and used.

In the classes I taught, I found it helpful to quiz my students on real-life psychological puzzles. "What was this person's motivation?" I would ask about a problem I had just presented. Time and again the brokers would declare they didn't know. When I asked them to guess, they would correctly solve the question 85 percent of the time.

The information is there latently; if you give yourself time to relax and let your feelings come out, you'll likely recognize many of your own personality characteristics as well as those of others. As you get deeper into self-discovery you're likely to find a variety of motives for business ventures.

In order to find some real-life examples we need to take a close look at the roles of an investment advisor or stock broker. The first role we would ascribe would be that of a leader. The leader role is important because people (clients) need help in maximizing their investments. A logical, composed leader will set a good example for the client to follow. This is particularly important for younger investors.

The second and very major role of an advisor or broker is to educate clients. One doesn't casually buy and sell and collect a profit. There's a great deal to learn, yet many clients don't even know what they need to learn. To invest without adequate knowledge is sure to impair investment performance.

Case 1: A good example was broker Debbie, a very energetic, pleasant, hard-driving person who tended to feel down when her investment advice failed to produce a profit. Debbie liked people and always tried to do her very best. However, she had two major weaknesses that hampered her performance.

The first was that she overinvested herself in the educational portion of her professional role. She often repeated things in order to be sure she was getting her point across. The trouble was that because people didn't like all that pushing, they tended to tune her out. It was an automatic reaction, so they didn't realize they were doing that. Then she would become angry and pout. Because clients now felt they had offended Debbie, they also withdrew. As a result the education failed.

Moreover, if the investments started going down Debbie became anxious. As the anxiety became clear to the client, the client in turn became very concerned. When anxiety got high, people wanted to do anything they could to shut the anxiety off, so they often sold when their investments were on the low side. Here was a vicious cycle.

Because Debbie was very conscientious and highly motivated to do good work with others, at times her feelings of anxiety and depression were very high. At that point she often became distant from her clients. In addition, with no one being aware of what was taking place, there was a further drop in communication.

Debbie's problems were like those of many well-meaning people who try to do too much. Overidentification with the client is one cause. An advisor who feels personally responsible for all that happens will put undue pressure on herself. With failure the client may become depressed because he senses that it was his investments that caused the advisor's self-recriminations. Now both client and advisor are punishing themselves. To make it up there's a tendency to go for the "big gainer" all in one move.

Obviously there are major differences among the personalities of brokers or advisors. I can still remember the time I was wakened by a stock broker calling me from New York. It must have been 6:30 a.m. I'm more of a night person. It took me a few seconds to pull my thoughts together but the caller went right on.

"Harry, have I got a deal for you! I know it's early but this opportunity can't wait."

By now I was wide awake, headed for our automatic coffee percolator. I was just too stunned to simply hang up. But I must also confess that my curiosity was piqued. I wondered what could possibly be so important that it prompted such an early call.

I never got a chance to ask, or even to comment. The caller went right on. I soon learned that if I had $30,000 I could invest in some stock I had never heard of. That stock was certain to go up. The caller was extremely confident, rattling off seven reasons why this one couldn't miss.

When I finally got a word in, I told the caller that I don't buy stocks that way but I wished him luck. The last thing he said was to watch this stock "skyrocket" and then remember him next time. All the caller's remarks were in a loud tone. I felt like saying, "Please don't shout, I can hear you."

Maybe because of the unusual characteristics of the call, I did remember the name of the stock. It went down like a World War II dive bomber. I thought to myself that it's fortunate that I don't make investments that way. I was sure that some others might be stampeded by this energetic, enthusiastic approach. The caller was absolutely convinced he had something spectacular. That amount of certainty can convince those who are more impressionable—another example of how those in authority can often convince someone else.

I was sure I would never hear from that salesman again, but I did. What was amusing was that he now claimed he had given me another stock, which had gone up. Someone else must have given me the other stock tip that didn't do well. He said he called this time in order to give me another tip. This time the conversation was notably short!

Case 2: There are many different styles among investment advisors. The best illustration I have seen came from two of my clients, Lisa and Gerry. They weren't related and in fact didn't at first know each another. Oddly enough, they both came for therapy because they wanted to take charge of their lives. Another coincidence was their interest in stock and bond investments.

That, however, is where the similarities ended. Lisa was a very relaxed but aggressive businesswoman who always wanted to be in control of her life. As she came to realize, she didn't really trust others very much. One of her favorite sayings was, "If you want something done right, do it yourself."

Lisa had early life experiences that made her do-it-herself philosophy appealing. Her father was the type who constantly made promises but seldom carried through with anything, like the time she told him that she was to be the starting pitcher on her softball team. Her dad promised he would be there and she told all of her teammates. He never showed.

Her mom was similar, although she never promised much of anything. Her favorite phrase was, "We'll see." In the final analysis, whenever Lisa had a problem she had to deal with it herself. Without adequate guidance she made many mistakes but she learned from them. Lisa was a bright, resourceful woman who could make her own decisions, but she also admired talented people.

Gerry was also a young and bright young man and very busy and able to make his own decisions. He recognized that there was more to life than just work. He came from a very happy family where freedom was deemed important. His parents were highly interested in his activities and had been ever since he was a youngster. They didn't push but did help whenever he asked for help. Because they were not critical of their son, he could admit when he had made a bad decision. At that point they stepped in and offered advice. Gerry became a business consultant, traveled a great deal, and commanded a big income.

Both Lisa and Gerry invested with the same investment house. Both were unhappy with their advisors. In order to get a sense of what was wrong I asked each to tell me what they didn't like about their advisors. I had become tired of hearing Lisa complain every Tuesday at 10:00 and then hearing the same thing from Gerry three hours later.

Yet Lisa and Gerry had different complaints. Gerry wanted his advisor to make decisions herself; he didn't want her to call him all the time to get his approval. He mentioned that once he was in a very important meeting in Europe with many hundreds of thousands of dollars at stake, and here comes her call. She had found a low-price stock that could easily go from $2 a share to $10. Well, fine, but was it really that important? He told her that she should go along with her own opinion. She did and he registered a good gain. But then she went back to her same procedure.

When Lisa's broker called her but found she was in a meeting, he went ahead and made the purchase. Though it turned out well, Lisa was still angry because she had wanted to make the decision, or at least to be consulted.

Lisa started therapy partly because she found that many of the people she dealt with made decisions without consulting her. Even the men she dated did that to her. A former boyfriend, for example, had made a dinner reservation at a Mexican restaurant to celebrate the couple's one-year anniversary of when they started dating. It was a nice place with good food and nice atmosphere, but Lisa felt that because this was a very special occasion, she should have been consulted. Her boyfriend couldn't see her point, which partly why they didn't have a two-year anniversary to celebrate.

After listening to the complaints I decided it was time to become more directive. I suggested separately that each consider a different advisor. After all, different personalities may match up better with different people. This turned out to be a wonderful change. With the improved communication both Lisa and Gerry found investing more pleasant and financially rewarding.

Another important factor for an advisor is the attitude he projects. Let's take two personality traits to see how each affects our impact on clients.

The extremely confident, highly verbal person loves his work and is sure that everyone will find it as interesting as he does—at least they sure will after he explains how it works! He never allows a failure to upset or slow him down. He's sure that the next purchase will be the big success that we all look for. Having great self-confidence, he's an eternal optimist and the consummate salesperson. He's up to date on new stock issues.

Who wouldn't be influenced by this personality type? Clients are likely to feel that they better get on his bandwagon quick. They may be somewhat disappointed by the way he seems to ignore losses, but they tell themselves that he really cares and is talented, so they enthusiastically follow his advice. Self-confidence is necessary to all kinds of success and this broker seems strong with knowledge, too. He needs, though, to realize what he projects because there's risk that his enthusiasm may encourage someone of lesser resources to pursue an unsuitable investment path.

At the other extreme is the advisor who lacks confidence and doesn't fully realize it. He will see himself not as a worrier but as someone who is careful. He will be very sensitive to market or investment highs and lows. When there's any kind of loss or drop in values, his tendency will be to get out quickly.

At the high end there will usually be one of two opposite reactions. The more common one would be to take the small profit and run. People who lack confidence usually see the world of investments as precarious. They don't feel there's much chance to gain mastery so they get out quickly. The second approach is to jump on the bandwagon. When you have low confidence, anything that helps bolster your self-esteem seems extremely powerful. The tendency to overdo a good thing could subtract some profit. Again we find moods having a major impact on our investments.

Another personality trait affects how available the advisor is to his client. Availability may be real or projected. Real means that you're actually, physically, available. You're not out of the country. You have a phone or pager system that allows clients to reach you. Projected availability means literally how others perceive you.

Case 3: A few years ago Nancy, a long-time friend of the family, commented that her advisor was very unavailable. She told me his name and, knowing Joe as I did, I couldn't believe he would be unavailable. It was near closing time and just on impulse I picked up the phone and called. Joe answered immediately. I smiled and asked Nancy if she had any questions; while I looked at her, she became obviously anxious. She stammered and had troubles organizing her thoughts. She nodded her head yes and I handed her the phone. She asked her questions and Joe apparently answered them.

When she hung up I asked if she felt Joe answered her questions. She shook her head yes but her expression said something still troubled her. I asked about her feelings. She paused and then attempted to describe how she felt. What finally emerged was her description of Joe: He was well organized and he hated to waste time. He always knew how to express what he wanted briskly. He was a private person who almost never told anyone much about his private life. He was highly respected. He was very assertive. If you asked him his opinion he gave it, but if you tried to argue he would withdraw.

Nancy was a quiet, controlled woman from a male-dominant background. What gradually emerged was that Nancy brought out Joe's assertiveness. When she became nervous, she couldn't organize what she wanted to ask. That wasted time and Joe resisted wasting time. However, once he realized what he was bringing out in Nancy, he was able to alter his approach. As Nancy relaxed more, she was able to communicate much better. When we know how we affect others, we are in a good position to make changes.

Some people would like very much to be very dominating. Much of what takes place in the lives of many people involves a power struggle. Since money can often be part of someone's attempts to look powerful, we can see how easy it is for advisors to lock in on power struggles.

Those who need to have a powerful aura may work very hard to create an impression of hero worship by the multitudes. This need can have a major impact upon a broker's behavior. If money creates a feeling of power, you want big profits. That could well suggest searching out glamour stocks and other flamboyant investments.

The major problem for the client is that unless she has abundant investment funds she may not receive as much attention as others. That may mean she won't receive maximum help in making the initial purchase and then optimal sale because she will get information late. She may also find himself pushed into more risky investments.

There are many situations where the advisor or stock broker may be put in a terrible position. People will say they are committed to a particular course of action. They may spontaneously state that "if the stock market does this, I will do that." But they don't.

Case 4: An acquaintance told me that he had bought a stock that had immediately started up. He had paid around $10 a share and now it had gone to $19. I listened, along with his broker, to his statements that if this stock hit $25 he would sell. His broker reminded him that originally he had set the goal of doubling his money. He admitted that but had then called his broker to say hang on. The order was, "Don't sell at $20."

Checking the stock in the newspaper, I noticed that the stock had gone up to $30. A nice little profit for Marshall, I thought. I wondered, too, what game plan he had used. Did he sell at $25 or higher? I recall that his broker had favored a sale in the early twenties.

I didn't pay much attention to the stock market for quite some time after that. Other things seemed to need more attention. When I did open the market news section, I chanced to look at that stock. To my utter shock it was now selling at $5 a share. Now I really wondered how Marshall had done.

As I was leaving my office the following week he came over to say hello. We talked about little things and then my curiosity got the better of me: "Marshall, I'm really curious about the price that you sold that stock for, the one we were talking about last time I saw you."

"Oh, Doc," he began, "I should make an appointment with you. I did a real stupid thing."

I could have guessed: He hung on to the stock all the time it went up. Then he hung on and watched it drop. From a potentially big profit he now had a loss. Marshall had gone for the big one, had it, and let it drift away. My reverie was interrupted by Marshall's frantic tone. I realized that he was suffering great self-recrimination: "Am I crazy, Doc, or is this just pure unadulterated greed? I really wish someone could tell me. I'm fine till I think of my stupidity with that stock. I'd really like to know."

I thought about how often I had heard stories about people going to casinos, placing bets, being ahead and then putting it all back. It's so hard to know when to quit. Maybe here was an opportunity to learn something that had always been of interest to me. I was always fascinated by sport competition and wondered why players or teams switch their approach when they're well ahead. It's almost as if they don't trust an approach that puts them ahead. My own policy was more "if it's winning, don't change it."

So with these thoughts in mind I asked Marshall if he and his stock broker would be interested in meeting to talk about his stock experience. He expressed interest but said he'd need to have more information to sell his broker, Matt, on the idea. I explained that our goal was to analyze what was involved in his recent stock loss. I reminded him that he'd asked me if it was caused by greed and I had said I didn't know.

So Matt, Marshall, and I set up some early evening meetings to go over this experience. I asked Matt if he knew how this whole thing started. Marshall and Matt looked at one another, as if to say neither wanted to take the responsibility. Marshall said it was Matt who got it started and Matt disagreed: "No, Marshall, if you remember you asked me first to check out a stock that you said a friend gave you as a 'hot tip.' But as soon as I started to check it, you purchased the stock through my assistant."

So that became the first interesting factor. Matt may have checked the stock but he didn't get a chance to (1) share his information or (2) advise Marshall. Matt said he probably would have suggested buying a few shares but not as many as Marshall bought. He felt there was considerable risk with this stock and he wanted more definite goals set, such as what they expected as a high, when they would sell, and how long to stay with it if it didn't move up as well as how far it might drop before they sold.

So now it was clear that Matt wanted some definite rules or goals. Why were they not set? I asked Matt and he looked sheepishly over at Marshall. For a few minutes no one answered. The silence told me that a problem existed because of the way the two people interacted. "Matt, when Marshall and you have a difference of opinion, how does it get resolved," I asked. "What typically happens?"

After a pause Matt said, "I guess I give in because Marshall is more enthusiastic and certain he's correct." With a little more encouragement Matt elaborated. He said that Marshall had a large account and he didn't want to lose him as a client. Matt also stated that the two had become friends. They socialized. And Matt admitted that it was hard to disagree with Marshall's business success.

Just to be sure there was no misunderstanding, I asked, "Matt, is it difficult for you to tell friends or successful investors you disagree with them?" Matt was emphatic in stating that it was. So now we had one important ingredient of the interaction. Matt was lacking in aggressive leadership. He felt intimidated by Marshall. We had to end our first session there but we raised some important questions for our next meeting.

We met again a few days later and this time we started with Marshall. Having done some thinking, Marshall immediately said he couldn't understand anyone being in awe of him. When Matt pointed out the success of Marshall's business Marshall had a ready retort: "That's what people always seem to think. But I don't feel all that successful. It was my father and grandfather that deserve all the credit. They started the business and then my dad put me in charge. But every time I do something wrong, dad rescues me."

Matt was surprised. He commented that Marshall always looked very confident. Marshall countered that it was all put on to hide his own insecurities. Marshall then showed some insight: "So my actions to look secure intimidated you? I wouldn't have guessed that."

Marshall went on to explain that having had such successful parents, there was great pressure upon him. Yes, it was true that his dad was kind and easygoing, but at the same time dad and grandfather were successful. So was his grandmother, who also worked in the company. Marshall said he tried to be successful to be like them but everything he tried failed. The family bailed him out but his pride was hurt.

At first he stopped trying to be so outstanding, but then he had a few successes in the stock market. He loved to study stocks and he had many business friends who, seeing his interest, gave him tips. Then he met Matt and they started working together. They had made some profits, but not the big ones Marshall yearned for.

That brought our discussion to the contemporary situation. I asked Marshall if he had set game plans or goals for the stock we were discussing. Did he know what his expectations were?

Marshall reminded us that his first goal was to sell around $20 a share. Then he changed his mind and said to go for $25. So Marshall had a plan, which by the way was doing well. The stock had now gone to $20. He had reached a goal. Marshall said he knew Matt wanted to sell, but he changed the goal.

I suggested a problem there. Many people do a lot of planning, are traveling the road to success, and then on impulse alter the plan. Had there been new information (e.g., a major profit increase), that might change the game plan, but that had not been the case here. Additionally Marshall wasn't going to listen to Matt and Matt didn't feel comfortable warning Marshall as he should have. Matt recognized he had to become a stronger leader.

Then I turned back to Marshall: "Can you remember how you felt when your stock started going up?"

"I sure do! I felt like for once I had a real chance to prove myself and do something great. I remember feeling scared. But each point higher gave me a feeling of power and I never had that before. I was on a high and I didn't want to listen to anyone else. I just wanted to win a big one."

Marshall then went on a self-punishing excursion until I pointed out that didn't help. What was important was to find out why; then it would be less likely to happen again.

We decided to have a few more sessions just to cover all facets. In them we learned some interesting facts. One was that after a certain point in Marshall's stock rise, his anxiety rose to the point where he didn't want to make a decision about selling. He felt that he might sell and then the market and his stock would go up yet more. So he didn't make a decision.

Neither Marshall or Matt could understand. I explained that many people who are afraid they'll make a bad decision turn it over to fate. Like flipping a coin, it removes responsibility—but also reason—from decision making.

Marshall looked puzzled for a few minutes and then asked, "Can taking added risks also be a way of dealing with anxiety?"

Marshall had come up with an astute question, probably based on what he felt. With a little support he described feeling anxious because his big winner could be taken away. He didn't know when this might happen and he described a compulsion to keep testing fate. Marshall described the feeling as "you know the ax will fall but you don't know when—the anxiety of the unknown is less than the feared event, so you keep pushing or tempting fate."

I complimented Marshall and said there are hundreds of examples of that: fast driving, drinking, threatening a spouse, and especially gambling.

Marshall felt that now that he understood his motivation, he would be more rational and thereby more successful. He could see where his question about whether the motive was greed was oversimplification. Often many motives play a part.

As the months went by Matt became a strong and well-informed leader. He developed skill at expressing his opinion even when the client disagreed. He saw his role as a professional one and he felt pride. Many of his clients thanked him for his warnings.

Matt experienced another change, too. I had commented that anxiety causes stereotyped behavior. Matt realized that he had been in a rut. As his anxiety went down, he made more varied investment suggestions. He used some funds, recommended bonds at times, some expensive stocks, some low-priced stocks. All that added to his flexibility and to his success.

The meetings that my friends and I had were very enlightening. They were fun, too, perhaps because we never labeled anything "sick" or "abnormal." Knowing yourself does increase freedom. Matt, for example, told me many months later that he had an assistant who became testy when clients failed to take his advice. That didn't make for the best investment attitude. Matt later observed that this same assistant tended to push a stock sale when he was notably anxious—almost like Marshall trying too hard to prove himself. That approach was corrected.

Matt became a very skilled and successful advisor. He kept trying to know himself better and better. He identified that when he felt down he didn't keep up with new information. On an emotional high he took a little more risk and held stocks longer. On an emotional low he sold quicker because he was less optimistic. He found that when he identified a pattern, he was able to control it. He could read his confidence levels and accept that we all have swings.

Matt also found that he enjoyed educational sessions with clients, so he scheduled them in the morning because he realized that he was a strong "morning person." Matt became a leader in his company and enjoyed talking about the effects of the sort of image we project to others. He learned, too, that people have different personalities that may not be compatible with a certain client. In that case a referral may be in order. The better you know yourself, the better you'll be able to know others.

Here is another chance to gather more information about yourself. On the following select what you feel is the best answer and see what it tells you.

1. At what time during the day do you feel your best?
   a). morning
   b). late night
   c). after lunch
   d). later in the day

2. When do you sell?
   a). early, well before the top value is reached
   b). toward the end, seeking maximum profit
   c). stay past the point where the value goes much lower
   d). at variable points.

3. How do you feel about investment purchases generally?
   a). highly enthusiastic
   b). very calm and quiet
   c). often uncertain
   d). happy to wait and see the results

4. All of us have some mood variation – describe yours
   a). stay in the middle range
   b). moods mainly go to a high
   c). moods go up and down rapidly
   d). mainly lows

5. Thinking of an outstanding success, what was your emotional state?
   a). non-emotional
   b). anxious
   c). on a high, much like in a competitive state
   d). very calm and quiet

6. How do you feel about seeking advice?
   a). I hardly ever seek advice.
   b). I feel we all need advice.
   c). People seek too much advice.
   d). I resent people who usually go to others.

7. What are your thoughts about a "bad streak?"
   a). When in one, do you feel a need to do something major?
   b). Is it easy to visualize a bad streak?
   c). Do you quickly modify your approach?
   d). Do you just wait it out?

8. Do market conditions substantially affect you emotionally?
   a). very little if any
   b). somewhat
   c). I feel down
   d). I feel an upswing coming on

9. How do you feel working with the opposite sex?
   a). highly challenged
   b). same as other clients
   c). uncomfortable
   d). it's okay

10. How do you visualize success and failure?
    a). Failure is easy because it occurs more often.
    b). Change is inevitable, so it's easy to visualize both.
    c). Losing has a greater impact.
    d). Failure should not be visualized.

11. How do you look at investment tips?
    a). almost never use them
    b). sometimes helpful

    c). always seek them
    d). often helpful

12. My approach is best described as:
    a). always long-term
    b). depends on the client
    c). depends on market conditions
    d). essentially the same no matter what

After selecting your answers, go back to see what the pattern tells you. For example, the answer designated "a" will usually show a conservative and self-reliant approach, doing mainly what he feels is right, e.g., question 12. The "a" is mainly guided by what the client wants.

If you go through this little quiz you may add to your self-knowledge, and that is sure to increase your success quotient.

Chapter XI
Avoiding Liability

Until now our emphasis has been on how to know your client so you can meet her needs. Now we add one more ingredient to this mixture: how to keep yourself from getting into trouble.

People don't yell and scream like they did in the old days and they don't talk out problems. They simply file a law suit. In many respects this seems a shame to me. There is often a great waste of money that could be spent for better purposes. A major loss, I believe, is that people will not want to do for others what they did in the past. It's difficult to help someone in need when you know that person may turn around and sue you. There seems a great danger that we may turn into a society made up of people who won't get close to one another.

Let me tell you about something that happened in another profession and you will note the tie-in to the investment profession.

Case 1: A nice, hard-working, dedicated doctor, Dr. Helper, had a habit of giving out medication without charging for it. On one occasion an acquaintance from his golf club was having what he diagnosed for himself as "minor aches and pains." These pains didn't bother him greatly in his day-to-day activitiies, but they did hinder his golf game. So he asked Dr. Helper for a specific medication, one that had benefited him in the past.

This man, Scott, had never gone to Dr. Helper before. Dr. Helper asked him if he had ever had any problems with that medication and he said no. So Dr. Helper gave him the prescription, Scott thanked him, got the prescription filled, and went out to play golf.

At some point during that round Scott got a terrible reaction that looked as if it might have come from Dr. Helper's medication. Scott went back to his own doctor, who reviewed all of the medications and foods that Scott had during his sudden illness. Ultimately it was discovered that

Scott had taken another medication that he had not mentioned to Dr. Helper. Scott had always tended to do that: he would supply information only if directly asked. The two medications together had caused the reaction.

A lawsuit was filed. Those defending Dr. Helper pointed out that it was not directly his medication that caused the reaction. It was also pointed out that Dr. Helper didn't know of the other medication. The lawyers representing Scott claimed that Dr. Helper didn't know Scott and shouldn't have given medications without more information.

Apparently a settlement was made. Dr. Helper felt very hurt by what had taken place. His whole approach to people changed and that was somewhat of a loss for all.

Was Dr. Helper in the wrong? You won't get me to answer that. It does seem to me, though, that generally you need to know the client in order to serve him well.

I can still recall a situation embarrassing for me even though it didn't involve a client. A fellow professional asked me whether if one twin boy develops schizophrenia, the other is likely to. I answered (and quoted) that research shows a positive correlation. At that point my questioner said, "That's bad, because I've a twin brother who was just recently diagnosed with schizophrenia." I felt terrible. Yet there was no way I could have known, and I thought this was one professional talking to another.

What comes of this is an edict: Know Your Client. New York Stock Exchange Rule 405 clearly emphasizes this principle. I believe it should be the cornerstone of all professions. It's very difficult to do for others when you're not sure what they want.

Case 2: J. J. and Ilene had been a married couple right out of high school and within a few months were on their way to financial success. J. J. sold cars where Ilene worked as a bookkeeper. Eventually J. J. owned a good part of the agency and Ilene had a fine-paying job, also with the agency.

The marriage was successful from all angles. They made good money and saved a lot, they were emotionally close, and they reared two fine boys. Everything went along very well until they were in their mid-thirties. At that point Ilene began to be influenced by what she referred to as "women's liberation." At first she joked about it but increasingly there was a serious tone to her voice. "Wives have rights, too" she said, adding that women shouldn't be left out of financial affairs.

Years earlier J. J. had stated that the money Ilene earned should be hers. At first Ilene had a savings account in her name and bought some

CDs from time to time. J. J. teased her that her "little nest egg" wouldn't grow much that way.

There came a time when the family really didn't have to worry about money. At age 39, the couple had children in their late teens who would soon be through college. Their own parents were well-to-do and had decided to leave all their money to J. J. and Ilene, who had already planned well for retirement.

J. J. began insisting that Ilene use funds from her account to have fun—travel with some lady friends, buy a luxury car, whatever. She refused. J. J. finally convinced her that she should buy some stocks.

Ilene was always a very conservative person where money was concerned. She even said "I just don't trust the market." But Ilene liked J. J.'s broker and even regarded him as a friend. Finally J. J. had the broker open a separate account for Ilene and told the broker that she wanted to buy a few blue chips. Other than the standard client agreement forms that he gave to J. J. to have her sign and return, the broker asked no questions about her investment objectives.

The broker recommended a few well-known conservative stocks and J. J. said he would bring back a check from her with the client agreement form, adding, "Go ahead and buy those three stocks you recommended for her."

The broker suggested that she should give J. J. limited trading authority for her account, but J. J. said, "Oh, you know her; she wouldn't want to be bothered with all that stuff."

The stock market was strong and J. J. was trading more with stocks that had a lot of upside momentum. The broker often called J. J. and chatted with Ilene about the kids and how well things were going. She used to joke, "Just make me a lot of money" whenever he tried to talk to her about investments.

J. J. told the broker that since he was doing so well trading stocks that "we should get Ilene going, too." The broker objected because he knew Ilene was conservative and that would be inconsistent with her investment profile.

But J. J. was a good salesman and he ran some powerful arguments against his broker. J. J. pointed out that he put nearly all the money in Ilene's account. There had never been a problem with their joint account: "You'll see, if we make her some money, she'll be happy as a lark."

Finally his broker gave in to J. J.'s demands and they began to buy and sell according to the firm's trading recommendations. Without thinking about it, they had now violated two of Ilene's rights. They had no right to buy and sell securities without her authority and no right to change her investment profile.

Some time later, Ilene began to feel that J. J. was dominating her and that she needed to find her own identity. She felt that she had to separate from J. J. in order to find herself. She contacted a lawyer, who wanted to know what each party was worth. When he discovered what had happened to Ilene's account, he suggested a lawsuit, telling Ilene that what J. J. and their broker had done was illegal and that this might be used to push for a bigger settlement.

Probably Ilene's lawyer pushed her to be much more ruthless than she really was. J. J. and his broker spent a very anxiety-ridden six months. Then, a kind of miracle took place. J. J. got Ilene to go to a counselor with him in the hopes that the situation could be corrected. The counselor put Ilene and J. J. in some group sessions with two other couples on the brink of divorce. In that group there was a pert blond woman who showed an interest in J. J. as soon as she met him. Ilene saw this and immediately went over to her and said, "Mary, I don't like you flirting those eyes at my husband."

From that point on, there was a reversal as far as Ilene was concerned. Maybe with the threat of loss she realized J. J. was quite a catch. They were able to get back together again—but J. J. never again tried to dominate Ilene as before..

Probably all of us have made decisions at times that later we wished we had not. This usually happens because we depart from our usual form of behavior. Again, therefore, we come up with the word of caution: Watch for changes.

Case 3: That was noteworthy for Nelson. His behavior began to change around the time he reached 45. He had always shied away from any high-risk investment. He was teased about being very conservative, though he probably wasn't. It was just that because he hated risk he usually was moderate where risk was concerned.

When he hit his forties he began to look for more bold investments. His broker noted the switch but he couldn't get Nelson to talk about it. That made him uncomfortable because he was never sure he was following Nelson's guidelines. The only thing the broker noted as far as a behavioral change was that Nelson was much less talkative than he had been. He didn't ask his broker's advice as often and he was more specific about what he wanted.

One day Nelson called his broker and asked him to make three purchases. His broker was upset because he felt these were rather high-risk and their purchase would also use up nearly all of Nelson's ready cash.

Because this was not like Nelson, the broker decided to talk to his office manager. The manager immediately asked two questions:What were the objectives Nelson had stated? How was this current purchase initiated?

The broker described what had taken place but added that he really didn't get a chance to offer any advice. The manager did react to that: "Gary, I suggest that you call Nelson back and tell him how you feel. See if there's anything major going on in his life."

Gary was able to get Nelson's attention and get him to come in and talk. When he arrived, however, he was sullen and didn't seem interested in talking about his life. The more Gary observed and listened, the greater became his concern for Nelson.

Then Gary got a call from Nelson's wife. She too was very concerned. She had seen differences in his basic personality. In a short time Nelson did go to see his doctor. The news was disturbing. Nelson was showing a dementia and was ruminating about how he didn't want to be old and not have money. A major sign of the disturbance had been the change when Nelson became impulsive.

The next party to this case was Nelson's attorney. Those last few stock purchases had not turned out well. There were indeed losses, so the question became, "Who had the control of the trading?" The answer is that the client does if he initiates the trade and if the trade was not solicited by the broker. But also of importance was whether the client, Nelson, had the intelligence to understand the advice given by the broker.

There were a few gray areas. Gary had not had much opportunity to offer Nelson any advice, at least with that very first phone call. Later he had tried to point out that Nelson was changing his approach to investing but Nelson didn't react. A thought-provoking question was, could Nelson understand the situation? was he responsible? After much consideration the lawyers decided that Nelson could at that time understand what he was being told and what he was doing. No lawsuit was initiated, but what could have happened if the dementia had been advanced?

Case 4: Another case sheds light on this issue. The client, Rex, had tended to be rather impulsive his whole life; he was known for making quick decisions, so it came as no surprise when he switched investment houses, bringing much enthusiasm with him. He started with George as his broker.

Rex was usually very explicit in telling his broker what to buy and sell and when. He arrived on the scene so quickly that people were caught up in his activities and no one gathered information about him and his investment style. Consequently, when Rex started making one trade after another, no one thought anything of it. Many of the stocks that Rex bought could be classified as high-risk.

After a flurry of activity, for several weeks Rex didn't put in an appearance. He called his broker a few times, but whenever he was asked he always said he wanted to hold all the stocks he had. His broker pointed out that he had several issues that were substantially down. Rex just said "okay" and hung up.

Over the following week Rex's stocks went much lower and he had to come up with cash to reduce his margin account. When he made an appearance at the brokerage house, he looked terrible. Where once he had been neat and stylish, now he was unkempt and sluggish. No one could pin him down about his plans.. The office manager even came around specifically to talk to him. Rex didn't get involved in conversation; he looked right and then left and he mumbled.

After quite a while the office manager began to conclude that Rex was emotionally ill. When he called Rex's wife, he found that she was as concerned as he was. With his support she called the family doctor and after one visit Rex went into the hospital. He was diagnosed as suffering from a major depression. He didn't recognize how disturbed he was or that he couldn't make decisions.

Rex was in inpatient psychiatric treatment for three weeks. When he was released he found horrendous financial problems. He certainly had a series of big losses on the stock market but he had problems everywhere. He hired a lawyer to try to straighten out his life.

He had known his attorney, Bill, for quite a few years. Bill could see an enormous change in Rex and wondered why others wouldn't have had the same perception. He visited the brokerage house to talk to the office manager. Bill asked why no one in the office noticed that Rex was becoming irrational and very depressed. The manager said it was probably because he had not been well known there.

Then Bill started questioning why no one saw the change in Rex's investment strategy. The office manager became more defensive. He said that no one had known what Rex's approach was because he had just recently transferred his account to this brokerage.

That gave Bill the information he wanted. He now knew that when Rex came to this investment firm there had not been a New Accounts Information Form that would have described Rex's investment objectives and approach. It was true that Rex had always been a quick decision maker and somewhat impulsive, but he wouldn't have gone to high-risk issues and he wouldn't have hung on to stocks that were dropping.

Rex's lawyer decided that Rex's new firm should pay for not having recognized that Rex was not up to making sound decisions. When this case went to trial, the court felt the same way.

Case 5: Family turmoil can be another force that has major impact on financial assets. Bryan and Sally had been married, seemingly happily, for quite a few years. Seventeen years his wife's senior, Bryan had somewhat of a paternal approach toward her. As he was a very successful businessman, he had been an excellent provider. He established an independent investment account for her but, seeing her lack of interest, he made the investments for her. Bryan loved the world of finance and investing; it was his hope that Sally would grow to love that world as he did.

He tried to show Sally how money is invested in stocks and bonds and how sharp investors made money. He even tried to get her interested in the business section of the morning paper: "Look, honey," he often said enthusiastically, "your stock just went up three points!" Sally didn't really care. She always said, "I'll get excited when you put the money in my hands."

Bryan always worked through the same broker, B. J., a very skilled advisor. B. J. always said that he gave little advice to Bryan because Bryan knew the market and what he intended to do. Sally just couldn't share Bryan's excitement and Bryan came to accept that.

Those who knew Sally well felt that she loved fun and cared a great deal about her appearance and about the world of entertainment. She also liked to travel and often did so without Bryan because he hated to be away from his business activities—although he sometimes did accommodate her at times and traveled with her. There were many other things this couple shared, such as theater, fine dining, and dancing. They seemed to have a happy life. Throughout Bryan carried on his little game of building Sally's trust with large deposits and successful investments.

Things went very well until Bryan was beset with health problems that made it impossible for him to keep abreast of his businesses and his investments or share many activities with Sally. Travel was risky and Bryan didn't enjoy dining out as he once did. Being well off financially, he could hire excellent people to stay at their home and look after him. There were rumors that Sally had found companionship and was less and less at her home.

When Bryan died, Sally was in Europe. She returned immediately for the service and she appeared genuinely upset by the loss. She seemed uninterested in talking to old friends but did begin a long confidential conversation with the family lawyer, Ed Grimwald.

Ed suggested a meeting to go over all of the accounts. He recalled that Sally's trust had been in her name only. Bryan had set things up that way as protection for Sally. He always had said, Ed recalled, that he should go first because he was older. He often joked that he had planned it that way because "I wouldn't want to live without Sally."

Ed arranged a meeting at Bryan's investment firm to go over her account. The meeting was attended by B. J., Bryan's valued friend and skilled investor. Ed requested that all of the stock in Sally's trust be put into three groupings, one pile for those investments that had done well, another including those that had stayed the same, and the third to include those that had showed notable loss. B. J. complied in short order. He even provided information about each stock and what its present prospects were.

At that point Sally dropped a bomb. She stated that first this was her trust and it always had been. No other names were listed as trustees. Sally stated that no one had ever asked her opinion, permission, or her advice as to what investments might be made. She further stated that no one had ever asked her about her investment goals and approaches. She went on to say, "Where is my new account information?"

Sally the little fun-loving, don't-bother-me-with-business girl, had suddenly become very business oriented. She stated that she was pleased with those stocks that had gone up, even though they could have gone higher. The ones that stayed even she wasn't going to "make a fuss about." She added that she felt some loyalty toward B. J. and his company. But she was very aggressive in her condemnation in all those stocks that had dropped in value: "I don't see the point in purchasing stocks that are likely to drop in value. No one ever talked to me about those stocks and I wouldn't have agreed to their purchase. I am not, therefore, willing to accept these loses."

It may sound unfair but that is actually how it works. Sally won her case and was reimbursed for the stocks that had dropped in value.

When the legal struggle was over B. J. took a look at where the mistakes were made. He saw that his firm and he had made a mistake right at the very beginning. No one remembered Rule 405; that made it more difficult to get to know Sally. Her identity for them was fused to Bryan's. With Sally's lack of interest in investing, she further slipped through the cracks.

Then B. J. rose from his chair and walked over to the office manager. Both men were very sad about all the losses they had suffered in a business they both loved. "I realize, too," B. J. said, "that we failed to know what Sally was really like. Bryan was such a considerate person and he worked in a very casual manner. We all just assumed Sally was the same and yet there were warnings she wasn't."

Case 6: How about another situation? I've heard of cases, for example, where a discount broker/dealer was held liable for losses incurred by a client even though all transactions were unsolicited and the firm offered no investment advice.

Let's look at a hypothetical case based on real life occurrences. John is a wealthy man who has made a fortune in business and as a stock and bond trader. Mary, his wife, also has a knack for investing in stocks, even though she never really needed to work. John was a very generous man who spent lavishly on his wife.

Relatively late in life the couple had a son. His birth was very difficult and their doctor was sure that Tommy was going to be retarded. Their doctor made this comment when Mary stated that Tommy didn't seem as responsive as most infants. Because Tommy was her first-born, she had limited opportunity to compare him directly to other children.

Tommy fooled everyone at first because his early development was rapid. He walked, stood, and spoke early. Mom and dad doted on him because he came at a time when they were sure they wouldn't ever have children. Both parents were very active in Tommy's life and he had a great deal of intellectual stimulation.

Tommy developed as a very friendly sociable boy who enjoyed being with other people. By the time he reached fifth grade, he had established himself as a fine athlete and he was liked by everyone. However, it was also clear that Tommy was lacking some very important cognitive skills, especially in "executive functioning," which meant he had a weakness with abstraction, organizing, and planning activities. He could learn many things but there was much that he couldn't do.

After Tommy was evaluated his parents were told of his limitations and their implications for his future. John could realize that Tommy wouldn't be able to take over for him in business. That was a source of disappointment, but as John looked at Tommy, he saw a really happy boy. "That should count for more than how smart someone is, especially when he's so nice to other people," John said to himself.

John tried to get his son interested in the stock market and went over accounts and transactions with him. Tommy could understand many things about the investment business but organizing and following abstract, complicated rules was difficult.

Over the years John made many deposits for Tommy. Sometimes Mary made her own investments but much of the time John directed the stock transactions in her own account. Things went along very well from a financial point of view and the three formed a happy family.

When he was 23, Tommy was offered a job on the west coast, quite a distance from his Midwest birth place. Tommy was particularly close to his parents, primarily because they were kind people but also because of his mental handicap. The thought of going that far away caused him some anxiety, but his father pointed out that they could fly back and forth and stay in touch on the phone. Before Tommy left, his father explained that Tommy should change his investment objectives; "At this point in your life, Tommy, you don't need to purchase the high-risk stocks I bought for you. You've built up a good investment fund." John told his son to find a broker he felt comfortable with and assured his son he would monitor his fund.

When Tommy arrived in California he had many urgent things to do. His residence had been picked out by a friend with his new company, but he still had to put things in order. He finally got around to visiting his new brokerage house and enjoyed the broker he met. He informed him of the advice his father had given as far as a changed set of objectives.

No further conversation took place that day but there were plans to meet again soon. A week after his initial meeting, Tommy had a call from the broker he had just met. He told Tommy he was very sorry but he was leaving this firm to go back to a managerial position in Michigan. Tommy asked if he could recommend another broker and he was told that he really couldn't. It was suggested that Tommy come in and meet the staff. Then he could make his own selection.

At the investment house Tommy met a very aggressive man who proceeded to tell him how much money he could make for him. This man, Phil, had been in the brokerage business for about 15 years. He could easily be described as a high-pressure salesman. He made promises galore.

Tommy had the feeling that he should leave but he wanted to show his dad that he could handle his own affairs. Phil took Tommy to his office and showed him some figures that purported to show Phil's investment record. He then explained to Tommy his "successful method."

Tommy tried to say that he couldn't follow many of the procedures that Phil was advocating. Tommy tried to reach his father but John was out of the country. When Mary asked if there was anything wrong, Tommy answered no because he didn't want to upset his parents.

Phil kept the pressure up and even added to it, saying that unless a deal was made very quickly big profits would be lost. Tommy decided to go ahead; at Phil's direction he made a rather substantial investment.

Then Tommy got very busy with both his new job and his apartment. He had also met a young woman with whom he spent a good deal of time. Consequently, he didn't pay much attention to his new broker or his investment.

A month later John visited his son in California. During a conversation Tommy brought up Phil and his investment account. He explained about what had happened with his former broker and described Phil's approach to him.

"Do you really understand Phil's approach?" John asked.

"Not really," Tommy answered, "but you know I'm not too good at that kind of thing."

There followed a lengthy conversation as to the roles of Phil and Tommy. After that conversation John contacted his lawyer and shortly filed a lawsuit against Phil and his firm, based on three primary allegations: (1) Tommy's investment goals were not pursued and in fact were not even inquired about. Had the firm checked, it would have been very clear that Phil was buying stock not consistent with Tommy's goals. (2) Phil did in fact solicit Tommy in regard to his own investment directives. (3) Perhaps most interesting, the broker had an obligation to give advice and words of caution in such a way that the client could comprehend them. Tommy never hid his limited intelligence. Clearly, Tommy didn't follow the explanation of Phil's investment approach or plan. Phil had not gotten to know the client. The investment firm and Phil were responsible for the transactions that had not worked out well. Tommy's losses were paid off because the firm lacked knowledge about the client.

Case 7: A similar problem occurred at a small investment firm in the mid-south. Broker George had done business with client Norma for over 10 years. He had known Norma to be very cautious about her investments, usually calling for advice before making any purchase. She was not as likely to call for advice when she sold a stock because it was usually then on the profit side. Norma knew that George would generally advise Norma to hold on for a little while—except that George had become tired of giving that advice because it was seldom followed. Norma was very conservative and quick to take her gains.

George often thought about that account and the changes that had taken place after the death of Norma's husband, Walter, some six years before. Norma and Walter were as different as two people could be and yet they got along beautifully. Walter would take some risks: in fact he loved to do that. "Where's the fun of investing if you can't gamble a little bit?" Walter would ask.

Norma would retort that she'd take her risks some way other than with money. Once she took over the account, she did reduce the risks every way she could and she always asked advice.

One day when George was away entertaining a new client on the golf course, his son, George Jr., was assigned to stand in for his father. Junior had done this before and he was planning to become a full-time stock broker, so when Norma's call came in, Junior took it. He listened to her describe a stock that she was quite excited about. She told Junior that she knew it to be a speculation with a greater risk than the stocks she always bought.

Junior asked if this purchase was advisable. Norma responded, "Junior, I've always been conservative, as you know, but I feel very sentimental. Today is the anniversary of the day, many decades ago, when I first met Walter. He liked to gamble, especially on a tip. Well today I got one. I feel it's an omen and I want to buy."

Junior felt there was nothing he could do but go along, so he got one of the regular brokers to make the purchase. That broker, feeling a little uneasy, made a note that this was an "unsolicited trade." That meant that the investment firm had not tried to push this trade. All recognized that this purchase was not in keeping with Norma's prior investment philosophy.

Norma's stock purchase turned out to be a real dud. She swore that she would never again depart from her usual approach, and she happened to make that statement again while she was in the company of a lawyer, Dave, she had started dating. Dave wanted to make an impression on her. He made the flippant comment that he would initiate a big "lawsuit in your favor." That's exactly what he did, but once all the facts were in, things were not so cut and dried.

In Norma's favor was the fact that there was no written account form change indicating that speculation was suitable to her investment objectives. She was still on record as a very conservative investor. She had given evidence to her broker that she was purchasing this "risky" stock on an emotional basis, e.g., that she was thinking of her deceased husband and his approach. Should she have been warned that buying that way is much more likely to make a bad choice?

On the side of the investment firm was the fact that they had not solicited the purchase of this stock. There had been some mild warning in that Junior had wondered about the advisability of this purchase. In the final resolution the major money loss to all parties was attorney's fees.

In this case, control of the trade was regarded as being held by Norma. But what about when there's a question of mental competence? We've all read about cases where team of psychologists or psychiatrists on both sides argue over competence—I've had my share of such cases and they're very challenging. The outcome is often determined by who describes what about the person's behavior. Doctors other than the family doctor will generally not have seen much of the client.

Case 8: Doug, a stock broker, was credited with being a wonderfully successful trader. By the time he reached 60 he was able to retire. He loved his work so much that though he reduced his client load, he went right on working. He basically kept those accounts that he really enjoyed.

Doug's wife, Gina, had been a social worker but she decided to retire shortly after their son, Bob, was born. Gina had one child, Greg, from a prior marriage who was about five years older than Bob.

As the years went by there were some interesting changes in the family. Doug, who had been a real city man, started to become a home body. An arthritic condition made extended walking painful; Doug often joked that he saved his legs for the golf course. Actually he used a golf cart all the time.

Gina had decided to use her social work skills again and began working part time. She became less and less interested in Doug's investment business and increasingly annoyed when anyone started talking about it. Her two sons began to have problems relating to one another, with Greg actually talking against his stepfather, Doug.

When Doug ultimately found paper work "impossible to deal with," he had his long-time friend, Tim, make the actual trades. On some occasions Tim suggested some trades and Doug usually went along. As time went on, Doug was increasingly prone to follow Tim's suggestions.

While all of this was going on, Bob and Greg began to have more severe conflicts. Some people said that Bob punched Greg in the mouth for saying that Doug was an "old fool who had lost all his stock skills." That report was never confirmed.

No one was sure what caused the final severe family problem. Gina began to state publicly that Doug had lost his memory, and she felt that he couldn't reason well. Neither she nor Greg liked Tim ; Gina hinted to Tim that he was churning Doug's account. The implication was that with rapid buying and selling Tim was increasing his fees.

Somewhere along the line Doug and Gina had severe marital problems, probably starting with the increasing conflict between Bob and Greg. Gina had indeed felt that Doug always favored his own son and that made her defensive of Greg. With all these thoughts weighing on her, ultimately she felt she had to get away.

On sudden impulse she moved out of the house and sought a lawyer to claim that Doug was no longer competent. The claim also stated that Tim had been taking advantage of Doug and that Doug was not competent when he selected Tim. That put Tim in the center of the legal action because it was claimed that Tim had no legal right to do the investing because Doug couldn't rationally select someone to do his investing.

There was massive spending in the case with authorities being hired on both sides. What I can speak to is that psychological testing indicated that Doug was indeed very competent. He had lost a little of his short-term memory but he was well-oriented, able to reason, and able to perform tasks involving abstraction and organization.

But Doug had lost some of his ability to fight. He said that the family fighting had taken all of his energy and that he felt no matter what he did the fighting would continue. He maintained that he had always loved both boys and he felt that if he favored anyone it was probably Greg. He noted that Bob had remained loyal to the whole family, but that Greg had split and favored only his mother.

Doug was convincingly able to defend his competence and the man he had selected to help with his investments. In a very organized manner he produced his original form at his investment firm showing the type of stock purchase that Doug liked. He then went over his current stock purchases showing that they were of the same type. There had not been a change in investment approach, and the stock purchases were high quality.

As a psychologist I've seen many cases like this one and they can cost many thousands before they are over. I recall the case of the man who went into an investment firm claiming to be a "multimillionaire" and brandishing a check made out for $10,000. He wanted to make some really big purchases, he said, and he presented himself as highly affluent and important. Yet no one knew who he really was. He had never filled out the new account application form and so there was no other information. No one in this investment firm knew this client. Yet he looked affluent.

Probably because of the way he looked, one young broker said he would handle the order. He asked his new client to slow down a little. He told his client that he was talking so rapidly he couldn't get his order and he didn't want to make a mistake.

The next day it turned out that the new client had no funds and once he calmed down he didn't want the stock. The rest of the story was that the client was under treatment for a bipolar disorder. He was fine as long as he was on his medication but he was not on it while all this was going on. The argument prevailed that the young broker acted incorrectly as he didn't know his client, and didn't warn him about the low quality of the stock purchases.

What can you as a broker do when someone comes in demanding that you accept an order? Couldn't someone claim that you operated unfairly by refusing the purchase?

Case 9: One aggressive man came in with demands to purchase some very expensive stock. He was loud and he refused to give information about himself. He was secretive, but when his demands were not met he became boisterous and even threatening. The manager came and invited this person, Steve, to come and talk with him. He explained why he needed the financial information that had been requested and why he needed to know something about each investor.

Steve accused him of being nosy and said he didn't feel that anyone needed to know what he was worth, how much he earned in business, or what he wanted to do with his money. When Steve became more verbally abusive, the manager said he was sorry but he couldn't accept Steve's business. Steve left, threatening a lawsuit claiming discrimination.

A week later more information about Steve came from some brokers in another firm. Steve had done the same act in their firm and they had been intimidated. They let him make some purchases and then he didn't have money to pay for his stocks, which all went down. All agreed that a successful investment business requires a set of procedures and standards that must be adhered to. The manager pointed out that you can require a money deposit for a new account. He added, "If you feel intimidated, you may be headed for trouble."

One further case history adds a little more information about how things can go wrong.

Case 10: Bob and Meg were a couple who had worked hard all their lives. Both had been married before and they had established separate investment accounts because they had had financial difficulties with their first spouses (one had been a gambler and the other had been an alcoholic).

They had recovered from the bad marriages and had become very successful. They both invested their funds through the same firm and the same broker, Lillian. From time to time Bob made his own decisions about investments. Meg didn't because she always said, "If I pick it, I know it's going down."

In a casual way Bob would sometimes order a stock for Meg and usually he did well by her. She used to joke that as long as he made a profit he could do that. For the most part, though, nearly all Meg's investments were the product of Lillian's suggestions.

Then one of Meg's step-daughters-in law came to work at the investment firm where the couple did business. Stacy wanted as much business
as she could get and approached Meg for her account. Meg didn't want to
switch because she liked Lillian, finding her to be very talented; besides,
Bob and Lillian worked well together. Meg enjoyed the situations where
Bob made her a nice gain with one of his investment decisions.

Stacy became more and more bitter and constantly talked about how
rejected she was by Meg's side of the family. Next thing anyone knew,
there was a lawsuit filed with some odd accusations. It was stated that
Bob was not a trustee on Meg's trust and he was not, therefore, legally
allowed to make stock decisions for her account. Lillian was out of line
for going along with it. Meg, who also went along with this, was accused
of being incompetent. Stacy was trying to open a door to get Meg's first
husband back in the picture as one of her "responsible heirs." This came
from an agreement Meg signed when married to her first husband.

The action that followed was loud and very angry. It was clear that
Bob should not have been making stock decisions as he was not a trustee.
However, Meg had made no objection. Stacy had no legal rights to raise
the issue.

It's particularly important to understand the benefits and pitfalls of
joint tenancy and trusts. I've heard of cases that went to arbitration
because the broker had opened an account in a person's name without
asking if they had a trust. One client died shortly thereafter, leaving the
estate open to probate because these assets were not titled in the name of
the trust.

With jointly-held property, probate is usually avoided when the first
spouse dies. However, a surviving spouse who is incapacitated and
unable to manage his or her own affairs may be forced to face a guardian-
ship proceeding. This can be expensive, dehumanizing, and destructive to
families.

With an increasing elderly population, it's important to understand
how people can protect their assets. Some want to keep a lot of money in
the bank in case of illness. Understandable! Do they need more health or
life insurance? Do they need someone to pay bills? The better you understand a client's situation, the more you can assist that client.

Don't assume that a son-in-law, daughter, or anyone else has the legal
authority to handle mom's affairs. I've heard of cases where relatives
brought in letters authorizing the gift of assets from old mom to help her
children or "to reduce her estate." The signatures were almost illegible
and not notarized. Did mom understand what she signed—if she signed?

What does it all mean? Each case we presented showed the psychology of someone trying to do something more for his own benefit than the client's. Often they were bending the rules, probably motivated by a need for power.

Lawsuits are painful emotionally and financially. The best way to avoid them is to make yourself psychologically and legally strong. How?

We make ourselves strong by following some simple rules. In the beginning chapters we talked about knowing your client. That helps to serve her better, to know what she wants but also to note when there are problems developing in any aspect of her life. You need to know how experienced the client is and the extent of the client's ability to evaluate the risks of certain investments.

Now we suggest more specifically that you follow New York Stock Exchange Rule #405, which also tells you to know your client. This rule will help you clarify suitability standards for clients. For example, does the client have a conservative approach? one with moderate risk? an aggressive approach? Aggressive to the point of speculation? What is most important: income, growth, tax deferral, or liquidity? How sophisticated is the client? What about risk tolerance? All these factors are important to knowing your client.

Keep aware of inconsistencies in activity related to the stated objectives. If investment objectives change, send a letter to the client outlining the perceived profile and request verification, information about what is not correct, and notification of changes. Keep the new account application form up to date. This will help to provide information about investment objectives and the general financial situation.

Know who's listed as a trustee on every account you service, and make sure only they make trades. Along with that, know who has control when trading takes place. Keep an accurate record whenever there is a change, whether in investment approach or personal philosophy.

The question of competence will probably become more important as the population is composed of more elderly people. Know the signs of deterioration and know to whom you should speak if there seems to be a problem.

There are a number of further points I as a psychologist would make, among them:

1. People who are happy with someone are much less likely to sue. Listening to the client's complaints can reduce anger or frustration. It's better to get it out than hold it in.

2. Listen to clients when they talk about their investment complaints. Maybe changes do need to be made.

3. Listening to clients helps them feel important.

4. Educate your clients where possible. Informed people are likely to make more rational decisions.

5. Don't play the role of a parent; clients may worship you for a while but eventually they will turn on you.

6. Never brag about what you do for others.

7. Never promise what can't be delivered.

8. Keep clients up to date on important news concerning their investments, even if the news is bad.

9. Don't come on like a miracle worker so the client expects too much. Stress the value of long-term results, not short-term gains. Set goals.

10. Don't argue, empathize.

11. Have your own lawyer to turn to for advice as you need it, but don't give legal advice to clients.

12. Treat people as you would want them to treat one of your parents.

13. Try to be sure your client understands the risk of any investment.

14. Show joy when you make a good gain—joy is a reward.

15. Help people realize that there will be short-term market volatility and how to anticipate the market reaction to political and world events.

Chapter XII
Helping the Investor
Stay Psychologically Fit

I firmly believe that one of life's most noble desires is helping others to attain health, happiness, and the pursuit of what they want out of life. In my opinion we have had too many years of "think of yourself and forget the other person." While I dislike this approach anywhere, I feel it's even more inexcusable applied to a client. There can be no excuse for not doing all we can to give to those who in their business dealings give to us. As a matter of fact, I've always felt that giving shouldn't be one-sided. People who are in a relationship give to one another.

Some would say that all a broker needs to do is make money. I don't buy that concept. I well remember many years ago when a local broker who had two reputations: He was very successful at making profits from stock investments, but he was terribly unsuccessful at relationships with people. He had many nicknames but the most popular was "Captain Grouch." He had a way of being critical of people that often encouraged feelings of inadequacy.

For many years people put up with Captain Grouch; he did bring them profits. Then his extensive people problems began to take a toll. He used the same approach with his wife that he used on others. After tolerating it for a few years, she divorced him. Tired of his mouth, his parents pulled away from him. With all this isolation and rejection, the Captain's work began to suffer. He seemed depressed. He couldn't keep up with current events, so he was not well prepared for his work. As his ability to make stock profits dropped off, clients began to avoid him. His people problems had put him in a bad situation. Clearly, the conclusion that a broker or investment advisor only needs to make money is false.

What can a broker do to make clients psychologically stronger? It may seem odd but I believe the first step is to make herself strong. The broker needs to recognize that anyone who does things for others will to some extent be looked up to. Think how often you've heard someone rave about a doctor who "cured" a person who was very ill. That doctor is certainly looked up to and may be worshipped.

If the broker makes herself strong, the client will benefit in two ways; first because there is a positive identification, and second because the broker will relate better. As a result the client will listen more carefully and accept good advice wherever it comes from.

The first step for the broker is to recognize that the occupation generates great pressure. Feeling tense at times, you need to find acceptable ways to release your emotions. Physical activity is one of the best ways. Some people like walking, others favor workouts or swimming. Exercise on a flexible schedule, but let it relate to your moods.

We all know that talking is a good way to get your feelings out—if you have the right atmosphere to talk. By that I mean conversation where the listener is not judgmental. When we talk to someone to ventilate, we don't want criticism, we want empathy. If someone says, "You shouldn't let that bother you," you'll feel you're wrong for feeling that way, so you'll hold your feelings in more than ever. But if someone listens quietly, the emotion is reduced. Then at the right time the empathetic listener can try to offer suggestions.

Balance in life is very important for all of our health areas, physical or mental. Make time for a full social life, the family, and relaxation, such as listening to music or watching TV. Just getting away from the work situation will increase your productivity when you get back.

Accept the fact that you don't necessarily like every aspect of the investment business. Very seldom does anyone love every aspect of a chosen profession. But look around for someone to whom you can delegate some of the chores you dislike.

Support is something all of us need. It can come from many different sources. One source is friends, who also help gratify a social need. Another that I consider extremely important is support from fellow employees. They know better than anyone else what problems you face. They see what happens around the office and with clients. If you need help, they can often provide it. I heard about a woman who came into a brokerage firm demanding that her broker refund money she had lost on an investment. When he explained that he couldn't, she started screaming and said he had "pushed" her. Fortunately, a number of the other brokers saw what happened and confronted the situation.

A pleasant atmosphere in the work place in and of itself will help work productivity. I do believe in rewards; they encourage positive feelings of self-confidence and desire to do well. When there's a feeling that "all my colleagues wish me well," it strengthens the desire to do well. An office that's a happy or fun place to work will help bring success.

Along those lines I recall an obviously depressed patient who had no idea about the source of the depression. I asked questions about his wife and every time I got back an answer that all was fine. I believed him, because he described some wonderful activities they shared. Then I asked about the children, now nearly grown; and again there were no problems. Everyone in the family was healthy. They didn't have money problems, although he did speak of wishing he could retire.

That last statement made me wonder. I finally asked a more detailed question about his office. His whole facial expression changed; he looked more depressed. He rambled on about life at his office: One man constantly complained that he wasn't appreciated at "this dump and yet I'm the only person who knows what he's doing." A woman broker complained on and on about her "ungrateful kids" who never appreciated her and all the sacrifices she had made for them. There was a frail older man who verbalized every day about how his neighborhood had changed and how unfriendly the neighbors were and how lonely he felt. Another woman constantly raved about how bad her life was: one thing after another.

These people all complained about different things, but the sum total was a place of depression. My patient was lucky; he was offered another job and jumped at it. I didn't get another chance to talk to him at length but when I saw him he seemed much happier.

We all know that many key decisions need to be made in the investment business. This adds up to a pressure situation, and tension can contribute to lessened psychological fitness. One way to reduce the pressure is to secure advice from others. Again, support from coworkers can help relieve the tension of this type of decision.

This is not to say that there should be a shift in who makes the decisions. I remember a conversation with Al, a friend from a small brokerage firm, who had to make a decision about four stocks. Sell or hang on: he couldn't decide. When he consulted several coworkers, they all disagreed with his thinking. Al was surprised but thought the situation over. He delayed what he was going to do, re-appraised his approach, and then a totally different approach came to him. It turned out to be very successful. The fact that he sought other opinions didn't mean that he went with the majority. He didn't. But their disagreement signified to him that there might be yet another approach. It turned out to be a very good one —plus it took pressure off Al's shoulders.

A wonderful resource that often escapes our attention is our spouse. Unless we're newly married, our spouses for years have heard us talking about what upsets us at work. They know what our approaches are like and what we're trying to do. They know our little personality quirks and what that means for our adjustment. If you can cultivate this resource, the support you get can mean a great deal. One word of warning, though: you also need to listen to and support your spouse in times of need.

Another quality that will help you stay psychologically fit is a good sense of humor. One of my clients had suffered when a few stocks had dropped in value. He had wanted to sell but felt he couldn't after the declines. His broker, trying to lighten the moment, pulled out a yo-yo he had just purchased for his son.

"See this," he said, working the yo-yo. "This is just like the stock market." "Not like mine," said the losing client, "your yo-yo comes up again, my stocks don't." Everyone laughed.

Another suggestion for staying fit is not to do too much for others. If you take too much responsibility for the lives of others, they will surely become dependent on you. You must set limits, not only for your benefit but also for theirs. Some may actually stop trying on their own when they see people catering to their needs.

We also know that if we establish some time for study and reading, that will make us stronger. A person who knows that he is well informed exudes confidence and that will make him strong.

Now for the other half of this equation: The broker should want to make his clients as psychologically fit as he can. It should be a goal of everyone who works with people that the better you help other people become (without taking on responsibility for them), the better you will become. I like to put it this way: "As you have strong clients, so will you become stronger." Being around happy contented people rubs off. You as a broker will face greater but more positive challenges because your clients will know more and seek more out of life.

Well, then, the question emerges, where do we start?

Strength comes from knowing where you want to go. This translates to being able to set reasonable, meaningful goals. It doesn't help very much to have a very long-term goal like, "I want to be a millionaire." Sure, we all do. But we need more timely, more specific goals. How are you going to make that million? Many, if not most investors, have no clear cut plan or short-term goals.

So the first suggestion goes back to what we have said over and over: Know your client. Try to elicit from her how she sees her goals, short-term as well as long-term. When you believe you have an ongoing relationship, you will want to have some idea as to what her earnings are, and her spouse's earnings, if any. It's important also to have an idea about savings. Indebtedness, too, is important because it undermines available investment capital. All this information will help you together to develop an investment picture. But again much of the planning must emanate from the client.

Case 1: Sometimes people fool you about what they want. Many years ago a very hard-working man, Ted, married an equally hard-working woman named Sylvia. I knew those two people socially and I was impressed with their ability to work together. Although both had demanding (but well-paying) jobs, they purchased rundown homes and rehabbed them.

One day they were talking about how much they enjoyed remodeling homes. In the group was Stan, their stock broker.

Stan later confided to me that he had a problem investing for them because he really wasn't sure what their goals were. When he asked them about stock purchases, they just said, "Use your own judgment." They wouldn't even point him in a particular direction, long-term, low-risk, whatever. After a few moments of silence, Stan ventilated some pent-up frustration: "You can't guess how much tension I experience because they don't tell me what they want."

I couldn't help but ask, "How do they react?"

"Well, I don't know exactly. Not with a lot of emotion, but they always seemed pleased."

As the conversation continued, a number of things became obvious. First, clearly Stan needed structure and didn't know how to attain it, at least from this couple. Second, equally important, Ted and Sylvia were giving Stan a message he wasn't getting, that they didn't much care about investments.

Later I learned Sylvia had put it into words: "Well, naturally, we want to make money, we all want that—but we love working with houses. To us this is play and that's why we do it so much."

We can see how the broker's personality shaped his interaction with Sylvia and Ted. Stan needed to understand himself and not try to force his approach on others. Make the investment decisions as Ted and Sylvia want you to. Don't spend a lot of time discussing the stocks' performance.

We can see by this case how knowledge of the clients' goals will make both client and broker psychologically stronger. Stan could have helped the couple learn what their goals and needs were. I seriously doubt whether Ted and Sylvia had ever communicated their goals to Stan.

It may well be that we will see more older persons who prefer to have someone they trust make the investment decisions. I've seen many hundreds of people in nursing homes and that seems to be what many want.

So our initial plan will be to get a clear idea of what goals attract the client and then to check regularly to be sure there's consistency. I've seen people who said money is not important but their life style said otherwise. This may need to be discussed. Goals must be reasonable.

The client's overall financial position is important because it will help determine what can and cannot be accomplished. Keep in mind that it's the unknown that causes the greatest turmoil. Many investors see things as much worse than they are; having a broker who goes over their accounts clarifies things for them. Greater strength for the client can come from clarification of goals, understanding what the portfolio is like, and deciding what goals are reasonable.

Strength also comes from knowledge. Many a broker educating a client sees immediate benefit. I've seen any number of clients who were very upset by some facet of the stock market. When they found a well rounded broker and got the information they needed, they became more relaxed. It's advisable for you to do the educating because you're in in a position to see how the new knowledge influences the client's behavior.

There are a couple of other interactional factors that need to be dealt with. The first is how active the client wants to be. This is like a definition of the rules of the game. It's exceedingly important.

Case 2: Burt always had wanted to pass on all of his broker's investments. Adding to the problem was that Burt enjoyed working with low-priced stocks. On one typical occasion, Burt's broker, Randy, started trying to reach him early in the morning and kept trying 'till noon. His wife said he had left the house very early and she didn't know when he would return. She knew he had gone out to play golf but she didn't know where. He just couldn't be reached.

Finally at 1:30 in the afternoon Burt called back. By that time it was too late. Randy had been calling because a stock had just come on to the scene, it had good earnings, and it was selling for a mere $1.50 per share. Randy expected this stock to easily double but then fall back as investors took their profits. The stock went to $3.50 but then did drop.

Burt learned from this experience. He realized that if you're going to deal from a strong position, certain things are necessary: decisions about when to invest and how often and when to communicate. Do you, the broker, call every day at a certain time or just when needed? Burt and Randy altered their approach so that Randy would make purchases himself if he couldn't reach Burt and if a stock investment was in keeping with Burt's general investment approach.

Another source of psychological strength is partnership with a spouse. I recall a fellow professional, Mary Kay, who loved the thrill of investing. She was very good at it but she said it bothered her to take certain risks because her husband was so against stock investing. Several of us suggested that she try working with her husband again. "See if you can't educate him a little about the investment game," someone suggested.

Mary Kay decided to use a soft sell. She bought him a short book on investing and she gave it to him right after she had prepared his favorite meal. He read the book and began to talk to her about investments. As he learned more, he became very interested; now he often invests alongside his wife. These two supported each other and the added strength seemed to increase their success ratio.

That brings to mind another way the broker can help his client gain strength. If you have ever seen two nervous people interacting, you've probably noticed that they feed off one another. I had a supervisor during my early days of training who talked about some of the traits in a psychologist that immediately help the patient. He enjoyed teaching by anecdotes and he said to me: Imagine the following. A patient comes to your office and says, "Oh, my God, doctor, I don't know what to do." "Now," he said, "how would that patient react if you said 'Oh, my God, I don't know either'?"

The point is that we become role models. If we're calm, it will tend to calm the client and help him become more logical. As you know the client better, you will make him stronger because you learn what his sensitivities are and how to help him through difficult times. I've seen it happen often that people who are anxiety-ridden or upset don't see any approach that could help. When they see a relaxed person who relates to them, they begin to feel that there must be a solution.

It will also help your client feel strong psychologically to realize that someone cares and is interested in his feelings. I believe that all young psychology students, and probably most brokers, fail to realize how important listening is.

I saw that early in my training. I was doing an "intake interview," which is an interview in which we try to find out what's bothering the client. This was a very verbal young woman who came with a list of her problems and with obviously deep hopelessness. She described each problem in detail and gave its impact on her life. I was afraid that at any moment she would ask if it didn't seem hopeless to me. At that point it did. I just kept listening. After 40 minutes of her talking and me listening, she stopped and I thought, "Here it comes." Instead she said, "Thanks. I feel a lot better now."

Then, to my surprise, she followed with a question: "Where do we start?"

That I could deal with, because there seemed a number of things in her life that could be easily changed. We worked on those and her life became more joyful, but it all started from listening to the client.

I believe this will work in the investment field, too! Much of the client's investment self-concept or business ego comes from his interaction with his advisor. It's important that he be treated as if his account is very important. Sometimes it may be difficult to be highly enthusiastic about a small account with a very questioning client, but the true professional will work at it or make a referral. I knew one broker who worked very diligently with a couple of small accounts; those clients then referred some very large, active accounts to him.

We all know many people who become exceedingly excited when they feel they're about to make a big gain. Perhaps there's a little of the gambler in all of us. One way of looking at it is this: When the client makes a big gain, it's all his money. Even if the broker chose the stock that makes a big profit, the money belongs to the client.

So the broker is in a less emotional, more objective position. That means that in most situations the broker can be stabilizing. Sometimes a client becomes so excited that he goes outside the range of good judgment. Usually if he does so, his excitement creates a psychological attitude of "this can't fail."

Case 3: Michael had a broker who constantly warned him about overbuying when he was presented with a good prospect. The broker tried to be a stabilizing force to slow Michael down, but Michael would push until he got his way.

Sometimes the stock would move up rapidly and sure enough Michael would buy more. He was of course betting that the stock would go higher. Jim was his primary broker-advisor but when Jim was tied up Michael dealt with George, Greg, or Tom. Since the last three did little more than buy or sell for Michael, they had little idea of the overall plan.

Michael and Jim had recently had a lengthy conversation about maintaining a "position of strength" in the market. Jim had stated that an investor with a good cash reserve is in a strong position should there be an upswing. An investor who is totally invested has nothing left to invest unless there are other stocks in the portfolio that have reached their peak.

Some may disagree with that approach but Michael generally agreed with it—until his excitement and optimism elevated. A short while after this agreement Michael again placed his investments in an inflexible position. The trouble started in March when Jim was away on a vacation. One of Michael's stocks dropped precipitously and Michael called Greg to talk about it.

Michael had taken out of context Greg's remark that the stock was a good buy at the present time. Later Greg recalled saying, "If one bought this stock at the current price, it would probably be a good purchase price." Very different from Michael's interpretation. Michael wanted to buy more of the stock and Greg asked for a delay until he could study Michael's investments.

Michael agreed to a "temporary" delay but said that if the stock started going up, he wanted to jump right in. Michael called back later because he heard the stock had gone up (it did—by one fourth!). He couldn't reach Greg, so he spoke with George and told him to buy several hundred shares of the stock. He repeated his interpretation of what Greg had said to him. George made the purchase. George did, however, say that a quick look at his portfolio told him that Michael would then be totally invested. He knew Michael and Jim didn't favor that sort of program. Michael was too excited to pay much attention to George's warnings, and George also knew that Michael often went out on his own.

Back in his office several weeks later, Jim took a look at Michael's account. He didn't like what he saw. The stock that had initially moved rapidly higher had now dropped. When Michael bought more of this stock at what turned out to be the high, he erased the profit he had on the original purchase. As a matter of fact, with further decreases in this stock's value he had placed his overall position at a loss. At the same time his purchase of a stock that was low also proved to be a bad move. That stock had gone yet lower.

Jim immediately called Michael and asked that he come in to meet with him: Michael came in right that day because he was worried about the position he had put himself in. He was indeed very humble but Jim also felt uncomfortable.

Jim said right away that he felt changes needed to be made. He pointed out that as a broker or advisor it was his job to help prevent this kind of situation. He pointed out that now there were no funds available should an excellent investment come into view. (That did happen, as a matter of fact, but much later.)

Jim went on to explain that he felt it was his duty to stabilize Michael's approach to the stock market. Michael said that he was aware that he became very anxious and often excited when there was notable activity in stocks he held. He also was aware that he became overly excited over stocks that looked as if they were going to move up. In this discussion Michael also saw that his view of stocks was one-sided: He looked at only a few of the yardsticks that are usually deemed important.

Jim expressed himself this way: "My job is to try to put you in the strongest possible market and investment position. If we're in a strong position, we feel strong psychologically and that confidence helps us behave more rationally. A balanced account also gives us strength because we have more confidence and flexibility. Then we aren't likely to feel trapped in one investment position." . . . Like the current situation, which proved to be a good learning experience for Michael.

Yes, they did find another stock that looked almost like a sure thing. It tripled, in little more than a month. They got out when they needed to. With his other two investments, Michael had lost both with the one purchased at what looked like a low and with the one bought at the high. What all this shows is that a stabilizing force can be the difference between success and failure.

Another area where the broker can help keep clients psychologically strong is in recognizing which investments are best for a client.

Case 4: A broker friend told me he had a very stable, hard-working client, Marco, who was a classic worrier. Life had not been easy for Marco but he was moving to a point where he began to have money to invest.

Marco worked as a tree trimmer and had at one time had a bad fall. He had gone into tree trimming because he could command a higher hourly rate than in other landscape work. As long as he was able to work, he was happy. His fall and the resultant injury intensified his already high level of anxiety. Now he had to be more of a supervisor and let his brothers do most of the physical work.

His brothers were not as hard-working or as skilled as Marco. Pedro, his broker, tried not to bother Marco with additional financial considerations but he often had to confer. He often found himself in a difficult situation. Because Marco might need funds from his investments at any time, Pedro had to focus on short-term investments. What became very clear was that now, more than ever, Marco was torn apart with anxiety over financial problems. The resultant anxiety crippled his functioning in all areas.

Marco began to follow some of his stock investments more than he ever had. Pedro noted that whenever Marco saw one of his stock investments go down, he called with extensive anxiety. This didn't help Marco function well in his tree-trimming business.

One day Pedro decided to talk to Marco about his investments. He suggested that for Marco, low-risk stocks were much better. This lowered his anxiety level and allowed him to be more efficient and comfortable in his life.

One of the ways a broker can help his client be strong, therefore, is by keeping investments in line with what the client finds comfortable. Someone who is a great worrier probably needs investments that don't increase anxiety.

Closely related is the situation where the client begins to change his investment approach. He may suddenly begin to buy higher risk stocks after having been very conservative.

Case 5: I recently heard about an investor, Sam, who did just that. There was no explanation but the change was significant. The broker told me that he had called to ask Sam about it, but all he got were denials.

With patience Sam became more talkative. He thanked his broker for bringing this to his attention and for trying to protect his investments. It took quite a while for Sam to get around to telling the rest of the story.

The change in Sam's approach was due to marital problems. He was very much in love with his wife, Charlotte, and their marriage had been a good one for both. They had shared many interests until some unknown factor had put distance between them. Sam felt that perhaps they were not as close as they had been because they couldn't afford many of the pleasures they had had before. So Sam was trying to find ways to make more money in the hopes that he could keep his wife. "I felt that if I could be more exciting, maybe she would stay with me," Sam said.

The funny thing was that Sam's broker got a call from Charlotte three days later expressing her concern that Sam was working hard in order to get enough money to leave her. She called the broker because she didn't know where else to turn. Charlotte was considerably more composed when she heard what the broker had to say, and it wasn't long before their marriage was be very happy again. The problem was resolved because the broker noted the change in investment approach. Sam has now gone back to his previous investment philosophy.

Here is another important principle that can be learned from prior experience that once again demonstrates the value of knowing your clients. Knowledge of the client needs to be kept up to date. This could become crucial if client and spouse, children, or whoever becomes involved in estate planning.

Being aware that psychological strength can come from many sources can make a broker even more valuable. Usually when you work with someone on something as important as money, it helps establish a bond. Then if the client has, say, a family illness to deal with, a call from the broker may pick up the client's spirits. At this point the broker is calling not so much as a financial advisor but as an empathetic person. Knowing that someone cares does provide strength.

There's one area of helping your client become strong that's very challenging: dealing with something involving the client's health. Many might say that the health of the client is none of your business. I disagree, for several reasons. One is humanitarian. If you see someone who looks ill and doesn't seem to realize it, shouldn't we say something? What if a comment could save someone's life?

Years ago I played golf with two people I hadn't known, one a doctor and the other a hard-driving general contractor who had just finished some very demanding apartment buildings. Dr. G. J. saw something in Jake that alarmed him. Though he asked a whole series of questions, Jake didn't seem to mind. At the end of the round, Jake thanked Dr. G. J. and wrote down the name of a doctor he recommended.

I learned later that Jake had very nearly died of poorly controlled diabetes. Now it was partially controlled, but only because Jake had begun treatment. Had Dr. G. J. not alerted him, Jake probably would not have survived.

Since that time I've heard of a number of situations where doctors made suggestions to people who were not actually their patients. They did it as a kind person wanting to help someone stay healthy.

I've heard of similar acts not involving doctors, one a warning about electrical usage and another about carbon monoxide. I recall once a stop light being warned about a tire by the driver next to me. When I looked, I noticed a big bulge that could easily have blown. Undoubtedly many lives have been saved because some interested person gave a warning.

Is such a warning required of an advisor or broker? No, I don't believe it should be demanded and, yes, I know it's often a very difficult thing to do. You might worry that someone will tell you to mind your own business. You may even fear losing the client.

Getting away from the humanitarian aspect, what about the possibility that if you don't recognize a person's state of health, your stock transaction may be questioned? What about the question of your client's state of mind when she bought or sold some of her investments?

At this point you might want to review Chapter XI. Here we're referring only to those factors that increase the psychological strength of those
in the investment business. Knowing someone cares about your health
adds to a person's feeling of well-being and giving. A warning can save
someone from unnecessary trauma.

We've mentioned that it may not be easy to bring up a question about
health. A lot depends on your approach to the other person. Without being
pushy I've found that most people respond well to a gentle question,
"How are things going?" A little more aggressive question might be, "Are
you feeling all right?" I personally have never had anyone become angry
over questions like these. The client may be firm in telling you all is fine.
If he does, at least you've tried and he may respond later.

As people become older many have an increased fear of losing their
mental faculties. I've seen nursing home residents who worried that they
might make a bad decision and "squander what I've worked very hard to
save." Often they realize that they need someone to help.

Among all these fears a source of strength can be the fact that someone shows interest in your financial well-being. We're not suggesting that
the broker or financial advisor should become a counselor or therapist and
take on a treatment role, any more than a treating professional should take
over any of the client's financial life. But you must be prepared in case a
client loses some ability to function. At that point you may have a very
difficult choice about who to talk to about the client's mental status.

Case 6: A broker friend, Bill, had a very alert, logical, highly verbal
client who was very active in the stock market. No one knew the specific time when this client, Joseph, began to lose some of his memory.
Recognizing it to a mild extent, he chose to talk to his broker about it. Bill
suggested he mention it to his doctor. Joseph didn't want to do that. He
said his doctor was always busy and that it took too long to get an
appointment. "By the time I get the appointment, I've forgotten why I
made it," Joseph said with his little smile. He still had that sparkle in his
eyes. His broker smiled, too, and thought about how lucky he was to have
clients who were fun.

Shortly after this episode Joseph started calling the brokerage to order
the purchase of a stock. Then he began to call twice in a day, placing a
second order for the same stock. He couldn't remember in the afternoon
that he had called in an order in the morning.

Other than this short-term memory problem Joseph was alert, well-
oriented, and logical. He loved trading stock and he was still very gifted
at it. He did, however, work out a deal with his broker that he would be
told if he was double-ordering purchases or sales. Joseph made his bro-

ker promise to tell him when he began to "lose it all." Joseph used to joke that if his broker hadn't stopped one double order, Joseph would have been wealthy. That particular stock tripled in value.

The same broker, Bill, undertook to protect another client, Janet who admitted to a drinking problem. Her broker had recognized that some time earlier and had been able to talk her out of what would have been a very unwise purchase. She was appreciative and said that none of the treatment programs she submitted to had effected a cure, though she was better in that she didn't become violent or abusive.

Janet was able to define some of her behavior when she was under the influence. What usually happened was that she felt on top of the world. She didn't believe she could fail and her stock choices reflected that. She felt that Bill could effectively act as a stabilizing force because she could accept his directive that she not make investment decisions under the influence.

My last suggestion for an approach to helping the client gain psychological strength is also my favorite because it involves a team approach, something I strongly believe in. Life in this age is simply too complex for anyone to do it all. The professionals whose help I suggest will clearly add to the feeling of psychological fitness. The following are the ones I feel your clients need:

1. *A financial advisor.* An investor may enjoy making his own investments and he may be very good at it. He may even prefer to buy his stocks at the lowest possible price. If that works for a particular investor, fine, but I think strength comes from not feeling all alone in the investment world and from knowing where you can go to at least get another opinion.

2. *A tax accountant.* Tax law changes constantly. It becomes more complex all the time. You need someone in this crucial area to help make financial plans that work around the tax laws. I've also found that accountants are very talented at figuring the rate of gain or loss. That helps you know which investment is profitable and what is not.

3. *An attorney.* Help is needed whenever a contract is being negotiated, when a home is sold or bought, and of course if there is some kind of liability or threat of one.

4. *Insurance agent.* Insurance is another way to protect yourself and thereby feel strong. We all worry from time to time that some cat

astrophe may run through our savings. We certainly need all the protection we can get.

There is one more person who can promote psychological strength: a spouse. This is someone to share with and ventilate feelings of frustration.

With all these sources of strength anyone is well equipped for success.

Chapter XIII
The Broker's Quiz

We gave the following quiz to a small sample of brokers and discovered some patterns that appeared prevalent among the successful. It became the "Broker's Quiz." We have some suggestions for interpretation after the quiz. Pick the response you feel is most accurate.

1. What do you do when angry?
    a. talk to a friend
    b. confront the situation
    c. ventilate through sports
    d. hold it in

2. Business dealings with the opposite sex are:
    a. like any other investment
    b. okay
    c. challenging
    d. much more difficult
    e. keep me on edge

3. How does stress affect your body?
    a. feel keyed up
    b. headaches
    c. muscle tension
    d. fatigue

4. What do you do to maintain relationships?
    a. communicate verbally
    b. look at what others are feeling

    c. talk about problems
    d. hold back all negative feelings

5. How do you look at defeat?
    a. learn and go right on
    b. look at what others are feeling
    c. talk about problems
    d. hold back all negative feelings

6. What type of client is most likely to anger you?
    a. no specific type
    b. overly quiet
    c. bad-mouthing type
    d. argumentative type

7. What type of client do you work best with?
    a. one interested in learning about the why of investments
    b. a challenging one
    c. one who seldom argues
    d. a quiet one.

8. Who would you like to see control your client?
    a. the client
    b. the investment counselor
    c. anyone who gets his attention
    d. the spouse

9. From what you can tell, how do you affect people?
    a. they become talkative
    b. they ask too many questions
    c. they become quiet
    d. they often seem jealous

10. How do you feel about teaching?
    a. enjoy it
    b. only with certain types
    c. okay if paid enough
    d. no interest

11. How do you feel when things go well?
    a. ready to invest more
    b. the same as usual
    c. ready for a turn-around
    d. hold back on investing

12. How well do you recognize the moods of others?
    a. very quickly
    b. it varies
    c. it takes quite a while
    d. I don't notice

13. What type of client is most difficult for you to work with?
    a. those who seldom talk
    b. those who question a lot
    c. angry people
    d. negative people

14. How much would your spouse say you like your work?
    a. very much
    b. some
    c. a little
    d. very little

15. How difficult is it for you to sell a stock that is significantly down?
    a. not difficult
    b. I feel discomfort
    c. very difficult
    d. I usually put it off

16. How often do you make changes in your investment approach?
    a. often
    b. some
    c. seldom
    d. very, very rarely

17. When a client bad-mouths you, how do you handle it?
    a. try to get him to talk about it
    b. challenge him
    c. ignore him
    d. yell at him

18. Someone threatens you with a lawsuit. What would you do?
    a. contact my attorney
    b. try to get him to talk about it
    c. refuse to talk about it
    d. have no idea

19. How much do you re-appraise your investment approach?
    a. regularly
    b. sometimes

   c. not often
   d. rarely

20. How many close friends would you say you have?
   a. many
   b. some
   c. a few
   d. not very many

21. How good are you at keeping up with the news?
   a. never miss a day
   b. very good
   c. sporadic
   d. only fair

22. How would your spouse say you handle feelings of anger?
   a. talk them out nicely
   b. get the other person talking
   c. don't often deal with them
   d. hold them in and later explode.

23. How often do you seek the advice of others?
   a. as needed
   b. regularly
   c. seldom
   d. rarely

24. How well do you generally know what your clients want?
   a. very explicitly
   b. pretty well
   c. somewhat
   d. probably not well

25. How clearly do you know your client's investment history?
   a. very well
   b. pretty well
   c. somewhat
   d. not well

   No definitive scoring is suggested but the highest correlate of success is a significant number of "a" answers and the lowest a significant number of "d" or "e" answers. You can make your own appraisal.

Chapter XIV
Dealing With Obnoxious
People

No matter what your occupation, you will be called on to deal with people whose behavior is not acceptable. Much of the time there will be a need for diplomacy because you don't want to lose clients. As I've reiterated, the first step necessary is to recognize what's taking place.

What if we just decide to do nothing? I don't recommend that for a number of reasons. The most striking is the buildup of tension. The world of investments is already a high-pressure world. Any time money is involved, there is great potential for major emotional upheavals ranging anywhere from rage to happy excitement. Both advisor, and client, not only have to deal with the threat of investment loss, they also have to work with the extensive emotions of other people. If you don't come to terms with the turbulent emotional life of others, you'll often find your work disrupted.

Secondly, a broker who doesn't find a way to let her feelings out is likely to find herself one day with a bodily disorder. It's impossible to keep holding feelings in and escape illness.

A third reason for dealing directly with unacceptable behavior, is office decorum. Customers who see irritating behavior unchallenged, lose respect for a place of business. The assumption is that if people turn their backs on one problem area, they will do so with other areas. A professional atmosphere helps make everyone more confident about the business. So we will try to describe some of the troublesome types and situations you may encounter and some techniques to deal with them.

Charley Casanova is the overly confident type who can't accept a "no" from any woman. He finds ample opportunity to pursue women in the investment world because there are plenty of women in that occupation. To Charley this creates a challenge. He may feel in a power position because he knows that his business is needed in this highly competitive world. He will often push for a date and continues to ask even when refused.

This situation is potentially dangerous. If Charley and a woman broker do get together in a romantic way, the professional relationship may become more subjective. Then if mistakes are made, Charley may become angry enough to take action. At that point it will become clear that investing and romancing don't readily mix.

What can you do? Be diplomatic but always very businesslike. Don't respond to the little provocative messages Charley sends. For example, one of my clients told me about Charley's hints, like, "I've to have ready cash because I like to spend money on my girl friends."

Don't respond. Focus only on the needed cash. If asked out, simply say thanks but it's a policy not to date customers. The main helpful ingredient is the manner you project, which says in effect, "I'm all business." Be as firm as you feel you need to be, but try to not allow him to get you angry.

Sometimes male brokers may encounter equally seductive female clients. This can become difficult because men often respond without realizing they're doing so. This may encourage the client to become more seductive and to feel that she is in control. Sometimes she actually is.

It's not our goal to be moralistic about people's social behavior. If the seductiveness is pleasant to both parties and the work situation not interfered with, well, that's up to the broker and client. The problem comes when work is interfered with and when one objects. If the broker wishes it stopped she must do it right away. When behavior is encouraged once, even if it's rejected the next three times, it's more difficult to stop. It must always be ignored if the message is to get across.

It will not work to mention the seductive behavior because the client will deny it. The best way to stop this behavior is to not respond, maintaining a businesslike approach.

There are many stories to demonstrate that one of the quickest disrupters of business decorum is alcohol. I still recall an Illinois investment firm that had a regular client Henry, who seemed highly changeable. Friday afternoon when he arrived it was already clear that he had started celebrating the weekend. He weaved, slurred words, and even appeared confused from time to time.

This was quite a departure from his usual mood. Consistent with that, one of the brokers who had been at parties with Henry on at least three occasions reported that often on Saturday Henry appeared under the influence, while on Sunday he was a model of sobriety. When he wasn't drinking he was quiet and serious, very poised. If anything he was regarded by most of those who knew him as overly proper. He appeared to be the sort of man one couldn't imagine saying anything with even a tinge of impropriety.

Until Friday arrived! Alcohol made very substantial changes. Henry was boisterous, overly talkative, demanding, and even a little rude. If he felt a need to communicate something he felt was very important, it didn't matter what others, including his broker, wanted to say: Henry decreed that his opinion was more important. At those times Henry interrupted to demand that he be heard.

Henry's drinking created another interesting dilemma. When he was sober Henry was an extremely conservative investor; when he was under the influence, he took high risks. Moreover, when under the influence Henry was very generous (so long as he wasn't irritated with a person). So he sometimes put money in his wife's account without telling her.

We can see the grave potential for liability here. Sometimes it seemed that that might be what Henry was trying to create. He also often espoused an investment philosophy that said, in effect, "We should all have the inner freedom to make any kind of purchase."

Henry usually conducted his investing business through a broker named Barry. Sometimes Barry felt like pulling out his hair in frustration. "Which is the real Henry?" he often asked, at his wits end.

Barry didn't want to start an argument with Henry, but he wanted to establish a more clear and consistent idea of what sort of investment philosophy Henry wanted to follow. The trouble was that on Fridays Henry often selected stocks that did rather well. In fact, when Barry checked, he found that Henry's more risky Friday purchases did better than his more conservative investments during the week. Notably, Henry was self-directed on Fridays while he was guided by his broker during the week.

There was one more aspect to this picture. On Fridays Henry was never subdued when he made a big profit. His loudness told everyone in the vicinity that here was a successful investor, and others wanted in. Consequentially Henry became an idol to many investors seeking quick profits. Soon Barry's problems were magnified hugely. Now there were suddenly eight to nine people investing in stocks on Friday that were not typical of their general investment approach.

Barry decided that he had to do something to be sure the investments were suitable. He decided that he needed a private meeting with Henry to discuss some of the problems. He presented the list of investments Henry had made in the last four months. It was obvious that there was much inconsistency as far as risk factors were concerned.

Henry immediately objected: "Well, Barry, as far as I can see, I've done pretty well."

"I readily admit you have. That's not what brings me to this conversation," Barry responded.

Henry of course wanted to know what the problem was, and Barry cautiously got into it. He pointed out that Henry was fast becoming an icon and many investors wanted to emulate his investment approach. At first Henry couldn't see any problem with that, but on reflection he changed his mind. He said that he realized that what was good for him was not necessarily good for others.

Barry went on to explain the concept of "suitability," which refers to how appropriate or suitable a particular stock is to a specific investor. Barry knew by the look on Henry's face that he understood clearly. He decided to move on to the rest of the problem, namely Henry's variable approach to investing. He explained that there was major concern in the brokerage because Henry seemed inconsistent. Advisor ethics demanded that Henry's broker know that he was able to maintain his usual logical approach.

Henry was subtle enough to understand what Barry was saying.

"I guess some might question my state of mind on Fridays," Henry said with a smile.

Barry very wisely didn't smile; he stayed businesslike. He knew that if he smiled it would add a degree of levity that could mitigate the seriousness of the situation. Barry went on to state that if someone had to undergo, for example, brain surgery, he would want a surgeon who was thinking with the utmost clarity. The analogy was well received and Barry quickly added that he and his staff all wanted to do the best they could for their clients.

"We feel that all factors in our lives do have an impact on investment strategy. Maybe we worry too much but our desire for the best for our clients does encourage that."

Henry did a lot of thinking about Barry's comments and began to understand. Barry had done a good job. He didn't complain, criticize, or make demands. He said his next approach would have been to set limits on the drinking and resultant behavior. Barry had allowed Henry to see the variability of his approach and expressed the dangers. He didn't lecture or get into areas remote from investing.

This approach can work with many people but nothing works for everyone. By attributing the placing of limits to "ethics" or "company policy," Barry took the rule-setting away from the personal issue, Barry versus Henry. He put himself in a more neutral position.

There may be situations where a client is not able to understand subtleties well enough to profit from this kind of a conversation. It may be worth trying humor or straight talk, but if it doesn't work, that client may have to be excluded.

A similar situation took place a few years ago when I was asked to help with an industrial setting. The business manager called me to say that there was a problem with employees who worked in one part of the factory. The company ran a metal stamping business; the jobs were organized so that men worked in teams. One team, for example, dealt with shipping, another with packaging, and so forth. It was the packaging crew that seemed unable to get along. Their work quality was uneven and so was their speed. I decided first to talk to the workers as a group, then to see each employee separately, hoping to get the employees to open up so I could look at how they were interacting.

My first meeting, lasting about an hour, gave me very little information. Not one person had any idea of what was wrong. No one admitted that there was a problem. I had the feeling that all of them were afraid to say anything.

The atmosphere seemed the same with the individual meetings until I saw the third man alone. He gradually began talking about one of his peers, Royce. Royce had an explosive temper and he intimidated people around him when his anger broke out. Otherwise he was quiet, even withdrawn.

From what I was told he was a man who had experienced many of life's disappointments and even some tragedies. His son had been born with many health problems, although he seemed to be doing much better of late. Royce and his wife often quarreled severely. Royce's parents had moved away, taking away a source of support, especially for the son.

After completing all the interviews I felt that I had an adequate picture of what was taking place. Royce was not a person who would ever resort to physical violence. What was described to me as "explosive anger" really related to words and angry gestures.

These outbursts, however, had a very negative effect on the group. People were afraid that any little thing they did might set off Royce's temper. This they didn't want to do. In addition Royce was generally liked and they felt sorry for him. Being afraid to talk out problems had a destructive impact not only on Royce but also on his fellow workers. They wanted to keep things quiet because they didn't want to hurt Royce.

Corrective measures were easily put in place. It was explained to the group that one person can have a very negative impact on the group and that made the work place unpleasant. The first approach was to help Royce learn other ways to express his frustration. He was told by the group that they wanted him to stop his outbursts and start talking. This meant refusing to respond when Royce behaved in an unacceptable way. It helped that the staff quickly came to understand that letting Royce behave that way was not good for him either.

The same general situation can happen in an investment house. If the explosive one is another employee, the solution might be very similar. If it's a client, the solution may be different. An employee is right there everyday and you as a manager have some control of him. As a rule the client is not at your office as much and your concern is not with his work but only with his behavior.

That doesn't mean that a client's angry outbursts are any more acceptable. They too, may disrupt business. I remember being in an investment house and listening to a client in the next office berate a broker. I was quite unimpressed with that firm for allowing that to happen.

So what can you do?

I believe that some people are just not made to do things together. We can call it a "personality clash," but whatever they try, they never seem to fit together. If a broker finds that a particular client is erupting with anger much of the time, they should both consider that they might do better with someone else. True, this is not likely, if the client gets angry all the time. That tells us the problem is within the client.

Once we have eliminated a personality clash, we need to try other measures to stop anger toward innocent people. You can, for instance, immediately stop the tirade by letting the client know that you will not allow him to express such anger toward you. I don't favor that approach because I feel that it will only increase the client's frustration.

I prefer to try to redirect the anger. Re-direction can in fact work with a number of emotions.

Ellen was a young woman well known for her temper. She often expressed this anger without any warning. Since she was usually not prone to talk about her life, no one at the brokerage house knew much about her. They did have, however, have a clear picture of her financial situation. She was very explicit that she wanted only blue chip, low risk investments. Ellen often called in her orders, and she had instructed her broker to never buy or sell without consulting her. Ellen did ask her broker's opinion of all stocks that she bought, seeking an opinion about how long it might take for a stock to show a profit.

Ellen went through many different brokers over the first four years. She lived in the area. What generally caused the problem was that stocks didn't do what her various brokers expected.

For the last year Ellen had worked with only one broker, William, with whom she was generally very satisfied. Her profits were high and she felt he kept her well informed. He was a cautious man and he spelled out the limitations of his predictions. His advice always centered on the suitability of an investment to Ellen's investment goals.

One Friday morning Ellen came in, all smiles, and announced that she needed to take some funds out of her investment account. She wanted William's opinion about which investments would be the better ones to sell. There was a little disagreement but for the most part William and Ellen agreed.

William didn't inquire about Ellen's plans until he was sure she wanted to tell him, but he recognized a new sparkle in her eyes. She was in the happiest mood anyone had seen in quite some time.

"Are you taking a trip or planning something special?" William asked.

"I guess you could say that: I'm getting married Saturday and then we're going to Italy for our honeymoon." She added that her future husband was currently highly invested and therefore wanted some help with the honeymoon cost.

"I don't know when I've felt so happy," she said to William. She asked him not to tell anyone else, because the couple wanted privacy. William said he wouldn't.

Ellen didn't come into the brokerage house for three weeks, and when she did her mood was greatly changed. It was clear from a distance that something was wrong. She was angry. She bit her lip. She was wide eyed and jumpy.

"William, I am very angry at you," she exclaimed from the door leading into William's office. Then she charged into the room. "Your advice was all wrong," she said with obvious, intense anger.

William raised his eyebrows. He extended an open hand, suggesting she have a seat at his desk. He walked over to a rack and pulled out a large notebook, opening it to her account. "I know it's no fun taking a loss: is that what made you angry, the market drop last week?" he asked.

Ellen nodded. By getting her to do that, William had started to redirect her anger. Instead of being just plain angry, she was now angry at something. She obviously felt that she had sustained a loss.

As William carefully went over each stock in her portfolio, it became very obvious that only one stock was down to any extent. Though he recalled that the down issue was one of the two he had recommended for sale if she was taking money out. William didn't mention that because a person who feels badly doesn't want to hear that it's his fault.

"Yes, this one is down," he acknowledged, "but how do you feel about the others?"

"They do seem okay," she said, looking sad but not so angry.

William waited a moment and then offered that he felt the market would recover. He didn't know how long it might take. Then he gently asked, "How is everything else?"

With that Ellen's whole countenance changed. She slumped forward in her chair and said, "Well, I guess that's the problem."

Her fiancé had decided at the last minute that he didn't want to get married. He backed out. Their trip was canceled. In addition to the humiliation, Ellen had lost about half of what she put down as a deposit for the trip.

When people share their good fortune with others and then it turns out badly, they feel very vulnerable. Knowing that, William said carefully that he was sorry, mentioning that some men have trouble making up their minds. He said casually, "There will be another day." Then he turned back to her investments.

A month later Ellen stopped in to see William. She had a very large diamond on her left hand and a big smile on her face. She had met Mr. Right and they had plans for a wonderful honeymoon, to Paris this time. Ellen appeared very happy. She was sure it would work this time and she wanted to thank William for his gentle support at a time when she needed it.

Though not explosive the behavior of Clara Changeable can also produce great frustration for brokers. Clara has always had troubles making up her mind. What she wanted one minute often displeased her the next.

Clara says that the reason for this inconsistency lies in her childhood. Her parents moved eight times during Clara's first eight years of life. Clara, however, with her good sense of humor says the problem started even before she was born. That was because her mother had six signs of impending delivery that proved to be false. Then when there were no noticeable signs Clara was born.

From high school on, Clara had changed career choices more times than she could remember. Ultimately she went into nursing and had a fine income and the respect of a number of doctors. Infact she was engaged at one time or another to three of them!

Clara was an excellent listener. She became fascinated by the number of doctors who complained about problems they had with collections.

After some extensive reading, she was ready for another career change. She established her own billing agency; then after 16 months she added a collection agency. With both businesses, she had excellent leverage to collect a high percentage of what was owed. Her business grew by leaps and bounds.

After a couple of years Clara had sufficient savings to make her money "work faster for me." She listened to her customers and finally found a good broker, "Mc Lavish." He was a very frugal, conservative, and studious broker who took his profession very seriously. The first thing Clara remembered about Mac was that right after he met her he asked her to fill out a form listing her philosophy about the type of stocks she wanted. Clara joked about this often. "I hardly knew this guy and he immediately gives me a test. I thought maybe he doesn't like my money and doesn't want to have me for a client."

Clara was not very specific in describing her investment philosophy but others told her she was on the conservative side. She gave Mac a lot of leeway in choosing investments but there also were many times when she called and told Mac or his assistant to make a particular purchase. She often got tips from doctors for whom she did the billing.

Watching her transactions, Mac declared, "This account is giving me a headache." At one time he said, "This behavior is obnoxious," but he later rescinded that comment because he really liked Clara. However, he had a major problem because of the changeability in Clara's tolerance for risk. On Monday she would tell him to stay conservative and then on Thursday she would direct a purchase that was very risky.

Mac decided to confront the situation directly. He called Clara to a meeting where he went over her transactions and explained the problem from his point of view. Realizing that Clara was immune to concerns about her investment strategy, Mac felt that if she was concerned about his own well being maybe that would cause her to be more cautious. It worked beautifully. Clara responded by telling Mac that she never had intended to be a bother or to increase his business liability.

Clara and Mac were able to work out their problems, although she still had periods of wanderlust. Mac told Clara that he probably had a bias toward solid, blue chip stocks and regarded himself as very conservative. He didn't feel comfortable with higher risk investments. He added that he found that he earned the highest percentage of profits with stocks that were mainly classified as conservative.

Clara decided, with Mac's help, to set aside a percentage of her holdings to invest in high-risk stocks. Then she found another broker who enjoyed working with higher-risk investments. The approach was very successful for all parties. Mac felt that he had handled the situation very nicely.

Another obnoxious behavioral pattern is seen in Peter. None of us enjoy seeing someone who is hurt but won't tell anyone why. I saw a classic Peter Pouter nine months ago referred by a broker friend of mine. My friend Jim felt that Peter had problems that needed attention not just for his sake but for the investment staff as well.

When Peter told Jim he had made an appointment with me, Jim asked permission to tell me what was going on. Peter gave his permission because, he said, he wasn't sure what problem he might have. In fact, he felt he didn't really have any problems; to hear him, he got along with everyone.

About an hour before I was to see Peter, Jim called me. He said that Peter was often a very frustrating person, but only when he was irritated. When that happened he would refuse to talk to anyone and he would literally pout. All the anger and frustration would be held inside and Peter would attempt to get away from everyone.

"How do problems and conflicts get solved?" I asked.

"They really don't," Jim said. Then he paused, "You know it's not a lot of fun working with someone who all of a sudden stops communicating with you. He's a really fun person when he's in a good mood. We all want to help him but we don't know how." Then Jim asked what I might recommend for the staff to do to help Peter.

I said I'd hold off suggestions until after I had seen Peter. When we did meet it was clear that Peter loved communicating with people. His problem was quickly identifiable. As a youngster from a large family he had been made fun of by older sibs whenever he became angry. He got to the point where he was afraid to show angry feelings. Whenever he did display any anger, he felt guilt-ridden and often anxious as well.

After just a few sessions Peter began to talk more about his anger. I know, however, that what helped Peter the most was that Jim kept after him to talk it out. "Tell us what's wrong," became a very common phrase.

Peter apparently began to feel more comfortable at the brokerage house. Jim's insistence that it was not fair to the staff when Peter didn't talk had a great benefit. I know this because Peter has now decided that he will train to become a broker. He has also found that interpersonal problems away from his business have been greatly reduced.

Then there is the very frustrating person, Sue Super, who endows certain people with special abilities. This may sound very flattering to those who have not experienced it, but living it is not much fun.

A typical example took place the first time broker Willard met Sue. She immediately began telling him all the wonderful things she had heard about him, continuing even when Willard tried to play down all accolades. Willard knew that problems occur when people expect too much. He also knew that it's not ethical for a broker to make exaggerated claims about his abilities. He had never done that, but Sue was talking as if he were infallible.

Willard began Sue's investment program with four very good stock performances in a row. Two of the stocks very nearly doubled and the other two were up about 20 percent. Understandably, Sue was very pleased and expressed her excitement to everyone around her. Sue thanked Willard and told him that she was going to bring in yet more friends to invest with him.

For his own part Willard tried to de-emphasize his success. He carefully explained to Sue that they had been very fortunate and that they should not count on that high a profit much of the time. He carefully explained what were reasonable profits for which to aim.

All of Willard's comments were to no avail. He did realize that people do become excited when they hit a rapidly rising investment. In addition, of course, people tend to remember the first investments better than later ones, and Sue's were great.

Sue told all of her friends about what a wonderful financial advisor Willard was. She talked as if Willard was almost certain to perform this well all the time. What was even more troublesome, Sue stated that Willard was a very modest man who "plays down his great abilities." The good news traveled far and wide. Willard, hearing some of it, found himself cautioning people when they talked of great investment gains.

Willard's fame increased by leaps and bounds. Soon he reached the point where he couldn't take any new customers. That didn't stop his influence from increasing however, because his clients often shared Willard's advice with their own friends.

Fame can be very fickle; it can smile on you one minute and knock you flat the next. Such was clearly the situation for Willard. It was not that he did anything wrong, but it was the perception that he might have claimed too much for his investment skill. Willard tried to explain that he had not claimed anything except that he would do his very best and that he would listen to the needs of his clients.

A downward turn of the market produced a change in how Willard was perceived. He sold some stocks at a very slight loss. That was something many customers and their friends couldn't accept because they had come to feel Willard was infallible—all because at the very beginning one person's investments realized a quick, large profit.

There were a few complaints. The office manager, fearing a law suit, agreed to review the whole situation. Fortunately Willard had conducted himself in a very professional way. He had always insisted that clients provide information about their desired type of investment, he had denied that he could consistently predict the future, and he had, in fact, stated that his original large profits were not typical. He had even publicly stated that people need to realize that an investment that is appropriate for one person often is not for another investor.

When Willard's good name was restored, he had only one comment about his short lived fame: "It isn't fun being superman!"

I think it's fair to state that all of us dislike people who are constantly argumentative. I still recall a fellow classmate in high school who was probably the most argumentative person I ever knew. Fred had a little trick that he liked to play on people to start an argument rolling. He would prod you to give an opinion on some matter. Then he would start asking many questions about how you formed your opinion. Then he would attack the premises that formed the basis for your opinion. If someone tried to avoid the situation by stating he didn't have a clear opinion, Fred would attack him, implying he had no strength in his values.

Fred was never a popular person, especially with girls. He would use the same questioning approach when he called to plan what they would do on a date. He seldom found a girl who would go out with him twice. Eventually he had few friends, male or female, young or old.

After he graduated from high school Fred started his first real job as a shoe salesman in a small store. He immediately got into trouble by arguing with customers. One woman, for example, told Fred that she wore one size. Fred argued that she should wear a half size bigger. The customer got up and walked out—but not before she talked to the manager. Fred was soon let go after this incident. That became a pattern throughout Fred's life.

Generally, there is little to be accomplished by long arguments. If people are looking for another opinion they'll ask for it. Usually they don't. Most people are set in their ways. When irritated, they become even more set in their ways.

Recognizing all this, I suggest you try to avoid arguments. In particular, when you sense that the arguing person is emotional, avoid confrontation. Draw out the client's opinion. Often, the more a person talks the more evidence there is that his argument is illogical.

If he doesn't recognize his own lack of logic, you won't be able to convince him. Either avoid saying anything or just tell him you'll think it over. If he persists, try telling him you're busy. Generally, though, when an arguer gets no reaction from others, he'll stop.

Just as arguers are annoying, so too are those who constantly have negative expectations. These Nervous Nellies become very jumpy with any change in their investments. Though you might think that as long as their investments are doing well, they would be very relaxed, that is not the case, as can be seen from their phone calls. For example; "I see my TSA stock is up, should we think of taking the profit?" The frustrated broker tries to reassure his client that there's a good chance that TSA will go higher.

Before the broker finishes his comment, Nervous Nellie is at it again: "Well, if you think TSA will go higher, should we sell some of those other stocks that are down and put that money in more TSA?"

The broker explains why he doesn't think this is a good idea. He feels sure that now he's finally put all questions to rest. Nellie thanks him and the two hang up. All is quiet. Then the phone rings. It's Nellie again; he forgot to ask something important. The broker accepts the call. "I forgot to ask you, but you do think that my stocks that are down will eventually make a comeback?"

The broker hesitates, organizing his thoughts. He knows that he can't make a specific prediction, but says, "Well, Nellie, yes, I do think they're top-rated stocks. They've been well recommended by other brokerage firms. However, none of us knows for sure."

Nellie responds, his voice cracking with anxiety, "Well, then should those go up?"

"Again, Nellie, we can't guarantee what's going to happen. Do you remember what I told you at our planning session two weeks ago?"

"I guess I don't," Nellie responds. Nellie can't recall because at the time Nellie was so loaded with anxiety she had trouble focusing.

"Why are my stocks down?" is a very familiar opening to a phone conversation. Dealing with these frequent calls is time-consuming. Also there is no real answer to most of the questions, so the answers bring only temporary relief.

There are a number of ways a broker can help calm a client. The first is to maintain his own composure and recognize that anxiety is what causes Nellie's behavior. If the broker is calm, it will reduce the client's fearfulness. With some clients it may be advisable to focus on stocks that show little movement. This would need to be talked about and the client would need to be made aware of his own anxiety.

Another approach would be to meet with Nellie on a regular schedule to go over expectations, plans, and investment philosophy. Then the
program should be written out so that Nellie can refer to it from time to
time as she feels the need. Anxiety cuts into concentration; when people
see something written in their own handwriting it not only promotes concentration, it has a strong measure of authenticity.

Then there are those who feel dissatisfaction with some aspect of
their investment program but never direct their displeasure to their broker. Instead they talk to everyone else they happen to be around. The broker only hears about the complaints secondhand, if at all. That creates a
new problem because you cannot correct a problem without talking to the
one who is unhappy. About all we can recommend is that the broker
encourage the unhappy one to talk to him about whatever bothers him. It
may take some coaxing, however, because usually those who talk behind
someone's back don't deal with issues directly.

Another frustrating type is the compulsive questioner. Though it's
rewarding to find that people are interested in our opinion, there's a limit.
Often the person who asks one question after another does so for one of
two reasons: (1) He doesn't understand our answers or (2) he needs attention. If it's the latter, there's nothing much you can do. If it's the former,
you might try to watch his facial expressions to try to note when he understands and when he doesn't.

Understanding one another is a major world problem. Communication between people from different backgrounds can be weak. If we can
see that someone doesn't understand, maybe we can listen to the words
they use to see what they did get. Then we can change our wording to fit
what they comprehend. Sometimes a question may elicit from them
where the breakdown took place. Perhaps some education by the broker
may help communication and clarify investment philosophy and objectives.

Just as there are those who constantly question and complain, there
are those who never do. Without wanting to start any battles, I'd say from
my clinical practice that the second group is mostly men.

I've seen many examples of this in marital counseling. Typically, the
wife says that she can't easily please her husband because everything she
does is "fine". "What does that mean?" she asks with frustration. One
wife put it this way: "We were just married and I wanted to do something
special for him. On Monday I prepared a shrimp dinner, on Wednesday
Dover sole, on Thursday veal picante, on Friday lobster, and on Saturday
a filet. We both wanted a quick dinner on Sunday because we were going

to a play. I made hamburgers. And you know what? He responded the same way about each meal."

The problem when people never complain or specify a preference is that we don't know how to please them. If everything in someone's life is just fine or even okay, why try to do something special for him?

What can we do to change this pattern? Try to help the person feel comfortable with you. Ask about his life. Try to get him talking about himself and to establish some preferences. Never be judgmental, because that is one trait that will turn anyone off very quickly. People will talk only until they feel others are not really interested. When they do start to talk, give them as much support as is reasonable.

These are a few examples of what any broker faces, sooner or later, in her professional career. There are some general suggestions we think will help in dealing with the more challenging clients.

From the start, you must realize that you are a professional in one of the most important of vocations: helping others to make money. You also help improve clients' state of mind, because sound investment planning does help a person feel more carefree. The point is that if you think of yourself as an important professional, you're more likely to take pride in yourself and to set appropriate limits for others. You send a message that "this is the way I expect to be treated." Since you will be dealing with people at every point on the emotional spectrum, you'll be thoroughly tested, but you must stand firm.

In setting limits, the first rule is the important one:

- *Be consistent.* If there is one cause of parent-child and broker-client problems, I've seen it's inconsistency on the part of the parents. That tells children that if they push hard enough, they will get their way. They don't even think about it, it's simply automatic.

- Never send mixed messages, because that will make for inconsistent limits.

- Never allow people to make you feel guilty about a restriction you have placed on them. Many people out there have had a lifetime of manipulating through guilt: Don't allow it to work!

- When people around you start to express considerable anger, try to redirect it. Are they really angry at you? the investment? or some other area of their life? We all know about the man who kicked the dog because his wife was bugging him. Once the anger is re-directed to its real source, you'll be in a better position to look at the client's investment situation. That is the broker's area. A broker doesn't give marriage counseling or deal with children's problems.

An important key to adjustment is knowing yourself and what you can tolerate. Do you mind if people call you at home or after working hours? Is it all right for some but not others? You must decide and let those who intrude know what you will allow.

Humor can be a very important ally. I once heard a broker respond to an angry client by saying "Yes, I know that stock is like a yo-yo." Everyone laughed and then the client commented that overall his investments were good.

The fact that the broker doesn't become overly agitated is soothing. It encourages rationality, and it's easier to be soothing if you remember that you can please some people all the time but not all the people all the time.

Chapter XV
Overcoming Guilt Over Success

Just for fun, how about a little quiz? It might reveal some preconceived ideas. Or it might show great insight into this topic. No one has to be told how you did.

If you accept the challenge, just select what you consider to be the best answer and then read the analysis at the end of this chapter.

1. Society places a heavier burden of guilt on women than on men.
    Agree   Disagree

2. People tell me I am a dependent person.
    Agree   Disagree

3. I am a very easygoing person.
    Agree   Disagree

4. I get upset when people describe morals different from mine.
    Agree   Disagree

5. I hate to disagree with others.
    Agree   Disagree

6. I hate saying no to other people.
    Agree   Disagree

7. It's difficult for me to stand up for my decisions.
    Agree   Disagree

8. I feel embarrassed when praised.
    Agree   Disagree

9. Most people describe me as overconfident.
   Agree   Disagree

10. People say I push my ideas.
    Agree   Disagree

11. I am always helping people.
    Agree   Disagree

12. I am severely annoyed by the immoral behavior of others.
    Agree   Disagree

13. I worry when things go too well.
    Agree   Disagree

14. My parents had most of my life planned.
    Agree   Disagree

15. I was seldom sure I pleased my parents.
    Agree   Disagree

16. I feel upset when my opinion clashes with the opinion of others.
    Agree   Disagree

17. All of us manipulate at times.
    Agree   Disagree

18. It hurts when you don't live up to someone else's standard.
    Agree   Disagree

19. If I win too much, I fear hurting someone.
    Agree   Disagree

20. It upsets me when I see jealousy.
    Agree   Disagree

21. Social attitudes shouldn't change.
    Agree   Disagree

22. Fun, joy, rewards, pleasure—all are suspect.
    Agree   Disagree

23. Women should not play an assertive role in financial matters.
    Agree   Disagree

24. Guilt is self-punishing.
    Agree   Disagree

25. When people feel free, they're likely to be more creative.
    Agree   Disagree

26. Some people suffer guilt when they do something better than others.
    Agree   Disagree

27. I often agree with others so as not to hurt their feelings.
    Agree   Disagree

28. When I make a mistake, I remember it forever.
    Agree   Disagree

29. Feeling guilty can block some great deeds.
    Agree   Disagree

30. If people don't do anything wrong, they have nothing to worry about.
    Agree   Disagree

You'll find an analysis of the quiz at the end of this chapter.

Now we come to guilt and anxiety, emotions that rob many of us of our productivity and joy for life. When we try to seek out the source of the sabotage, we're soon forced to the conclusion that the person who does this to us is—US.

Of the two emotions, anxiety is much the easier to understand. We mentioned earlier that when there's a threat of any kind, we experience anxiety, an emotion described as a vague fear. We've all had the experience at one time or another of being afraid we couldn't do something. We may feel that we don't measure up or that we can't take the pressure of failure. We fear having people laugh at our poor performance.

But guilt over success? How could that be! And why should women be more vulnerable? . . . because they are.

People can feel guilt about anything. Many people believe that you only feel guilt when you do something bad or wrong. Yet directly from my clinical practice I could cite many examples of people feeling guilt-ridden after having done something very worthwhile. I once saw a young girl who was encumbered by guilt because she could sing better than her mother. There was a young man who felt bad when he started to have lower golf scores than his father. There was a woman who felt guilty when she aged better than her younger sisters.

My clinical practice tells me that people suffering from guilt feelings usually don't get much support from others. If people see someone suffering from anxiety, they immediately try to help by reassurance and anything else they can think of. But if someone is suffering from guilt, others want to stay away, as if this were an area too dangerous to enter. Of course, some people *think* they're offering support when they say, "There's no reason to feel guilty about that." That makes the victim feel, along with everything else, that now he's stupid for feeling as he does.

What is guilt? It's a strong, negative emotion similar to anxiety in that there's a perceived threat. A major difference is that usually anxiety is stimulated from the outside; guilt comes almost totally from the inside. Like nearly all psychological statements this is a generalization. There's an important distinction that needs to be made to clarify our position. In most cases where anxiety is present, we would be happy to destroy the threat. In the case of guilt, we would not, because we would fear harming someone who is nearly a part of ourselves.

Look at the following dilemma, for example: As a child Jane was taught by her parents that she shouldn't do certain things. Being a child she didn't want to rebel, so she automatically went along. Having reached adulthood, she now wants to behave differently but parental directives still stand in her way. She wishes she could dispose of the threat but she can't easily do that, because the threat still comes from her parents. She doesn't want to offend them but she doesn't want to lose her identity either. She also doesn't want to make waves in our society. That little voice inside her that causes conflict can be very punishing, besides being behaviorally restrictive.

At this point we can provide some descriptions of guilt. We know that a primary quality is a feeling that we've done something wrong, probably one or more of the following:

1. We've said or done something to hurt someone else.

2. We've accepted something we feel we didn't earn.

3. We've not given to another what that person needs.

4. We've given to others but not to a degree appropriate to what we've received.

5. We've violated a religious or moral position of a private nature. An example might be cursing. I will not deal with this here because it refers to a private act not related to business. (If you curse a person with whom you do business, you're harming a business relationship. That means behaving in a self-destructive manner.)

Keeping in mind that this is a book relating to business investments, we eliminate not only category 5 and in most cases also category 1. Sometimes we offend someone else because our views differ. Often someone becomes upset just realizing that someone else has a different opinion. We can all recognize that a new idea can be threatening at times. It might be wise to use care when giving advice or criticism. If your advice backfires, your guilt will probably encourage you to proceed more slowly next time, but new information can also help avoid tragedy. No one is forced to listen if information or an opinion causes a threat.

Let's move on then to the second category, taking something under false circumstances. Perhaps you have a talent that enables you to perform a service. Low self-esteem, however, may cause you to feel that you aren't competent. You're a fake, a fraud, a cheat.

I once saw a young woman who had a great deal of talent but had such low self-esteem that she was sure others would see her inadequacies. She was so compulsive in checking her work that she couldn't get it done on time. When her bosses praised her, which was fairly often, she felt panic because she was so sure they would find something wrong. She was ridden with guilt long before anyone said anything critical.

People with this orientation generally have major weakness in negotiating. Since they must view themselves as defective, they also view their product or service as inferior. Advice is given so passively that others don't even recognize it. For this kind of person the focus is not on winning but on avoiding failure.

What if a person with this orientation is working in a brokerage? This is a person who does not trust his own decisions. What he did today he may change tomorrow and again the next day. Usually his approach is ultra-conservative no matter how the market is moving. Sometimes the person may rebel and actually take a chance, but then guilt will set in. That inner voice will say, "You shouldn't do this—you aren't that spectacular." Then there will be flight born of panic to change. That is not likely to bring success.

We must realize, however, that guilt feelings don't always cause inactivity; they can cause very rebellious behavior. Deacon Jr. could well attest to that. His father, Deacon Sr. was a very imposing figure with strong opinions and rigid attitudes. He hated change. He probably would have preferred that the nineteenth century had never ended. He was constantly suspicious of anything modern; everything new was a "fad" to him.

Deacon Jr. often said that he had an easy childhood but a difficult adolescent and adulthood. Childhood was easy because "all you had to do was what dad wanted and he always made it real clear what he wanted." As a child Deacon Jr. may have felt he had to conform to dad's expectations, but as an adolescent or adult he felt that he just couldn't. He would be giving up too much of himself.

So father and son began a long battle; they disagreed whenever possible, and it was usually possible. Their major areas of disagreement were politics, investing, and borrowing money. Father was in all areas ultra-conservative. He called his son "a flaming liberal."

Deacon Sr. fostered tremendous guilt feelings in his son by pointing out some other boy who "always makes his father feel proud of him." Deacon Sr. also used the threat of heart attacks to control his son. When they argued politics, for example, Deacon Sr. would get red in the face, grab his chest, and say, "You're going to drive me into my grave." Sometimes he would even claim "heart pains."

By the time Deacon Jr. reached 22 he had some very conflicting feelings. He knew he was guilt-ridden and controlled by dad, but he felt very inadequate even admitting that. He didn't want to hurt dad,but he hated giving in. The latter motive turned out to be stronger. When he began to openly support the most liberal politicians, that really got to his father.

What was even more frustrating to Deacon Sr. was that his son started to become a very active investor, particularly favoring the stock market. Junior found an excitement there that he had not found elsewhere in his young life. All the investments he made were in high-risk issues, sometimes exceptionally high-risk. He wasn't altogether sure why this was so exhilarating, but he mentioned later that he felt more of a man after one of these investments hit.

The trouble was that usually they didn't hit. Then Deacon Jr. felt very guilty. But he would go right back to high-risk investing. However, he was losing money very rapidly and that led him to seek help.

Many people rebel against control by others and in the process rebel against guilt. Just look at the large number of violent people who report that as children they had extremely strict, punitive parents. A person who feels guilt-ridden knows that he's in pain and he hates that, so he may rebel against the one who caused the guilt feelings. Unfortunately, rebellion can be very self -destructive. Deacon Jr. depleted most of his investment funds until he learned more about himself. He still rebels at times, but in a more rational, constructive way.

The major emphasis of this chapter is not only on what guilt does to people in the investment world, but also on why I believe women are more pressured in our society to feel guilty.

Look at the list of five guilt-producing categories above. These categories basically say, "Lady, your job is to give and give and not demand full value in payment."

Child-rearing practices encourage some very key gender-driven characteristics. Boys are taught to go out into the world and win. Try to follow the rules, but basically win at nearly any cost. Girls, however, are told that their job is to nurture everyone—husband, children, parents, and anyone else who wants something. Achieve only or primarily through caring for others. Our society has been very consistent on this point.

Now look at the guilt potential! The girl who acts assertively offends others, especially men. If she offers an opinion it may be unwelcome and for that reason offensive to some. If the girl is cut from a different mold (is an individual!), society may become very punitive.

It gets worse. The girl grows up, feels encumbered in work, but seeks nevertheless to get a career going. She tries to find her own identity. She tries to find activities that she enjoys. Every inch of the way she's likely to hear about someone she's neglecting

The pattern completes itself like this: The girl is told that sure she can have a career, but her career is taking care of her husband and children. She can maybe join the PTA or be on a school committee. She's warned that men aren't going to like dating her if she's assertive. Sometimes she'll be told, "Women are suppose to nurture, not be competitive."

The maturing girl finds little support if she wants to be a businessperson. Other women who have surrendered to the pressure will condemn her assertiveness—generally because they want to convince themselves that they made the best choice. After all, when you see someone who's still fighting, it reminds you of what you might have become.

When anyone hears the same thing over and over, there's a tendency to believe it. You begin to feel that you're neglecting everyone when you're doing your thing. If you make a profit on a deal you suffer guilt because it was too big a profit. When things go along very well with little effort, you feel so guilty you're sure something bad will happen. Sometimes we can provoke bad happenings just with our negative expectations.

Case 1: One of the most rewarding professional experiences I ever had was in counseling a young woman with many of these burdens. Georgia had been in one of my sport psychology programs, where she had caught my eye because she was so extremely self-critical. Though she had a good golf swing, to hear her talk she was hopeless. Often she would play so conservatively that she missed great opportunities. I recalled saying to her that we had to change her attitude if she was to become a consistent winner.

Much to my surprise she called for an office appointment, arrived early, and had a list of specific things she wanted to work on. That was very impressive! On her list were things like "improving my self-concept," " being able to make up my own mind," and "not always having to make everyone like me." She said she was tired of everyone walking all over her. (Later I found that it was mostly her boyfriend and a few close friends who were the offenders.) Georgia had a number of important goals and she started working on them right away. She supplied a very thorough history that afforded many insights into her behavior.

There was one problem that had to be counteracted. Georgia pushed so hard that she often raced through information so rapidly that she couldn't learn from it. She stopped that when I asked her to slow down so I would be able to read my notes. She demonstrated that she had a good sense of humor.

Georgia started by telling me about her parents. Father was a self-made man who took the first job he found after high school. He attended college in the evenings and graduated in seven years. He was a hard-driving man who offered his motto to anyone who would listen: "Life ain't easy. You have to suffer and push, push, push to get there—and then you gotta push harder 'cause someone else wants it, too!" Georgia said he always bragged about how he never took the easy way out.

Georgia's mother was the opposite, except when it came to entertaining. Then everything had to be perfect. She was also very careful not to offend anyone, especially business prospects. Her tool to deal with tense social situations was to laugh. Her life goal was to have children and support her husband as he tried to become more successful.

There were some other interesting facts about Georgia's parents. Her mother, Joan, seemed to have never had any activity that was special to her. Sports were "okay." So was dancing. Sometimes she liked to draw. But nothing really excited her. Over and over as a child Georgia heard her mother say that "my life is my family."

Dexter, her father, didn't take kindly to new ideas. He was rigid on what constituted acceptable behavior for girls and, for that matter, women. The man was the head of the family "because that's what our creator decreed." In to his own life, duty and responsibility were the driving forces. As a child Georgia had often asked if he enjoyed his work. He always responded by saying in effect, "Enjoyment is not part of the human condition." Then would follow a lecture on how life is a challenge and is not meant to be fun. "People who seek fun are childish people who don't care about their families," he would say.

Both of Georgia's parents said they had "faith in her." Her father often said there was no excuse for her to ever fail at anything: She had supportive parents, adequate financial support, good schools, and proper training at home. Her parents could never understand why she would feel pressure or harbor self-doubt.

Georgia wanted to please her parents. When she did well, she came running to them to share. Once she recalled getting an A in geometry at the mid-term. She was sure her dad would be proud. She showed him her test and he was pleased but he had to comment: "Don't get too sure of that A, honey. So often we start fine but then end up being unable to continue the effort. In baseball, we call that choking."

So Georgia was learning some major lessons. If you do well at first, don't assume you will continue to do well. If you don't handle pressure, you fail. You have built others up and then let them down. If you enjoy an activity, you're probably seeking rewards that are unimportant. You have no excuse to fail because you have such a supportive family. Never be satisfied with an accomplishment because that's when you fail.

Georgia didn't fail, however, in either grade school or high school—not with her studies at least. But there were problems with extracurricular activities. In grade school the swim coach discovered Georgia's talent and at first Georgia seemed to enjoy the competition. She tried to get her father to come and watch but he couldn't seem to find the time. The coach called him and told him how much it would mean to his daughter. He said "maybe," but he didn't come. A second call was less well-received. Dexter said he really didn't think he wanted to watch a bunch of muscle-bound girls compete. "Why not put them in a sewing class?" he joked.

Georgia happened to hear this comment. She got the impression that there was something wrong with swimming for girls, so it marked the end of her swimming career. She still continued her involvement in sports but she showed guilt feelings when she did well. It was as if she were daring to put time into an activity that just wasn't important.

In high school things begin to get crucial as far as the shaping of a life is concerned. As a young adult Georgia could think of things she wanted in her life. She also increasingly looked forward to some decision making of her own. Finding an interest in business, particularly marketing, she secured a part-time job with an advertising agency. By the time she was a high school senior she was spending many long evenings at the agency. She began to feel excited about advertising as a career possibility.

Georgia also kept her golf game up; she played on her high school team. At first her father showed some interest, because golf can help with business. Then be began to reconsider. "If you get too good at that game, honey, no young men will want to play golf with you," Dexter declared, "and then they won't date you either."

This was followed by questions about a career versus being a housewife. Then came the inevitable comments that golf couldn't help with your business unless you have a business. "Surely you wouldn't pass up a family just for golf," Dexter said.

Georgia began to recognize that she always felt worse after she talked to her parents. It usually turned out that what she wanted was all wrong. When it came time to choose a college, she just asked her father for a range of what he could afford, then did all the other checking on her own. She knew her dad wasn't happy about her desire for college. He preferred that she find a temporary job and wait till someone proposed to her. These wishes were ignored, because this was at a time when Georgia no longer asked advice from her parents.

Away at college, Georgia adjusted very well. Her grades were excellent. She got along well with her roommate, a journalism major. Her professors also related well with her; one in particular kept telling her how talented she was.

Georgia was bothered by this. " I wish he wouldn't say that all the time," she told Marcy, her roommate, "I'm afraid I'll do something to let him down. What if he finds out I'm not that bright?"

Marcy just laughed. "You're that bright," she stated with a broad smile.

Georgia's professor continued to support her. Under his tutelage she learned a great deal about marketing, a field she soon began to love. Her professor realized that Georgia had little emotional support from her father. Georgia had told him of Dexter's comments about college: "I think all this is a waste of our money—you're just going to get married anyway." He also said, "A woman's place is with her kids" (never mind that she had none at the time) and "You can't be a mother and a career woman, too, you'll have kids with all those problems."

Sometimes Dexter mentioned how much it cost to send Georgia to college. Professor Murry heard some of those comments and in Georgia's third year he found her a scholarship. Georgia was convinced she didn't deserve it, but Marcy helped to convince her she did.

The rest of Georgia's college career was pretty much the same. She and Professor Murry became very close and she showed much professional growth. She also continued to grow closer to Marcy. Marcy was such an assertive person that Georgia liked to watch her interact with people. "She knows what she wants," Georgia said over and over to herself. Georgia was popular in school. She had many friends, both male and female, but she never seemed to get close to any of them. Learning was what "turned her on."

Underneath it all, though, Georgia had problems from childhood and adolescence that were hidden by her positive college adjustment. A year after she graduated from college she had her first romance. Fred, her boyfriend, wanted to be her fiance but a little voice held Georgia back.

There were other problems that marred her adjustment. Georgia had fallen in love with marketing, advertising, and art work. Marcy and she were working for the same little ad agency with plans one day to have their own agency. Marcy was a consistently good worker who shone under deadline pressures. Georgia didn't, largely because she didn't trust her own judgment. Marcy kept telling her to just trust herself but Georgia couldn't. "What if I make a mistake and screw things up?" she asked, her voice shaking with tension.

"But you have a good track record," Marcy insisted, flashing her supportive smile.

"Yeah, Marcy, but I bluff a lot and in the long run your weaknesses come out. I just know mine will."

There were problems when Georgia had a success. "Maybe I overcharged the client. Maybe they didn't get what they really wanted. Maybe I charged too little and unfairly competed with other agencies." All these torturous thoughts weighed heavily on Georgia

Not surprisingly, one day Marcy had a confrontation with Georgia. She felt that Georgia wasn't carrying her weight and that things were getting worse. She couldn't stand to see Georgia fail, but that's where things were headed. Feeling that Georgia's golf experiences might provide a good opening, she directed her initial comments there: "Georgia, you don't see it but you're wrecking your golf game."

"I know, Marcy, but I don't know how or why," Georgia said.

"Okay, Georgia, let me point out some examples. If you get ahead, you feel sorry for your opponent and you lose concentration on your game. You reassure your opponent until she gets going and beats you. If things go well, you think about failure until it happens. You constantly say you don't deserve something until I could scream. I bet you feel guilty about feeling guilty."

"Well, yeah, you're right," Georgia said laughing a little, "because when I feel guilt I let people down and that makes me feel guilty. My last name should be guilt."

It was around then that Georgia decided to call me for an appointment. The list of things she came with was very rational, but it was obvious there was much more.

In therapy Georgia talked abundantly about both Fred and her father. Both seemed to attack in similar areas. For example, both said over and over that a woman's nature is nurture, not competition or worldly achievement. Georgia said that to think of herself and her personal goals caused powerful guilt feelings.

I raised a question: "Georgia, are women selfish when they don't immediately think of nurturing a child or a husband?"

She laughed. "It doesn't sound right, does it?"

A role model has been thrust on women. Both men and women have many needs and both are likely to feel unfulfilled if a variety of needs are not met. I agree that most women have a need to nurture but that is clearly not a woman's only need. I certainly don't believe that one needs to or should nurture 24 hours a day.

But let's look at the word *nurture*. It means to provide an atmosphere conducive to growth. Can't women also grow? Can't *they* profit from being nurtured? Don't men have any need to nurture? They seem to when they have a coaching position.

Georgia learned over the weeks in therapy how someone else can often create a model for you to emulate. Once internalized, that model then provides an inner voice that becomes your guide. Whose model should we allow into the inner portions of our mind? Should people have the right to choose their own models?

Georgia made some important decisions over the next few months. Fred was long gone. Georgia had seen that he blocked her from self-actualization. He liked it when she lost on the golf course; he pouted when she beat him. He wanted a "full-time wife," which Georgia saw as being dominated.

Fred was easily replaced with David, a man in the same business who was assertive and confident and helped others be the same. He listened to Georgia's and Marcy's ideas—oh yes, he eventually helped the two start their own agency.

Georgia found that as her confidence level rose, she wasn't so dependent on others. If people objected to her opinion, well, too bad. She didn't let the opinion of others hurt her, though she didn't intentionally hurt others. She now saw her talent and appreciated her gifts to others. She felt good about herself. She was in balance and in love—David, advertising, golf, marketing, and (a little later) two happy children. She realized that some members of society would never completely accept her life role, but she chose it and it works for her. She wanted to have that inner voice be hers, not someone else's.

Georgia's investment approach has also changed. She no longer feels she doesn't deserve a big profit. She doesn't suddenly sell when there's the chance of a better profit. She can go for the big gainer. She can make up her own mind, but she can also get information from others. No longer does she express that she won't understand what some expert is trying to explain. Now people often come to her for advice.

Another case is compelling because I had an opportunity to know the chief participants over a number of years.

Case 2: Martha first brought me her daughter, Renee, when Renee was a junior in high school. Martha said she was concerned for a number of reasons but the chief one was Renee's "independent, aggressive, and competitive style." Her concern, it turned out, was that "men won't date her and she won't be able to marry." Martha felt that Renee was, or at least had been, a "tomboy." When I asked a few questions, Martha also objected to Renee's desire for a career, even though Renee didn't know what career she wanted.

Renee's father had left the family shortly after Renee was born. Martha said that it was rumored that he didn't want a daughter. He never came back except to complete divorce proceedings. Martha didn't remarry. She said that when she realized she couldn't get Ed back, she decided to devote her life to being a good mother. I noted that her concept of motherhood was that you were there 24 hours a day. She showed guilt feelings because she had been forced into a job after Ed left her.

When I saw Renee I immediately noted that she didn't have any noteworthy problems. Her mother was her problem. I worked with Martha along the line that values change, too. What's moral in one generation may not be in the next. I started to talk about fulfilling our personal talents and drives. I mentioned self-actualization.

Martha interrupted that line, saying that if I thought Renee was "normal," that was acceptable for her as the mother, and she thanked me. That was the last time I saw either of them for seven years. I did read about some of Renee's athletic successes. I also saw that she had won an artistic contest for advertising a charity outing.

Then I got a call from Renee asking for an appointment. She came to my office looking bright, cheerful, and worried. She said that she had done well academically but her mother had been on her case a great deal, saying that she would create problems for her family and "not be a very good mother one day." To appease her mother she had tried to prepare herself to be a secretary, an occupation that Martha said would "allow you to attract a man because you're not competing with them."

She did attract a man, a teacher of history from the local college; they had married nearly two years before. Renee had taken courses as she could and became efficient not only in typing but also with computers. Starting out as a secretary at a large brokerage house, she had pursued her training and become a full-time stock broker.

Renee's husband, Jess, wasn't pleased by his wife's sudden success. He continued to talk about "us having kids one day but what kind of mother would you be with your career?" Martha had again been on Renee's case for the same reasons.

Renee realized that she was becoming so guilt-ridden that she was having trouble making decisions at work. She began to feel inadequate, guilty for making big profits, and mercenary because Jess told her she was "just pursuing the almighty buck." She said, "People are right, I can't give to others."

"What people?" I asked.

"Well, my husband and my mother," she answered. I asked about the circumstances when such comments had been made. Her mother apparently had said such things a number of times, her husband less often. Most recently the couple had been at a large party and two men walked over to meet them. They addressed Jess as "Mr. Renee" and proceeded to tell him about the "great success you've had in the market from what I hear." Both men had friends who had invested through Renee. She was developing a reputation for being a very sharp advisor.

Jess was noticeably angry. Both men apologized and then left abruptly. Jess pointed out that Renee's success was squashing his identity. Renee as usual felt guilty. That increasingly handicapped her at work. She more often sought advice now, sold quicker, and second-guessed her decisions. She thought about leaving the business she loved.

That's when she called me. Feeling at odds with her mother and husband, Renee recognized that she was carrying a lot of anger around with her. Her fear that she would explode at some innocent person also caused guilt feelings.

So Renee came for therapy while Jess went to one of my colleagues, trying to find a way to save the marriage. There was ample evidence that they cared deeply about one another and their problems didn't run as deeply as it might have seemed.

Renee's situation presents a typical picture of guilt from both childhood pressures and what happened to her as an adult. The treatment steps we took proved successful:

1. We recognized that her mother, unbeknownst to her, was also loaded with guilt feelings. Renee reported that her mother sometimes leaned on her, wanting to be supported as a "good mother." Renee felt that she had to do what mother wanted or mother would feel very hurt. Renee perceived that her mother felt to blame for her husband leaving and thereby depriving Renee of a father. She was afraid to have more in her life because she might lose that, too,

so she never dated or sought another relationship. Renee had to realize what caused mother to feel and behave as she did.

2. Knowing this background we could see that Martha worried about her daughter losing a relationship with a man. Martha never realized that Renee could pursue a different type, namely a man who supports his wife's growth and freedom.

3. Renee did have emotional strength and achieved some degree of self-actualization. But she was vulnerable. In knowing what she wanted, she was inwardly directed towards growth.

4. Renee felt inadequate and undeserving at times because she felt she had failed her mother. I had a suggestion for that: Compile a list of all those things that you like about yourself, including your accomplishments. Add to the list regularly. Read the list regularly.

We then came up with the following directives:

1. When you feel guilt-ridden, ask yourself where the guilt feeling came from. Who told you that you should feel guilty about some behavior, thought, or idea? Whose values are you following?

2. When you identify the source, ask why that person seems to feel that way. Is the person indoctrinated and trying to force that on you? Is she trying to pressure you in order to convince herself she's right?

3. Ask yourself if the guilt is currently rational or just related to the past. For example, people used to insist that pregnant women should not be exposed to the full moon because it could affect the unborn child. We wouldn't have that concern now; what was moral and good then would not be now. Of more recent vintage I've seen several teenagers who were afraid to cross a street because they felt guilt-ridden for disobeying parents. This came from parents saying when the youngsters were seven that it would be wrong to cross that street. Things are often dangerous at one time and not at another. What a child can't handle, an adult often can. Ask what reason lies behind the directive. It may no longer be valid.

4. Make a judgment as to the outcome of the action that helps cause the guilt. For example, the striving, aggressive career woman will be able to find any number of men who like women like that. They're will be men who like to share and to see people grow, and

who enjoy challenge. The consequences don't have to be bad. The world has many different types of people.

5. Realize as a woman that while you enjoy giving it should be reciprocal. You want to nurture growth, not foster dependency. As the other person gains in strength, he will enjoy doing more on his own.

6. Realize that to be fulfilled you must find what's right for you. Everyone is unique. The world can't afford to lose anyone's creativity. Don't let anyone put you in a mold; find your own pattern.

7. Never give more than you feel able or willing to give. If you feel that you honestly can't give enough, share responsibilities with someone else. For example, a busy career mother may need some help from husband or hired help. Give quality, don't overstress quantity. Also, remember that if you give when you don't want to, you won't let go and you'll foster guilt feelings in the other person.

8. Ask what is right for you. You aren't going to commit a crime. You don't have to be compliant all the time. Society changes, too.

9. Realize that your identity cannot be given away; nor should the identity of others with whom you relate.

10. Seek others like yourself for support; you'll never get it from everyone you know. You don't need everyone to support you, just those you can trust to understand your way of life.

11. Don't argue. You won't convince anyone. Just find your own way.

12. Keep in mind that guilt feelings come from the past. What was right then may be wrong for you now, and vice versa.

13. Work constantly to grow as your own person.

14. Realize that how you feel with others is very important. If they support you and nurture you, you'll feel comfortable with them. If not, go where you do feel comfortable!

Recently a young woman in one of my workshops posed a most challenging question. She said during her childhood she was taught to hold feelings in. She never learned to identify what she was feeling at any given moment. She often heard her mother say, "Janet, don't look at me that way, I know what you're feeling." This caused her to repress her feelings even more.

Janet's question to me was: How do you know when you have a problem? I told her that I used a nine-step program to recognize and deal with guilt feelings:

1. You must feel some discomfort or pain, with the sense that you're missing out on something in your life. If you have no discomfort, then you're not missing anything important to you. Realize, too, that missing out can also mean that you engage in an activity but do not enjoy it.

2. Identify what you're missing out on. Is it the pleasure part that's missing? Is it a lack of success? Self-realization?

3. Identify what holds you back. For example, is it a feeling of unworthiness to even try? Is it a vague fear of some unrecognized harm?

4. In what areas of life are you being held back? Earning a large income? Being independent? Having power? Marching to your own drummer?

5. Identify the feelings holding you back. Are they guilt feelings? Is it a fear of being found inadequate?

6. Where do the feelings originate? Things parents said? A teacher? Society? What's the source of the discomfort?

7. Why did they tell you that? Perhaps there was a dangerous disease prevalent then, like polio, which was thought to be correlated with swimming. So swimming was wrong, then.

8. What are the realistic dangers now?

9. Find rational ways to deal with the painful feelings.

This approach has worked well for my clients. Janet wrote me a nice letter to say it had helped her.

Chapter XV Quiz Analysis

So what does it all mean? My clinical experience provides the following "right" answers:

1. Agree—Women are judged more severely and have more of an image forced on them.

2. Disagree—If you're a dependent person, you're more likely to be dominated by someone else's ideas.

3. Agree—That would suggest you're not overburdened by guilt.

4. Disagree—You want inner security, so you're not upset with differences.

5. Disagree—It's inevitable unless you're so guilt-ridden you have to just go along.

6. Disagree—Also inevitable, unless—well—you don't have a life of your own.

7. Disagree—Why make any decisions if you can't hold to them?

8. Disagree—Accept yourself as worthy of praise—it will do wonders for you.

9. Agree—We sure hope so!

10. Disagree—Learn to feel secure with your ideas and let others feel happy with theirs. It makes for popularity.

11. Disagree—This may be a shocker but "always" is the key word. You need to do for yourself, too.

12. Disagree—Be secure with your ideas. Live and let live.

13. Disagree—This is often caused by feeling unworthy and leads to guilt feelings.

14. Disagree—We need to feel worthy of finding our own way.

15. Disagree—Children grow confident through realistic praise.

16. Disagree—Be secure within yourself and learn not to feel guilty when your uniqueness shows.

17. Agree—Think of how you would hurt others if you were always truthful.

18. Disagree—Each of us must strive to live up to our own standards.

19. Disagree—If winning means taking food from starving children, okay. If not, it's part of our world.

20. Disagree—Learn to live with it; it's part of human nature.

21. Disagree—They do: The earth is not the center of the universe!

22. Disagree—Happiness can inspire growth.

23. Disagree—Check most households and see who pays the bills (mine too).

24. Agree—Severely so, and often the punishment is never-ending.

25. Agree—Yes, because creativity is always different from the norm.

26. Agree—Examples are in this chapter.

27. Disagree—Otherwise you'll be self-reproaching.

28. Disagree—We must learn how to learn from our mistakes.

29. Agree—Especially with the fear of being different.

30. Disagree—The guilt-ridden will always find something or someone else will find it for them.

So what does it all mean? How about the following scale?

Correct	28 - 30	Low guilt, high individuality.
	23 - 27	Good but some sensitive areas.
	19 - 22	Watch that inner voice.
	15 - 18	That inner voice may not be yours.
	0 - 14	Will it make you feel guilty because we disagree?

Glossary

Acute stress disorder—reaction to a traumatic event with feelings of being detached, numb, unstable, or helpless.

ADD—*see* Attention Deficit Disorder.

ADHD—*see* Attention Deficit Hyperactivity Disorder.

Alzheimer's disease—a type of dementia with significant memory loss and general cognitive deterioration.

Amnestic disorder—loss of memory resulting from organic causes.

Anorexia—fear of gaining weight out of proportion to reality.

Anti-social disorder—a disorder characterized by deceit, irritability, recklessness, inability to conform to the rules of society, and lack of logic.

Attention deficit disorder—a disorder that causes an inability to focus adequate attention on some tasks.

Attention deficit hyperactivity disorder—a disorder that adds hyperactivity to the ADD inability to function.

Avoidant personality—one that deals with problems by avoiding them.

Bipolar disorder—a disorder characterized by violent mood swings from elation to depression

Borderline personality—a disorder that produces impulsivity and erratic behavior, such as sudden anger directed at someone who was previously idolized.

Brief psychotic disorder—a disorder characterized by delusions and hallucinations lasting less than one month.

Catatonic state—a state related to schizophrenia of generally frozen activity or movement, though at times there is excitability.

Churning—excessive buying and selling in an account to increase commissions.

Cognitive functioning—intellectual functioning, e.g., memory, judgment, comprehension, and reasoning.

Cyclothymic disorder—mood swings that are less severe than in bipolar disorder.

Defense mechanisms—mental mechanisms used to protect against anxiety or threats to one's ego (self-esteem).

Delirium—disturbed levels of consciousness, often with memory impairment.

Delusional disorder—a disorder that features non-bizarre delusions, often seen in marital conflicts.

Delusions—false beliefs, one sign of a thought disorder.

Dementia—loss of both memory and other cognitive functions, e.g., abstraction, judgment, etc.

Denial—a defense mechanism that lessens anxiety and threat by disavowing something.

Dependent personality—one that hangs onto others, resists making his own decisions, and resists change.

Depression—*see* Major depression.

Dysthymic disorder—mild inability to experience pleasure that can last for several years, not as disabling or energy-draining as major depression.

Ego—mental mechanism that affords reality contact as well as protecting the self-concept.

Executive functioning—mental skills of planning, sequencing, abstracting, organizing, and using judgment.

Flat affect—severe apathy and thus a lack of emotional expression.

Flights of ideas—rapid jumping from one idea to the next, often without any clear linkage.

Hallucinations—false sensory experience with no actual external stimulus.

Histrionic disorder—need to be the center of attention, suggestible, displaying shallow affect.

Interactional problem—a problem created because of how people interact.

Intermittent explosive disorder—assaultive behavior or destruction of property.

Joint tenants—those who share results of and responsibility for an account.

Labile—changeable in moods and emotion.

Long-term memory—memory for events that happened long ago.

Loose associations—jumping from one unrelated thought to another without logical connection; a sign of possible severe mental deterioration.

Major depression—severe disorder lasting from two months on characterized by empty, sad, and worthless feelings, generally with loss of ability to experience pleasure and often a marked loss of energy; the person becomes withdrawn.

Manic disorder—a period of acute elation, often with rapid talk and jumping from topic to topic.

Mental status—a measure of how well oriented and sensitive to environment a person is.

Narcissistic personality—self-centered, grandiose, arrogant, seeks constant attention.

Obsessive-compulsive disorder—recurrent thoughts or acts that the individual cannot control.

Oppositional disorder—a tendency to express irritability toward people and to do the opposite of what they request.

Panic disorder—intense fear, often of bodily impairment, such as choking, chest pain, and death.

Paranoid—showing delusions of grandeur or persecution.

Passive-aggressive behavior—expressing hostility by refusing to act, e.g., failing in school as a means of hurting parents.

Personality disorder—a strongly ingrained pattern of responding maladaptively in work and social situations.

Post-traumatic stress disorder (PTSD)—reaction to a severe trauma with severe fear, frequent recurrent thoughts of the trauma, and feelings of helplessness.

Schizoid disorder—coldness toward people.

Schizophrenia—a disorder often featuring delusions, hallucinations, disorganization, and flat affect.

Schizotypal personality—odd thinking and beliefs, vague, eccentric, suspicious.

Selective memory—remembering only what fits one's needs or motivation.

Short-term memory—memory for recent events.

Suitability—how well an investment fits a client's investing philosophy.

Thought disorder—thinking not in tune with reality, often with delusions.

Transference—relating to others as to an important earlier figure, e.g., relating to a boss as to a father.

Index

For Product Safety Concerns and Information please contact our EU
representative GPSR@taylorandfrancis.com
Taylor & Francis Verlag GmbH, Kaufingerstraße 24, 80331 München, Germany

www.ingramcontent.com/pod-product-compliance
Ingram Content Group UK Ltd.
Pitfield, Milton Keynes, MK11 3LW, UK
UKHW021006180425
457613UK00019B/824